DEVELOPING MORE CURIOUS MINDS

JOHN BARELL

D0071724

Alexandria, Virginia USA

1703 N. Beauregard St. • Alexandria, VA 22311-1714 USA
Telephone: 800-933-2723 or 703-578-9600 • Fax: 703-575-5400
Web site: http://www.ascd.org • E-mail: member@ascd.org

Excerpts from the Young Naturalist Awards reprinted with permission. The award is a program of the American Museum of Natural History.

Cover art copyright © 2003 by ASCD.

ASCD publications present a variety of viewpoints. The views expressed or implied in this book should not be interpreted as official positions of the Association.

All Web links in this book are correct as of the publication date below but may have become inactive or otherwise modified since that time. If you notice a deactivated or changed link, please e-mail books@ascd.org with the words "Link Update" in the subject line. In your message, please specify the Web link, the book title, and the page number on which the link appears.

Printed in the United States of America.

February 2003 member book (p). ASCD Premium, Comprehensive, and Regular members periodically receive ASCD books as part of their membership benefits. No. FY03-5.

ISBN: 0-87120-719-2   ASCD product no.: 101246
ASCD member price: $21.95   nonmember price: $25.95

Library of Congress Cataloging-in-Publication Data

Barell, John.
  Developing more curious minds / John Barell.
    p. cm.
Includes bibliographical references (p.   ) and index.
  ISBN 0-87120-719-2 (alk. paper)
  1. Questioning. 2. Critical thinking. 3. Problem-based learning. I. Title.
LB1027.44 .B37   2003
371.39—dc21   2002151117

12 11 10 09   12 11 10 9 8 7 6 5 4 3

For my mother,
Elizabeth Ferguson Barell,
who taught me the value of asking,
"How do you know?"

SUSTAINABLE
FORESTRY
INITIATIVE

Certified Fiber Sourcing

www.sfiprogram.org

DEVELOPING MORE CURIOUS MINDS

Preface

The primary skills [learned in college] should be analytical skills of interpretation and inquiry. In other words, know how to frame a question. How do you evaluate the safety record of an airline? How do you evaluate the risk when you smoke? . . . In this is also the capacity for intelligent empathy, the ability to understand the other side even when you may not share it. You should not be dependent on the sources of information, either provided by the government or by the media, but have an independent capacity to ask questions and evaluate answers.

—LEON BOTSTEIN, PRESIDENT OF BARD COLLEGE, ON THE GOALS OF A COLLEGE EDUCATION, AUGUST 2002

The ability to pose good questions when we are confronted with complex situations contributes to our growing up to living our lives to their fullest potential. We cannot, however, wait until our students become freshmen in college. We need to cultivate their curiosities within the curricula from the first day of kindergarten through their graduation from high school.

Why is this even more important now?

Because of the terrible events of September 11, 2001.

For weeks following that day of infamy I was consumed with the question: "How could this have happened?" Some said we could have predicted the horrific attacks. Certainly, we had warnings, such as the attack on the *USS Cole* in Yemen in 2000 and the bombings of our embassies in Kenya and Tanzania in 1998 and the World Trade Center in 1993. Terrorists had left their calling cards across Europe and at home. But our leadership did not rouse us to national awareness.

Others have said we entangled ourselves with such bureau-cratic procedures and safeguards that it was too difficult to pur-sue foreign enemies living within our borders. We guarded their civil rights as equally as we guarded those of law-abiding citizens because, we say, we are a nation of laws.

And some have said we just couldn't conceive of any strike against our homeland. "We . . . suffered not from a lack of data but from a failure of imagination," wrote Lewis Lapham in *Harper's Magazine* (November, 2001, p. 40). We heard from some govern-ment spokespersons that information was available to different agencies, but no one "connected the dots."

When the first anthrax cases hit Capitol Hill and the offices of U.S. senators and representatives, no one thought, "We have to protect the postal workers. What if anthrax can spread through the machines even if letters containing it haven't been opened?" We should have had people thinking in these hypothetical fash-ions, but evidently we didn't.

We all know how to ask questions, but it seems as if some of us had not been asking the right questions in key situations prior to September 11. I wonder if our limited response to these events reflects a broader condition—a complacency and passivity, a lack of inquisitiveness among some of us.

Is there any evidence to support such a concern? I think there is, and I deal with more of this data in Chapter 1. Here at the beginning of this book I want to place the whole volume in a con-text far different from the one I imagined in writing it before September 11, 2001. The attacks on the World Trade Center occurred in my hometown. I live about five miles north of Ground Zero. The assault on the Pentagon took place not far from the offices of Stephanie Selice and Tim Sniffin, my editors at ASCD in Alexandria, Virginia, who shepherded this book toward publica-tion with masterful craftsmanship, intelligence, and a commit-ment to its ideals.

As Americans, we have been blessed with so many riches: a homeland bounded by two magnificent oceans and friendly neigh-bors to the north and south. Our soil has been productive enough to feed and sustain us as well as millions around the world.

But more than the precious gift of the earth we till have been the beliefs by which we live, beliefs for which we fought the Revolutionary War and which are to be found in our sacred documents, the Declaration of Independence, the Constitution, and the Bill of Rights, guaranteeing each citizen freedom of speech, press, religion, and congregation, and from unlawful searches and seizures.

Men and women of America have fought and died to preserve the freedoms we enjoy and cherish. In difficult times, we have been fortunate to have leaders who measured up to the difficult challenges that threatened our security and our ways of life.

But on September 11 everything changed. This was my first logical thought after the shock of witnessing the attacks on the World Trade Center on television. The lives we lead could no longer be the same. I didn't know then just how differently we would have to go about the business of living, but it seemed as if when terror hit our shores, nothing could remain the same.

Our senses of safety, security, and freedom from what others around the world have experienced for hundreds of years—such as warfare at home—have been obliterated.

This morning I watched a group of school children very happily being led by their teachers along a sidewalk across the street from my home in Manhattan. Perhaps they were joyfully parading to a playground near the East River or to a local hospital or fire station. I wondered what kinds of futures we are preparing for them.

What seems clear to me now is our need to be wide awake to the world around us, to the people with whom we live and the magnificence of nature that envelops us. All of nature is there for us to behold, to learn from and use to sustain our lives in moderation. Most of that world is friendly, but some parts of it are not.

In order to achieve this status of heightened awareness about our communities and the world, we need to foster and develop what makes us unique—that is, our ability to imagine, to think, to ask demanding questions of people and of nature. Our inquisitiveness is the beginning of meaningful learning about the world and ourselves. We become inquisitive when we are very interested in a certain subject and just want to find out more; we are excited about exploring new territories, whether they be the continent of Antarctica or the poetry of Wallace Stevens.

This book is for the educators and parents of the children I saw joyfully parading by my apartment building—the children in the New York City public schools I have the good fortune to work with. My goal is to ensure that our children grow up to be active citizens of our democracy, citizens who take seriously their charge to be what Barbara Tuchman said every government needs, "great askers" (1984, p. 384).

Every citizen of a democracy needs to be constantly vigilant to the status of her freedoms. One way to do this is to possess the capacity and will to challenge authorities whoever and whatever they may be—parent, teacher, employer, past practice, current philosophy, tradition, and folk wisdom. We do this with respect and with reason, not arrogance. How do we prevent such disasters from happening again? What alternatives to current policies are we considering? And how do we acquire the imagination to conceive of possibilities unthought of?

I do not have answers. But I do have a surpassing faith that the contents of this book can help us engage our children and students as my grandfather always tried to challenge me. Llewelyn Ray Ferguson would often say, "Johnny, did you ever wonder . . . ?" He was my model of an inquisitive person and, fortunately, I grew up with the ability to speculate in some areas of my life, but not in all. I need this book to help me become more of a critical citizen, so I ask the kinds of questions of leaders who present policies and programs that directly affect all of us.

Schools can become cultures of inquiry wherein all our children learn to conceive and cherish questions and to act on these curiosities beyond kindergarten, to speculate reasonably and with respect about what they are doing and about the natural and interpersonal worlds into which they are growing.

Nancy Cantor, chancellor at the University of Illinois at Urbana-Champaign, says, "There isn't a pat answer anymore to this world, so the best we can do for students is have them ask the right questions" (Flaherty, 2002, p. 26).

Inquisitive minds are the safeguards of our democracy, now and forever. But of even greater importance, inquisitive minds are the promise of living enriching lives; they are the energizers of our growing and thriving civilizations.

Leon Botstein concluded his comments, "A college education has to engender a lifelong habit of curiosity, as opposed to becoming more convinced that you are an authority" (Flaherty, 2002, p. 27).

I will add only that this "lifelong habit of curiosity" needs to be developed, nurtured, and cultivated way before college. We must start at home by acknowledging children's questions and helping them find answers throughout their public school lives. The daily curiosities of life can become the habit of mind we call inquisitiveness only by patient, loving, and sustained support throughout one's life.

What are the questions you are asking now? What questions are your students posing? And what questions will ensure that all human beings will live together in peace sharing the benefits of human rights?

—John Barell
August 2002

References

Flaherty, K. (2002). What should you get out of college? Interviews. In *The New York Times Education Life*. August 4, pp. 26–28.

Lapham, L. (2001, November). Drums along the Potomac: New war, old music. *Harper's Magazine, 303*, pp. 35–41.

Tuchman, B. (1984). *The march of folly: From Troy to Vietnam*. New York: Ballantine Books.

Chapter 1

A Culture of Inquisitiveness

The whole art of teaching is only the art of awakening the natural curiosity of young minds for the purpose of satisfying it afterwards.

—Anatole France (1932, p. 238)

The events of September 11, 2001, have changed the lives of Americans and of people around the world for the foreseeable future. Now we know that we need to keep our eyes and ears open to ensure our safety and security. Part of our new awareness is being alert to those situations that may seem abnormal, perplexing, or full of uncertainty. Such situations usually lead us to ask "Why?" or "What's happening here?" Anatole France saw youngsters as possessing a "natural curiosity," and it is this curiosity that can help us become more vigilant as well as lead us toward those personal landscapes of growth that will enhance our lives. And the more our curiosity awakens us to new possibilities, the more we will open our eyes to life in our democracy and see whatever inequities may continue to exist. One of the benefits of inquisitive minds is focusing upon the extent to which our cherished liberties extend to all citizens.

To understand how this book focuses on inquiry, we can examine other events that might have led us to ask a lot of questions. See if you agree that there are similarities among all

1

of these episodes and that they lend an urgency to the contents of this book.

"Bonfire"

On November 18, 1999, students from Texas A&M were building a three-story structure of timber they had cut down during that September and October. On that terrible Thursday, the log pyramid suddenly collapsed. Twelve Texas A&M students died; 27 more suffered injuries. There was no advance warning, as there seldom is for such a surprise disaster. There was no horrible storm, no tornado, no earthquake to set the assemblage of cut timber tumbling toward collapse.

Immediately, we want to know why this happened and how it could have been prevented. As we answer these probing questions, we encounter conditions that existed not only at this university but also in governmental agencies, in corporate America, and in our schools. What we discover is that our culture in many respects does not value one of humankind's most cherished gifts, the gift that separates us from other living creatures—our inquisitiveness. Our curiosity about ourselves and the natural world is what helps us develop intellectually and spiritually and provides the fuel for the growth of civilization.

The massive 2,000-log construction at Texas A&M was to have been set on fire just before the traditional football game with archrival the University of Texas, as previous bonfires had been for generations of Aggies. "Bonfire," as it was called, would rouse the student body toward victory and would represent the culmination of thousands of hours of work by the undergraduates charged with erecting it.

What happened?

The president of Texas A&M, Dr. Ray M. Bowen, ordered an investigation, and on May 2, 2000, the Special Commission on the 1999 Texas A&M Bonfire, headed by Leo Linbeck, Jr., as chair, issued its findings (Linbeck, 2000).

For decades, the administration had permitted students to work on Bonfire without proper supervision. "Student leaders made important design decisions and choices without understanding their impact on structural integrity" (Linbeck, 2000, p. 27). Indeed, students worked from plans handed down on scraps of paper, and they, the students, lacked proper knowledge of building such immense structures (the log construction was about 80 feet high) and the forces that keep them stable.

Most importantly, the commission noted, "The university has a culture that instills bias and tunnel vision in decision making. *No credible source ever suspected or thought to inquire about structural safety*" (p. 37, emphasis added).

Therein lay the problem. No one thought to ask, "Is this safe? Do these students know what they are doing? Why are we encouraging this bonfire in the first place? What are the risk factors, and how can we manage them?" Writing in *The New York Times* on May 3, 2000, Jim Yardley summed up the commission's report by referring to "an insular university culture that for years had resisted change and discouraged criticism" (p. A16). In other words, those in administrative positions of power did not create a climate or culture that encouraged continual inquiry and self-reflective assessment.

But Texas A&M administrators throughout the school's history were not alone in their failure to create a culture of curiosity throughout the university.

A Question at NATO

In May 1999, the North Atlantic Treaty Organization (NATO) was, according to Steven Lee Myers of *The New York Times* (April 17, 2000), "under tremendous pressure to escalate its war against Yugoslavia" (p. A1). In an attempt to bomb Serbian president Slobodan Milosevic into agreeing to withdraw Serbian forces from Kosovo and to provide safe haven for the Kosovars who had fled their homeland under pressure and threats from Serbia, NATO commenced a bombing campaign against the capital city. General Wesley Clark, the NATO supreme commander, demanded 2,000 targets in Serbia, a number many considered too high for a country the size of Ohio, reports Myers.

NATO enlisted the help of the Central Intelligence Agency (CIA), which hired an outside consultant, a retired Army officer, to find a suitable target. The CIA designated one target as number 0251WA0017, "a large L-shaped building located in the Novi Beograd district of Belgrade" (p. A10). It was supposed to be a warehouse. When the CIA submitted its target to NATO, one unnamed officer, who had no authority to review targets, looked at aerial photos of the target and immediately became suspicious. The building didn't look like a warehouse to him. The shape and the grounds made it look like some other kind of structure. According to Myers's account, "At that point he raised his concerns with military officers in Naples, but he did not make his questions official or sound grave enough to remove the target from the list . . . . Then he left work for three days to attend a training session" (p. A10).

No one picked up on this officer's questions, perhaps because it was not his job. Maybe he did not sound serious enough. It is also possible that once the CIA delivered a target, it came with such an aura of authority that no one thought to question it.

For whatever reason, NATO proceeded to bomb the Chinese Embassy, killing several people and ruining U.S.–Chinese relations for months.

A Few O-Rings on the Space Shuttle *Challenger*

Like many Americans, I can remember where I was on January 28, 1986, when the space shuttle *Challenger* exploded into two hideously white entrails of exhaust smoke billowing out over the Atlantic just seconds after liftoff. I heard NBC's Tom Brokaw describe the tragedy in saddened monotones as I stood in a restaurant at lunchtime.

It wasn't until the panel headed by former Attorney General William Rogers started investigating that some of us discovered that here was another tragedy that could have been averted had enough people heard the concerns of the manufacturer's two primary solid booster rocket engineers. Temperatures at *Challenger*'s launch time were below freezing, and icicles hung from the booster rocket exhaust funnels. Two engineers, Roger Boisjoly and Arnie Thompson, questioned whether it was wise to launch at the time. But their questions did not make it up the ranks to NASA officials or were disregarded. It was Nobel Prize–winning physicist Richard Feynman who asked these officials, in open inquiry sessions, if they had approved the launch. They said, "No" (Feynman, 1988, p. 163).

Chris Argyris observes in *Overcoming Organizational Defenses* (1990) that the *Challenger* accident is a case where engineers felt that questioning the managers' reasoning to proceed with the launch was stepping outside their spheres of responsibility. In other words, the engineers who knew most about the booster rockets thought they could question only so far and had no right to know why management proceeded to launch *Challenger*. Questioning the thinking of those who make decisions was not part of the culture at NASA.

FBI Agent Coleen Rowley

And, finally, we come to the terrible events of September 11 and the possibility of what might have been. Federal Bureau of Investigation (FBI) agent Coleen Rowley did question those in authority. She wrote a memo to FBI Director Robert S. Mueller III, raising questions about the bureau's handling of the case of Zacarias Moussaoui, who had taken flying lessons in the United States during which he exhibited strange behavior, like focusing on flying in midair and not learning how to land or takeoff. After Moussaoui's arrest on immigration charges on August 17, 2001, and after French intelligence warned the FBI of his alleged ties to al Qaeda, field agents in Minneapolis wanted permission to investigate Moussaoui's computer hard drive. However, officials at FBI headquarters and the Justice Department decided there was not enough evidence for a warrant. Here were dots that might have been connected, but the FBI did not pursue the lead.

"I do find it odd," Rowley writes in her memo to the director in May of 2002, "that . . . *no inquiry whatsoever* was launched of the relevant FBIHQ personnel's actions a long time ago about this case" (Rowley, May 21, 2002, emphasis added).

Realizing that transforming the FBI was a formidable task, New York Senator Charles Schumer asked Rowley before the

Senate Judiciary Committee on June 6, 2002, "How do you change the culture. . ." of the FBI? Rowley replied, "I go back to the 'don't rock the boat, don't ask a question' problem." Any question, she said, might be perceived as a "complaint," or "as a challenge to somebody higher up and they may get mad or whatever" (Excerpts . . ., 2002).

Agent Rowley did what so many whistleblowers have done; that is, they raise tough questions about performance and practice. This is not what was done, however, during the financial scandals that rocked corporations like Enron and WorldCom and sent the New York stock market plummeting during the summer of 2002. Executives, accountants, and reporters, by and large, failed to question the operating practices of large corporations and accounting firms like Arthur Andersen. One analyst noted, "You couldn't ask hard questions, because it was viewed as offensive" to Enron executives (Smith, 2002, p. C17). One auditor from Arthur Andersen who did ask probing questions about Enron's JEDI partnerships in 1999 was Carl Bass. Enron complained and Bass responded, "I am not into negotiating with the client over accounting" principles. Subsequently, he was removed from the Enron account (Hamburger, Schmitt, & Wilke, 2002, p. C1).

People who ask "hard questions" too often have been fired because of their challenges to accustomed ways of thinking and doing business.

In these incidents, we have specific examples of what is occurring in society and in schools: Not enough people are asking questions or voicing their suspicions or apprehensions about policy, practice, and performance.

Reflective Pause

At various points in our narrative journey I will pause and ask that you reflect on what you have just read. We know that good readers are actively thinking and questioning what they read, so my intent is to engage our minds about the text as fully as possible.

So let us begin our reflective pauses with these questions:

- *Given the events just described and those of September 11, 2001 (see the Preface), do you see patterns in some segments of society?*

- *How would you explain the seeming lack of a culture of inquisitiveness among some of us?*

Feeling Threatened by Questions

One seemingly superficial reason we don't question things is that being questioned about anything often leaves some of us feeling uncomfortable. We are threatened by questions, fearing loss of control of the decision-making process or over the entire situation. I once asked a high school teacher why he seldom posed open-ended questions where students would have to respond with their own ideas. "I'm afraid they'll get out of hand," he said.

Our egos are sometimes affronted by upstart questions that may reveal weaknesses in our knowledge and performance. One recurring fear that many of us have is that someday the world just might discover just how little we know!

Richard Hofstadter, writing in *Anti-Intellectualism in American Life* (1966), notes that early in U.S. history, certain religious groups feared education because it would reduce children's "reverence for parental values and religion" (p. 126). The same is true today, with some believing that too much learning and too many questions might undercut and diminish the role of those in authority—parents, teachers, or CEOs. During the latter decades of the last century, there were folks who thought that the curriculum ought to clearly differentiate between right and wrong. Not much room there for student questions and doubts.

When I have asked college students what facilitates the culture of inquiry in their classes, they often laugh and tell stories of professors saying, "I will determine which questions are worth answering here" or "I ask the questions in this classroom." Both statements mean that the students' role is to sit quietly, listen, take in the information, and then someday repeat it in more or less the same form on an answer sheet.

Preserving the Status Quo

Another causal factor in hesitating to ask questions is what is exemplified in the Texas A&M situation—the authority of accumulated tradition: "We've done it this way for all these years, so why change?" I've heard this argument in schools many times. When some of us encounter proposals for change, we respond, "But we've always done it this way." Fear of change and the unknown are some of our most powerful disincentives to taking action. We know our routines and we cannot predict or control what might occur if we change them.

A different facet of this social conservatism is the "Quigley" factor. Frank McCourt in his novel, *Angela's Ashes*, describes his catechism class where one of the boys asked, "What's Sanctifying Grace?" This student was "questioning Quigley," as the boys called him. Upon hearing these kinds of questions, the good priest went into a tirade about the status of those who ask them:

> Never mind what's Sanctifying Grace! That's none of your business. You're here to learn the catechism and do what you're told. You're not here to be asking questions. There are too many people wandering the world asking questions and that's what has us in the state we're in and if I find any boy in this class asking questions, I won't be responsible for what happens. Do you hear me, Quigley? (p. 118)

Quigley got the message: Do what you're told and preserve the status quo.

Cultural Inhibitions

Have you ever wondered why certain societies seem to advance more steadily and dramatically than others? Why, for example, does the United States garner so many more Nobel Prizes than other countries?

Is it the school system?

Is it something in the nature of how children are raised?

Are there few socially acceptable mechanisms for criticism?

There are probably several possible answers, but one that recently struck me as relating to our discussion came from a renowned climate physicist, Syukuro Manabe, who was born in

Japan and spent most of his life working in the United States: "The reason we have difficulty establishing a peer review system has to do with a kind of an Asian culture. You don't want to speak openly in criticism of someone else's work. It is a kind of a mutual admiration society, and that has real consequences." Another scientist, Okamoto Hitoshi, an expert in vertebrate development, notes that in Japanese schools, "Teachers still tell you that eloquence may be silver, but silence is golden" (French, 2001, p. A6).

It is significant that within our American scientific community there are expectations that all reasoning is to be challenged. Part of being a scientist is knowing that whenever you draw conclusions, they are openly questioned. Whenever we read of scientific discoveries or breakthroughs in the newspapers, there is usually a reference to one or more dissenting voices who say, "Wait a minute! We do not necessarily agree with these findings. Here are our questions." Albert Einstein is reputed to have said that he expected his theories to be questioned because that would bring him and everyone closer to a more accurate understanding of how nature works. Doing and learning in science (and the humanities) are a process of continual questioning, debate, reconsideration, and drawing tentative conclusions from evidence. This is not, however, the way in which we teach it!

Our legal system in the United States is built on adversarial confrontations. We do not accept one person's version of what happened. We ask hard questions of all witnesses in order to allow juries to draw their unbiased conclusions about the truth of what may have occurred.

My intent in this book is to break the golden silence of acceptance and allow our inquisitiveness to flourish and begin to mold our entire culture beyond what already exists in our scientific, legal, and media communities.

Acting "Like Cattle"

Finally, we can look to ourselves—those of us who gladly accept our subservient roles and do not question. Why? Because we prefer that others make the decisions, thereby absolving us of responsibility. We are more comfortable, says Fyodor Dostoevsky through his Grand Inquisitor in *The Brothers Karamazov* (1880/1995, p. 309), being led around "like cattle," not exercising our free will.

In *Escape from Freedom* (1941/1995), Erich Fromm provides one perspective on the rise of the Nazis in Germany and on other authoritarian regimes by observing that some of us willingly submit our wills to that of a superior power. "It seems that nothing is more difficult for the average man to bear than the feeling of not being identified with a larger group" (p. 234). We can see such identifications in our society today, and these relationships tend to reduce our sense of individual responsibility. We are following a superior group or leader, one we do not question.

Alexis de Tocqueville notes a similar phenomenon in his 1835 masterpiece *Democracy in America* (1835/2000). In a democracy with "the principle of equality . . . the human mind would be closely fettered to the general will of the greatest number" (p. 521). We can argue with his observations of our early democracy, but we do hear the phrase "the tyranny of the majority," and just maybe there is truth in his observation that some of us give undue deference to the judgments of the majority. De Tocqueville goes on to observe that some of us do not engage in deep analytic thought because we have a tendency toward "easy success and present enjoyment" (p. 526). We are, in effect, somewhat lazy and driven by other "interests," namely, the pursuit of wealth.

"Rude Questions"

All of these elements are evident in what we call "the command and control" structure of organizations: family, schools, and businesses. Those at the top of the organizational chart—parents, teachers, and CEOs—are accustomed to ruling through our decisions alone. We govern by the power inherent in our roles; we know what's best because of our experience, training, and intelligence. We have access to knowledge that will ensure good decisions and those below do not.

As Lewis Lapham (2000) notes, we as a nation do not want things to be different. We fear the "active intelligence [that] tends to ask too many rude questions . . ." (p. 9). Some educational

theorists go so far as to claim that schools, as presently constituted, perpetuate the race and class divisions already inherent in
society. The "savage inequalities" noted by Jonathan Kozol (1992)
have existed since the 19th century; students who challenge
authority, who ask impertinent questions about what they are
learning and about their passive roles in schools might just upset
this balance of power. "The schools as presently constituted,"
says Lapham, "serve the interests of a society content *to define
education as a means of indoctrination and a way of teaching people to know their place*" (p. 7, emphasis added).

Critics of schooling have long observed that schools social-
ize students into already existing socioeconomic strata. We have
known since the 1970s that teachers do most of the talking in
class, and most of that talk is telling. When teachers do ask questions, they have mostly been short-answer, recall kinds of
questions. Dillon (1988) observed that students pose very few
questions related to content during their classes. Have conditions significantly changed since then?

And the existing language patterns in classrooms support
their contention that many, if not most, students are not challenged to think productively or to challenge the status quo with
thought-provoking questions.

Reflective Pause

*Now, why do you think it is important for us to foster and
develop inquisitiveness in our children and students? Why do
we want them curious about the natural world, life in our
democracy, and their personal and professional lives?*

The Importance of Inquisitiveness

Life's Purpose

In Alice Walker's searing novel, *The Color Purple*, a young black
woman, Celie, becomes the wife of a man who is simply called
"Mr." throughout the story. At first "Mr." mercilessly abuses Celie

physically and sexually as she struggles to care for his children. Finally, as the two opponents grow older, they achieve a reconciliation of sorts during which "Mr." makes this extraordinary claim: "I think us here to wonder . . . to wonder . . . about the little things as well as the big things" (p. 290).

"Mr." has finally figured out that our lives are not necessarily governed by our physical appetites but by the innate naturalness of being curious, trying to fathom what life is about and why the crops do or do not grow in a given season.

Curiosity Stimulates Intellectual Development

Pat Wolfe and Ron Brandt (1998) note that "*the brain is essentially curious*, and it must be to survive. It constantly seeks connections between the new and the known. Learning is a process of active construction by the learner . . ." (p. 11, emphasis added). It seems as if at birth we are endowed with the mechanisms and dispositions to discover the world and to make it a meaningful place in which to live. Without a desire to look, to explore by hand, mouth, eye, and ear, we would not grow up to be the human beings we are.

Marion Diamond, one of the United States' foremost neuroanatomists, notes that brain growth is the result of interacting with enriched environments. These enriched environments are characterized by

- Novel challenges,
- Opportunities for free choice and self-direction,
- Stimulation of all the senses,
- Pressure-free social interaction, and
- Experiences of self-assessment. (Diamond & Hopson, 1998, p. 108)

What Diamond and Hopson identified are the elements that characterize a good play environment, full of novelty or strangeness, that challenges children to think, to ask questions like "What is this? What can we do with it? Can we make it into something we want and like?" Questions like these lead to individual or group sociodramatic play—House, Doctor, Construction, and so forth. From such research we can infer the basis for designing curricular experiences full of complexity, novelty, and challenge. Such experiences can be formed around problems to solve, rather than creating laundry lists of information to be mindlessly memorized.

Studies recently revealed that our brains do not necessarily deteriorate in later life. A good regimen of learning new subjects and exploring different challenges can continue to stimulate the brain and even lead to growth of neurons. Diamond and Hopson note that our brains possess "neural plasticity," a flexibility that allows us to grow and develop well into maturity (Wolfe & Brandt, 1998, p. 11).

No wonder that Samuel Johnson, writing in *The Rambler* (1751), notes, "Curiosity is one of the permanent and certain characteristics of a vigorous mind." Our minds thrive upon the driving process of inquiry—our striving to find and figure out what seems strange, unusual, or novel.

Leonardo's Fossils

Leonardo da Vinci is often viewed as the quintessential Renaissance artist, creator of the *Mona Lisa* and *The Last Supper*, designer of the first flying machine in his notebooks, and an engineer of water systems. He also might be credited with asking the kinds of questions that led to present-day studies of geology. Wandering around the hills of Tuscany, not too far from Florence, Leonardo made an amazing discovery: fossilized seashells.

When he reported this find to his friends, they said, "Oh, they must have blown up there." Or, a current theory suggested, they were driven upwards by "the violent currents of Noah's flood" (Gould, 1998, p. 26).

But Leonardo rejected that possibility. Had they blown up there, some would be chipped and cracked. No, there had to be another explanation. How could elements from the bottom of the world's oceans find their way to the top of high hills? That was the question that led Leonardo to consider that Earth was not a stagnant, dead mass of rock, but an everchanging, dynamic sphere. There had to be cataclysmic forces at work that raised up sea floors to the heights of mountains. Leonardo didn't know what they were.

Today we know that the Earth is composed of massive plates on which the continents rest, that these plates move—incredibly slowly to be sure (a few centimeters a year!)—and that mountains rise up as the result of collisions (the subduction) of plates, as in the Himalayan Range. Leonardo knew nothing about these subterranean forces that cause volcanoes and the formation of new landmasses, as with Hawaii's Mt. Kilauea.

Curiosity in Leonardo's case came in the form of recognizing something strikingly novel and wondering about it. Others just passed by those fossils, saying, "Oh, they just blew up here!" The problem of "fossils of marine organisms in strata on high mountains" had perplexed observers since the days of classical Greece. Leonardo's explanation focused on the movement and erosive powers of water, not on the dynamic forces within Earth that move the continental and oceanic plates (Gould, 1998, p. 43).

All learning progresses with this kind of natural curiosity about the world.

"Skepticism Is a Virtue"

Richard Feynman, the Nobel laureate in physics, was a member of the committee that investigated the *Challenger* space shuttle disaster. He was curious enough to place one of the solid booster rocket's O-rings in a glass of ice water and observe the results. What he found was that at low temperatures, these rings became brittle and snapped. Feynman thus demonstrated that low temperatures at launch time at Cape Canaveral played a major role in the *Challenger*'s explosion not too long after liftoff (Gleick, 1992). Feynman (1999) made some observations that expose the very roots of science:

> It is our responsibility as scientists, knowing the great progress and great value of a satisfactory philosophy of ignorance, the great progress that is the fruit of freedom of thought, to proclaim the value of this freedom, to teach how doubt is not to be feared but welcomed

and discussed, and to demand this freedom as our duty to all coming generations. (p. 149)

We should be proud to say, "I don't know!" Too often we are embarrassed by our ignorance. Unfortunately, schools do not always nurture that sense of being in a state of doubt and then searching for answers.

Even more, we should recognize when someone tells us something that perhaps we do not have to believe it—that, for example, surplus funds in the federal budget ought to help sustain Social Security. We should be ready with questions that would help us resolve our doubts and disbeliefs. Doubts should lead to questions, and this is what should be at the basis of living in our democracy: the freedom to question, to raise the possibility that there might be better ways to do things than the ways that are being proposed or implemented.

When we talk about schools educating citizens to live in a democracy, surely we are talking about the duty to question authority, to raise doubts about government policies, to express apprehensions about practices with which we do not agree. The government is *us,* and unless *we* question, we will end up in a dictatorship of the powerful over the apathetic, the passive, the led. This is what Dostoevsky's Grand Inquisitor in *The Brothers Karamazov* told the Christ figure who returned to Spain during the Inquisition: people do not want to make choices; they want to be "led like cattle" and to be told what to do. "Man's greatest need on Earth," said the Inquisitor, "is the need to find someone to worship" (1880/1995, p. 310).

Some people think that, in times of crisis, to question is unpatriotic. The point of view is that dissent can "give ammunition to America's enemies and pause to America's friends" (Ashcroft, 2001, p. 7). This, however, is the essence of democracy—the lively discussion and debate of all ideas and the questioning of authority. Leaders who fear dissent need to realize that what the United States stands for is freedom of opportunity and expression, even to the point of defending those who would burn the U.S. flag and march in our streets carrying flags of our enemies.

An advertisement on buses in New York City says, "Skepticism is a Virtue." Yes.

Izzy and the Road to Success

The late Isidore I. Rabi was a renowned nuclear scientist. In 1944 he won the Nobel Prize in Physics for his work on the electrical characteristics of the electron. During World War II, he worked on the Manhattan Project, helping to build the first atomic bombs.

Someone once asked him how he grew up to be a physicist. He answered:

> My mother made me a scientist without ever intending it. Every other Jewish mother in Brooklyn would ask her child after school: "So? Did you learn anything today?" But not my mother. She always asked me a different question. "Izzy," she would say, "did you ask a good question today?" That difference—asking good questions—made me become a scientist. (Sheff, 1988, p. A26)

If Izzy's mother had not encouraged him to follow up on his curiosities, perhaps he would not have gone on to MIT or done his prize-winning research.

Izzy's mother is really the reason why I am writing this book. She and Anatole France had the right idea. Curiosity should be the focus of education, and every day we should be challenged with novel experiences that beg us to pose wondrous sorts of questions.

But often our experiences with schooling do not reflect the concerns of Izzy's mother. We do not fashion our learning environments or our curricula to stimulate our children's curiosities. And very often, when they do raise fascinating questions, we have no strategies for incorporating them into our busy schedules made more demanding with the press to prepare for standardized tests that increasingly sap our instructional strength.

My own education outside of school has been characterized by intense inquiries about a strange and mysterious land, a continent enshrouded in mystery to the depths of two to three miles of ice, isolated at the bottom of the world, inhabited now by scientists trying to figure out questions about the solar system, the warming of the planet, and its effects on polar wildlife. This continent is, of course, Antarctica. I have spent many, many long hours trying to find out what explorers like Captain Robert

Falcon Scott, Roald Amundsen, and Admiral Richard E. Byrd did during their expeditions at the beginning of the last century. I was so captivated by their experiences when I was in the 7th grade that I started reading about their adventures. I wrote them letters, and met Admiral Byrd when I was 14. Eventually, I sailed to Antarctica myself, and to this day I am fascinated by scientific discoveries of geology, paleontology, and biology that affect the south polar regions.

But my life has not been a brilliant testimony to curiosity. Sad to say, I grew up with such respect for authority that I never questioned it. During the 1960s I saw the Volkswagen Beetles on the road with their anti-establishment bumper stickers demanding, "Question Authority!" I just laughed. Reverence for authority was just too ingrained within me. My life, perhaps, reflects the observations of Erich Fromm and Alexis de Tocqueville when they spoke of the need some of us feel for identification with large groups, with the majority. Many of us are conformists without really intending to be such.

And to this day, there are questions I do not ask in interpersonal situations, perhaps because of deep residues of anxiety about the answers or just my apprehension about being rebuffed.

Conclusion

So here is a book on inquisitiveness for all of us who care about educating the young to grow up to be thoughtful citizens who can use their imaginations to wonder, to speculate about possible futures, and to critique all these new ideas with the rigor of young scientists. These were the twin goals of education set forth by Carl Sagan: "Both skepticism and wonder are skills that need honing and practice. Their harmonious marriage within the mind of every school child ought to be a principal goal of public education" (1996, p. 306).

There is an urgency about education for inquisitiveness just now that stems from the events of September 11. No longer can we abide raising children who do not ask appropriate questions of themselves, of others, and of the world. We need an educated citizenry, and this means that we all need to be alert. Yes, we need to look around us for those persons and events that might harm us.

But more than mere vigilance, we need young men and women who are wide awake to the possibilities of alternative futures. Adults cannot presume to have fashioned a world that our children and students would wish to grow up in. We need inquisitive people to grow into this new millennium who can ask those rude questions so many of us shy away from. These questions will open new landscapes for exploration and discovery. Perhaps of even more significance, such questions will help move our society toward those days when all our citizens will enjoy the benefits of those sacred freedoms preserved in the Bill of Rights—freedom to doubt, to question, to worship, speak, write, and form communities of like-minded persons.

As Anatole France said, "The whole art of teaching is only the art of awakening the natural curiosity of young minds." That is what this book is about.

References

Argyris, C. (1990). *Overcoming organizational defenses: Facilitating organizational learning.* Boston: Allyn & Bacon.

Ashcroft, J. (2001, December 16). Quoted in "A time to speak up for American values." Public service announcement by The Open Society Institute. *The New York Times,* p. 7.

de Tocqueville, A. (1835/2000). *Democracy in America* (H. Reeve, Trans.). New York: Bantam Dell.

Diamond, M., & Hopson, J. (1998). *Magic trees of the mind: How to nurture your child's intelligence, creativity, and healthy emotions from birth through adolescence.* New York: Penguin Putnam.

Dillon, J. T. (1988). *Questioning and teaching: A manual of practice.* New York: Teachers College Press.

Dostoevsky, F. (1880/1995). *The brothers Karamazov* (A. MacAndrew, Trans.). New York: Bantam Classic.

Excerpts from Senate Judiciary Committee's counterterrorism hearing. (2002, June 7). *The New York Times,* p. A23.

Feynman, R. (1988) *"What do you care what other people think?" Further adventures of a curious character.* As told to Ralph Leighton. New York: W.W. Norton & Co.

Feynman, R. (1999). The value of science. In J. Robbins (Ed.), *The pleasure of finding things out* (pp. 141–149). Cambridge, MA: Perseus Books.

France, A. (1932). *The crime of Sylvestre Bonnard*. New York: Walter J. Black, Inc.

French, H. (2001, August 7). Hypothesis: Science gap. Cause: Japan's ways. *The New York Times*, p. A6.

Fromm, E. (1941/1995). *Escape from freedom*. New York: Henry Holt.

Gleick, J. (1992). *Genius: The life and science of Richard Feynman*. New York: Pantheon Books.

Gould, S. J. (1998). The upwardly mobile fossils of Leonardo's Living Earth. In S. J. Gould (Ed.), *Leonardo's mountain of clams and the Diet of Worms: Essays on natural history*. New York: Harmony Books.

Hamburger, T., Schmitt, R., & Wilke, J. (2002, April 1). Auditor who questioned accounting for Enron speaks to investigators. *The Wall Street Journal*, p. C1.

Hofstadter, R. (1966). *Anti-intellectualism in American life*. New York: Vintage Books.

Johnson, S. (1751). *The Rambler, 103*.

Kozol, J. (1992). *Savage inequalities: Children in America's schools*. New York: Harper Perennial.

Lapham, L. (2000, August). School bells. *Harper's Magazine*, 7–9.

Linbeck, L. L., Jr., Chair. (2000, May 2). *Final report*. College Station, TX: Special Commission on the 1999 Texas A&M Bonfire.

McCourt, F. (1996). *Angela's ashes: A memoir*. New York: Scribner.

Myers, S. L. (2000, April 17). Chinese Embassy bombing: A wide net of blame. *The New York Times*, p. A10.

Rowley, C. (2002). Memo to FBI Director Robert Mueller, May 21, 2002. Quoted in *Time Magazine*, May 28. http://www.time.com/time/covers/1101020603/memo.html. Accessed August 30, 2002.

Sagan, C. (1996). The marriage of skepticism and wonder. In C. Sagan (Ed.), *The demon-haunted world: Science as a candle in the dark* (pp. 293–306). New York: Ballantine Books.

Sheff, D. (1988, January 19). Letter to the editor. *The New York Times*, p. A26.

Smith, R. (2002, January 29). The analyst who warned about Enron. *The Wall Street Journal*, pp. C1, 17.

Walker, A. (1996). *The color purple*. New York: Pocket Books.

Wolfe, P., & Brandt, R. (1998, November). What do we know from brain research? *Educational Leadership, 56*(3), 8–13.

Yardley, J. (2000, May 3). Errors and poor supervision cited in bonfire collapse. *The New York Times*, p. A16.

Chapter 2

Models of Inquiry

How do we know it's DNA?

—Teachers attending professional development session
at the American Museum of Natural History, 2001

Recently I had the pleasure of coming close to understanding the thrill science teachers experience when they conduct an amazing experiment in class and their students are left in awe and wonder. The occasion was a workshop on inquiry that I conducted at the American Museum of Natural History in New York City during one of its summer institutes for educators.

We each took a tablespoon of water, swished it around in our mouths for 30 seconds, and then spit it out into a jar. This gave us a water solution full of our own cells. Then we added one teaspoon of a salt solution and the same amount of a soap solution. To get a better view of the mixture, we poured the contents into a test tube and watched the milky white substances floating around. Finally, we added a tablespoon of rubbing alcohol slowly so it formed a topping for the saliva solution.

All the students then held up their test tubes and watched as tiny white bubbles formed in the alcohol and, rather quickly, we all noticed the bubbles trailing tiny strings of white stuff.

"What's that?" someone asked.

"That's your DNA," I said.

We were all amazed at the sight of the code or blueprint of life stringing upward, being attracted into the alcohol (because it was of opposite charge to the DNA liberated from its cell membrane by the soap). There, right before our very eyes, were tiny strings of the 3.2 billion base pairs that comprise our human genome. There in the test tube was evidence of what makes us as humans different from one another.

What's amazing is that you and I and all the people on earth turn out to be 99.9 percent the same. We share about 98.7 percent of our genes with the chimpanzee! We have borrowed genes—those parts of DNA comprised of the nucleotides (adenine, guanine, cytosine, and thymine)—from bacteria, according to Eric Lander of the Whitehead Institute in Cambridge, Massachusetts (Wade, 2001). And, adding to the amazing similarity in the gene scene within all animals, Craig Venter of Celera (the private company that has sequenced the human genome) says that he has found only 300 genes with no counterpart in the mouse genome (Wade, 2001, p. A20).

Out of all 3.2 billion base pairs, we seem to have about 30,000 genes—far fewer than earlier estimates, which ran to over 100,000.

So in Linder Theater at the museum there were 20 educators, each gathered around several sparkling clean test tubes with this milky substance floating up into the alcohol. Adrian, a biology teacher from New York City, showed us how, by slowly twirling a wooden stirrer, we could lift the string of DNA out of the alcohol. Then the questions came.

"What is DNA?"

"How do we know it's DNA?"

"How are these molecules different from others?"

"How did we extract it? What roles did the salt, soap, and alcohol play in this experiment?"

And on and on.

We were modeling the inquiry experience that commences with a surprising, perplexing, and complex phenomenon that encapsulates major concepts, skills, and attitudes within the subject. We proceeded to work with an inquiry model that we shall describe more fully in a later chapter (Chapter 8).

This little scenario amazed me for several reasons. First, because for most of my educational career I've been a teacher of English literature and educational planning, I've had little experience with conducting scientific experiments! I saw how dramatic a demonstration could be. Second, this 10-minute experiment was relatively simple, even though I practiced it seven times before sharing it with workshop participants. Third, I was struck by its power to awaken the curiosities of participants. People were standing up and gazing in some kind of reverential awe at what makes them human. I'd just never found such instant "Aha!" kinds of experiences when teaching Shakespeare or Alice Walker. Here was an excellent example of what "Mr." says in Walker's novel *The Color Purple*, "I think us here to wonder . . ." (1996, p. 290). And that's exactly what we did.

Inquiry and Our Curriculum

Let me suggest that fostering inquiry and critical thinking is one of our most important curricular goals. We can justify this claim with all of the information presented in Chapter 1: Inquiry fosters intellectual and cultural development, and it is responsible for human development in childhood and for advances in science and all of civilization. If humans did not possess inquiring minds, we would die off as a species just as the Neanderthals did. Maybe that's what happened to that branch of our family tree; they asked too few questions about their rivals and themselves.

Wonder and skepticism—"their harmonious marriage"—ought to be a "principal goal of public education" (Sagan, 1996, p. 306).

Wonder, inquiry, skepticism, and doubt—the pillars of our civilization, the promise of our future on the planet.

Inquisitiveness as the Keystone

In our discussion of curriculum, we need to lay out a partial web of dispositions that are related to inquisitiveness. Wonder, speculation, and curiosity provide the foundation for the following significant dispositions, and perhaps others.

Openness to Mystery and Novelty

German philosopher Martin Heidegger describes thinking as, in part, an "openness to the mystery" of phenomena (1966, p. 55). This suggests that curious people are comfortable with a certain amount of ambiguity, doubt, and complexity. The world is not painted in black and white. There are shades of gray to be investigated, nuances of meaning and subtleties of interpretation that invite our inquiries. The inquisitive person is attracted to the wonders of the Big Bang, the personality of Hamlet or Mona Lisa, and the intrigue surrounding Thomas Jefferson, Sally Hemmings, and slavery.

Willingness to Take Risks

British philosopher Gilbert Ryle notes that thinking "is trying out promising tracks which will exist, if they ever do, only after one has stumbled exploringly over ground where they are not" (1979, p. 78).

The inquisitive person is an explorer, daring to forge ahead into new territories where he or she may make significant discoveries about new hominids, genetically modified foods, or wondering how Enron really made money, if in fact it did!

Collaboration with Others

Recently, I observed college students fascinated with little bugs called "rolly pollies" (pill bugs), supplied by Christine Muth of the American Museum of Natural History. These creatures were crawling around inside shoebox-like structures. "Look, they're crawling out into the light." "I wonder if they dislike darkness." "Do they avoid water?" "This one scrunches up into a ball when you poke it!" These observations and questions reverberated around the small group as the students speculated. Then they conducted little experiments to determine if their hunches about darkness and water were correct. They worked together in their observations, generating and investigating hypotheses the way teams of curious people cooperate in pursuit of knowledge. Here was a scientific community spurred on by their collaboration.

Empathy with Others

Empathy heightens our sense of wonder: "The imagination can, by a process of identification, extend the self into the world and into other people" (Engell, 1981, p. 159). Empathy is the ability to feel ourselves in the "variety of human experience" (p. 157). With such a capacity and determination we can experience awe and wonder about the drive to power of Macbeth and the determination of John Adams to see the Declaration of Independence accepted by the 13 colonies. Empathy provides inquisitiveness with a human heart.

When we speak of cultivating inquisitiveness within our young people, we are interested in developing an array of inter-dependent dispositions that also involve nurturing the confidence to speak up when appropriate, being persistent in investigations over time, becoming as observant as Sherlock Holmes, and being able to reflect on what we know and do not know. What other dispositions and skills can you think of that might be correlated with an inquisitive mind?

Curriculum Standards

We know leaders at the state and national levels consider inquiry to be important because they present standards of accomplishment that include learning how to inquire within all the major subjects we teach. In science, for example, we expect students in 4th grade to be able to "ask a question about objects, organisms, and events in the environment." Then we expect they should be able to "plan and conduct a simple investigation" (National Research Council, 2000, p. 19).

States such as Wisconsin have developed standards for new teachers that, for example, include an expectation that these professionals will become proficient in ways they acquire new knowledge in their subject. I find this a daunting challenge! What the expectation suggests to me is that both new and experienced teachers should know what kinds of questions we pose in history, math, science, literature, art, and technology in order to gain new knowledge and deeper understanding of complex phenomena within each of their several disciplines. I'm not sure that professional development programs prepare teachers (either pre- or inservice) to undertake these significant challenges.

However, we should be able to model for our students what scientists want to know about complex situations like the calving of huge sections (as large as the state of Delaware) of the Ross Ice Shelf in Antarctica, and we should challenge each of them to pose the kinds of questions that will lead to our understanding why those situations happen.

Curriculum content can be thought of as the knowledge, skills, and attitudes we learn while engaged in teaching students. Knowledge consists of those concepts, ideas, and facts we need to understand and use in appropriate classroom and life situations. Within these complex situations we also need to apply specific skills and processes. Attitudes become dispositions or deep-seated habits of mind—tendencies like being curious or being open to many possibilities—that affect how we live our lives. Inquiry and critical thinking/skepticism are two essential components of curriculum content and can be represented as in Figure 2.1.

Those twin components must be seen in relation to three major elements that have always been considered the foundation of what we teach in schools: knowledge, skills/processes, and dispositions and attitudes. You can expand this illustration to encompass your own priorities, but it is important to consider curriculum as more than the aggregate of facts we can memorize and pour into an examination booklet. Curriculum consists of all the experiences we design and implement for the benefit of our students' learning. Curriculum is more than what is found within Chapter 17 of a textbook! It consists of our classes, our assemblies, our field trips, and our open campus policies that permit students to leave for lunch or to enjoy other privileges.

Curriculum also consists of the social events, clubs, and sporting events planned under the school's authority. All of these planned experiences should help our children become responsible, curious citizens who can think productively, who can work

Figure 2.1
Curriculum Content

Knowledge	Dispositions/Attitudes	Skills/Processes
Of major concepts/ ideas Within our subjects: *"We know that—"*	Wonder/curiosity: *"What if?"* Healthy skepticism/doubt Openness to mystery/ ambiguity Empathy Collaborating with others Risk taking	Problem solving: *"What is the problem and how will we solve it?"* Critical thinking: *"How do we know?"* *"What are our conclusions and why?"* Hypothesizing/creating Ways of knowing

collaboratively with friends, and who can reflect in order to improve. Inquiry is a major element within all these curricular experiences, and we can plan, experience, and assess it as part of the school's overall program.

Several Inquiry Scenarios

There are so many ways we can encourage inquiry. I have had the good fortune of working with educators whose work exemplifies some of these strategies.

When I first began to work with inquiry in schools, I teamed up with a 3rd grade teacher named Peg Murray, who is from the Montclair, New Jersey, school system. In her classroom, we created all sorts of strategies and social groups to help students identify and investigate their own curiosities (Barell, 1992). I'll never forget two 3rd graders who in consecutive years came up with questions that led to serious research and helped us develop the models we subsequently used.

One year, a student named Keeven sat with a group of his friends trying to identify things they were curious about related to their school. Finally, Keeven asked this question: "Why do school buses always be yellow?" Everyone in the group looked at each other in some amazement at his questioning something they knew to be true, yet had never thought to ask about.

How do you suppose this 3rd grader answered his own question?

As I stood in the background of the principal's office filming the process, Keeven sat in the principal's leather chair and spoke on the telephone with the director of transportation of the Montclair public schools. His eyes widened, his smile broadened as he listened, and with a little prompting he said, "Thank you!"

Keeven then enlightened all of us about the time in the 1930s when school administrators wanted to find a color that would be the safest for buses to use. "They took a vote," he said, beaming with pride at finding the answer himself.

A year later, his brother Kerry worked in a small group in the same classroom while we elicited from all his friends what they already knew about the solar system and what they would like to know.

"Why do sun flares shoot out from the sun?"

His group looked it up in an encyclopedia. Even though they copied the definition of sunspots almost word for word, a conversation with them afterward told me they had a certain level of understanding about how the sun builds up energy "and then shoots it out into space." I asked them what sunspots were like, expecting them to mention volcanoes. "Like a fan shooting out air . . . Like a light bulb . . . ."

At the end, I asked Kerry and his classmate Diana what they liked about this kind of learning experience. They said, "You get to learn fun things and to do it with your friends."

It was here in Peg's classroom that we first began to experiment seriously with the inquiry strategies described in more detail in Chapter 8. The strategy depends on assessing students' prior knowledge, determining what they are curious about, and then helping them identify ways they can answer their own questions. Other inquiry experiences in Peg Murray's class focused on reading E. B. White's classic story, *Charlotte's Web*. Students like Diana had many questions about the spider, her environment, and how humans interacted with the animals in the story.

The story of brothers Keeven and Kerry introduces us to what inquiry can look like in our classrooms—students posing questions about subjects such as the solar system and *Charlotte's*

Web—and about life in school. What follows are several other stories of teachers using their curricula as platforms to encourage students to ask good and important questions that they can then investigate. We will begin with teachers who focused their inquiries on very specific content areas and will end with the story of one teacher who risks a far more open-ended kind of inquiry at the beginning of the year—a strategy that helps her design a year's curriculum.

"Who 'Discovered' America?"

For years, Jane Rowe, a teacher in Provincetown, Massachusetts, spent the summer before greeting her new 5th grade class by sending them all sorts of clues to a giant puzzle. The clues would include pieces of maps, excerpts from journals, and other evidence that explorers had visited a "New World" during the 15th century and before. What Jane wanted to do was to create a genuine sense of perplexity in the minds of her students. She wanted them to come to school in September, share all the information they had received, and then generate their own essential question: "Who do we think 'discovered' America?"

The curriculum for the next several weeks involved investigations of this central issue, with the students sharing their own conclusions as a culminating experience. Such investigations obviously gave students excellent opportunities to think critically about historical sources and to check them for reliability, accuracy, and believability. By the way, the Vikings often beat out Columbus, and the students saw Native Americans as the people who settled here first.

"Why Do Things Float?"

Cathy Brophy is a 5th grade teacher in Hampton, on the short Atlantic coast of New Hampshire. At the end of the school year, her students look forward to participating in "The Coastal Floating Lab." The purpose of the program is to learn about the complexity of the marine environment in their front yard.

Students learn the basics of oceanography from Cathy and from a program docent ashore. Then they embark with parent volunteers on the *Lady Merrilee Ann,* a local fishing boat, for a day's sail. The students began with general questions about water environments and their current conditions. After conducting observations and several experiments, they generate more questions about water clarity, plankton, currents, and the effects of salinity on water density. Students wondered why things float, why "pH paper turned different colors [and] what would happen if the estuary became contaminated with something that could change the pH of the water.

"Finally, the last observations were of live specimens that included sea stars, crabs, sea cucumber, and (after hauling an otter trawl) skates, lobster, flounder, and some other spiny, dangerous looking fish. The students left the lab experience with more questions than when they began—determined to find out more about ocean life." Students thought "this was the best thing they'd ever done! They loved everything about it—dragging the otter trawl and working as a whole group to haul it up on board was the highlight" (Brophy, personal communication, May 2001).

Classroom investigations can become wonderful collaborative experiences where we learn not only the content but also how to listen to, argue, and reason with each other.

High School Biology

Ms. Idoni annually conducts a field investigation at a lake in the city park. She takes her 10th grade students there after many months of preparation in the skills of conducting investigations—how to plan an inquiry, how to control one factor in an experiment, and how to draw reasonable conclusions. "The field trip," she tells her young biologists, "will help you decide what question you want to pursue" (National Research Council, 2000, p. 67).

At the lake, Ms. Idoni asks the students to walk around it, observe it, and think about questions that they may be interested in answering. She then asks them to record the observations and questions in their journal. The students develop a broad range of questions:

- "Is the lake water safe to drink?"
- "Can people swim in the lake?"
- "What kinds of plants and animals live in the lake?"
- "Have humans changed the lake?"

Students classify their questions, develop priorities and themes (change, stability, and how humans affect nature), arrange for small group investigations, and proceed with their inquiry. Students eventually settle on a general question: "Is the city park lake polluted? If so, how have humans influenced the pollution?" (National Research Council, 2000, p. 68).

Ms. Idoni's complex inquiry experience is an excellent example of how inquiry begins with direct observation and builds on prior knowledge—in this case, about ecological systems and the interdependence of organisms, two of the concepts in the science standards for students in grades 9 through 12 (National Research Council, 2000, p. 70).

During investigations, students need to use their critical thinking abilities, developed over years of schooling (we hope!) to answer their teacher's questions: "What explanation did you expect to develop from the data? [What other explanations could there be for the data you've collected?] Were there any surprises in the data? How confident do you feel about the accuracy of the data?" Students will become very sensitive to issues of reliability, representability, accuracy, and objectivity.

Open-Ended Inquiry

At the end of Cathy Brophy's Coastal Floating Lab experience, she contemplated opening the next year with her 6th graders (many of whom would be her current 5th graders) with questions like: "What interests you in science? What are you curious about now? What do you want to learn more about?" She would then take students' responses and relate them to "benchmarks within the science curriculum."

A teacher with experience in an even more open-ended approach to curriculum is Barb Johnson. She is a 6th grade teacher at Monroe Middle School who takes a far more risky approach to inquiry in her classroom.

At the beginning of the year, she asks her students two powerful questions:

- "What questions do you have about yourself?"
- "What questions do you have about the world?"

These two questions lead students to reflect on those experiences that have raised important questions about their young lives. As you can imagine, such opportunities would fill several chalkboards or flipcharts with a wide variety of questions! How would you handle such a spectrum of personal perplexities?

I'm sure you would do what Barb did and challenge the students to reflect on their lists, to organize them into categories, to search out similar themes and issues. Then they make priorities within the broad classifications of questions about themselves and about the world.

The student-generated questions then become the guiding objectives for the curriculum. For example, "one question, 'Will I live to be 100 years old?' spawned educational investigations into genetics, family and oral history, actuarial science, statistics and probability, heart disease, cancer, and hypertension. The students had the opportunity to seek out information from family members, friends, experts in various fields, on-line computer services, and books, as well as from the teacher" (Bransford, Brown, & Cocking, 2000, p. 156).

Barb Johnson sees these kinds of experiences as helping to develop what we all want in our classrooms—that is, a "learning community," one where we are bound together by common curiosities and the camaraderie that takes shape when curious minds become highly active in investigations and sharing information.

"We decide what are the most compelling intellectual issues, devise ways to investigate those issues, and start off on a learning journey. Sometimes we fall short of our goal. Sometimes we reach our goal, but most times we exceed these goals—we learn more than we initially expected" (Bransford et al., 2000, p. 156).

It takes a person with confidence and a breadth of knowledge about several disciplines as well as current intellectual issues of social, scientific, and personal importance to be able to lay out challenges like these to students. She must also be aware of how children learn and what kinds of strategies will work best under these circumstances. People who wish to follow in Barb Johnson's pioneering footsteps need, in addition, to be comfortable with a great deal of ambiguity and with multiple ways of inquiring into complex subjects. Above all, they need to be comfortable with helping students make hard choices, ones that will affect their entire school year.

Reflective Pause

What do you see as significant in these teacher vignettes?

One of the observations you might have made is that in these teacher models, there is a spectrum of inquiry from that which is focused on specific subjects and questions—Peg, Jane, and Cathy—to an approach that is far more open ended—Barb. Inquiry, therefore, can be closed or open, more teacher-directed or more student-directed (Figure 2.2). This spectrum suggests that there are times when we need to make most of the decisions regarding curricular questions to be answered; times when we negotiate these with our students; and other times when we follow the lead of students' interests and concerns, allowing them to make most of the decisions.

Student Investigations

Because it is our students who we want to pose questions, I want to share with you several examples of young investigators setting out to explore intriguing landscapes. These students have all been winners in a competition sponsored by the National Center for Science Literacy, Education, and Technology (housed within the American Museum of Natural History in New York City:

Figure 2.2
Spectrum of Inquiry and Control of Decision Making

Teacher Control ➤	Shared Control ➤	Student Control
Teacher makes most decisions about content	Negotiated decision making	Students contribute their significant questions for investigation

www.amnh.org/nationalcenter/youngnaturalistawards/). These "young naturalists" have obviously been guided by excellent teachers like those mentioned here and in subsequent chapters, but I want to highlight some of their questions and means of pursuing knowledge.

Think back to my DNA extraction experience. What was it that grabbed people's attention and led to their questions? What fostered inquiry? Why did workshop participants rise to their feet and focus their intense gazes at the test tubes?

Yes, it was the amazing and captivating sight of something strange, mysterious, and inviting: our personal DNA floating up into the alcohol. We were all mesmerized by this unusual, novel, and unique experience.

So it is with our young naturalists.

Tropical Fish in Fresh Water

In Reed Point, Montana, 8th grader Amber Overstreet noticed tropical fish living in a fresh water pond 157 miles from its natural home. "Tropical fish normally live in conditions of 66 to 76 degrees Fahrenheit and pH of 7.2 to 8.0. Montana has severe winters and I wondered how tropical fish could live here. How did they get in that lake? I decided to try to find out" (Overstreet, 2000, p. 32). With her teacher, Jenny Weigand, Amber discovered that a local pet storeowner introduced the fish to this pond 30 years ago "in order to supply his store." But how did they survive?

When Amber took a systematic look at water temperatures, she discovered a warm water spring feeding the high-latitude lake, thus providing a natural habitat for the tropical fish. She concluded, " . . . if the water temperature remains constant, the fish should survive" (p. 35).

The Fiddler Crab

Ninth grader Gaurav Gupta, of Alexandria, Virginia, has spent long hours investigating the marshlands near his home. On one specific expedition, Gaurav noted in his journal:

> We have come to the marsh today with one main goal, one sole purpose in destroying the serenity of the marsh morning. We are after the fiddler crab, a denizen of the marsh that will do anything to avoid getting caught, measured, and eventually thrown back into the marsh, seemingly miles away from its warm, comfortable, and secure burrow . . . our ultimate intent is not malicious. Our goal is to discover if the fiddler crab will experience substantive change over the coming decade. As I pensively observe the marsh, I ponder the many threats to this population of decapods during the next decade. (Gupta, 2000, p. 16)

His field journal, maintained under the guidance of his teacher, Jennifer Seavey, has these queries: "Will my children and grandchildren be able to come to the marsh and interact with the fiddlers as I have just done? Or will they find an area devoid of life, save the cordgrass swaying silently in the cold wind?" (p. 16).

Mystery and Majesty of the Palisades

Max Arno grew up in full view of one of nature's many marvels, the Palisades rock formations on the New Jersey shore of the Hudson River.

> I stand at the very edge of the cliff, looking out across a vast horizon. My eyes trace the ancient sill of lava curving around the land like a gigantic fortress. Glancing down, I can see the jagged wall of rock plunging straight down 400 feet to the Hudson River. I am fascinated by the thought that continental plates once collided and then pulled apart and huge glaciers swept across the very spot on which I stand. (Arno, 2001)

Assisted by his teacher, Daniel Brownstein, Max decided he wanted to investigate this wondrous structure that had dominated his youthful imagination. "Since my childhood, the high point of this sill has loomed directly across the Hudson River from my town [Hastings-on-Hudson, New York], mysterious and majestic. I have often wondered how a rock formation that is so enormous and has cliffs that are so vertical could have come to exist. Now I stand on the very top of the Palisades, my expedition is about to begin" (Arno, 2001, p. 7).

Max discovered that the Palisades resulted from the intrusion of igneous rock, called "sills," into horizontal layers of sedimentary rock about 200 million years ago. He also discovered what forces led to their becoming vertical bastions guarding the banks of the Hudson River (Skinner & Porter, 2000, p. 106).

After reading Max's account I am wondering if this is the whole "sill" or are there other similar components of the same sill elsewhere on Earth?

Hills Shaking Like Jell-O

In the heartland of the United States, 12th grader Megan Hagenauer of Verona, Wisconsin, stumbled on a strange phenomenon—earthquakes in the continent's midsection.

> I first ran across information about these quakes when researching the San Francisco earthquakes for the 1999 Young Naturalist Awards Essay. I was amazed that the most violent quakes in U.S. history had happened in the Midwest, of all places, and that I had never heard of them. The idea that an earthquake zone existed in the Midwest and that a recurrence of these fearsome earthquakes might be felt from my home in Verona fascinated me. We hear warnings about tornadoes and snowstorms all the time in Wisconsin, but earthquakes?

Megan became intrigued. "Fascinated, I abandoned all of my research on San Francisco to pursue some vague leads about 'the hills of Missouri shaking like Jell-O'" (Hagenauer, 1999, p. 30).

Megan and all Young Naturalist award-winners have set about doing what scientists do: identifying a fascinating question and figuring out ways to conduct investigations. They all ventured out into the field. Some waded through ponds, others climbed over rock outcroppings, and all conducted traditional library research and ventured onto the Internet in search of answers.

Reflective Pause

In reviewing the adventures of these curious young people, what is it that provided the spark for their investigations? What got them going? How are their investigations similar to our DNA extraction experience? How are they like what Ms. Idoni and Cathy Brophy have done? What got all of us under way on these marvelous adventures in curiosity?

Conclusion

I have presented model cases of teachers who have created instructional frameworks within which students can identify significant questions related to learning the major concepts and skills within their subjects. I hope it is clear that inquiry is one important way in which students become meaningfully immersed in learning not merely school subjects but, more importantly, about the worlds they inhabit. Inquiry is an essential element within our curriculum and is recognized as such at the state and national levels.

What I also hope is becoming evident is reflected in Megan Hagenauer's conclusion to her investigation: "To me, the New Madrid [Missouri] earthquakes are a reminder of a fact I often forget—that there is so much in our lives outside of our control. Even though I live in as seemingly safe a place as the Midwest, who knows when my whole world may shift out from beneath my feet?" (Hagenauer, 1999, p. 32). What started her on this marvelous adventure in learning was a surprising fact—violent earthquakes occurred not only along the Ring of Fire that borders the Pacific Ocean, but also in the midwestern plains of North America, where farmers grow corn and raise cattle and where there seem to be no intersecting continental plates.

This is what gets us started asking questions: some occurrence, observation, or encounter that seems strange, puzzling, or somehow perplexing to our way of understanding the world. These doubts, difficulties, and uncertainties create questions in our minds. The teachers and students we have met here have recognized and acted upon the questions that are important to them.

"Museum scientists go on expeditions to remote places such as the Gobi Desert in Mongolia and as close to home as Central Park in New York City" (American Museum of Natural History, 2001, p. 5).

Those of us who grew up becoming students of literature, art, and history set off on our own expeditions. Our questions and hypotheses may focus upon the actions of human beings; our field expeditions lead us through the pages of written expression or the examination of evidence in paintings, plays, and poetry. We search out the significance of William Blake's imagery and the ways Winston Churchill led England through the Battle of Britain.

Nonetheless, we are all seekers after meaning, scientist and humanist alike. We are all curious folks, wondering and speculating, searching for answers to questions we find fascinating, amazing, and perplexing. In the end, as Jacob Bronowski noted, "science is as much a play of imagination as poetry is" (1971, p. 50).

References

American Museum of Natural History. (2001). *Young Naturalist Awards 2001.* New York: American Museum of Natural History.

Arno, M. (2001). Shaped by nature and man: The geological history of the Palisades. In *Young Naturalist Awards 2001.* New York: American Museum of Natural History.

Barell, J. (1992). *". . . EVER WONDER . . . ?"* Columbus, OH: Zaner-Bloser.

Bransford, J., Brown, A., & Cocking, R. (Eds.). (2000). *How people learn: Brain, mind, experience, and school.* Washington, DC: National Academy Press.

Bronowski, J. (1971). *The identity of man.* New York: Natural History Press.

Engell, J. (1981). *The creative imagination: Enlightenment to romanticism.* Cambridge, MA: Harvard University Press.

Gupta, G. (2000). Fiddler on the marsh. In *Young Naturalist Awards 2000.* New York: American Museum of Natural History.

Hagenauer, M. (1999). The New Madrid seismic zone. In *Young Naturalist Awards 1999.* New York: American Museum of Natural History.

Heidegger, M. (1966). *Discourse on thinking.* New York: Harper TorchBooks.

National Research Council. (2000). *Inquiry and the National Science Education Standards: A guide for teaching and learning.* Washington, DC: National Academy Press.

Overstreet, A. (2000). Can tropical fish survive in a lake in southwestern Montana? In *Young Naturalist Awards 2000.* New York: American Museum of Natural History.

Ryle, G. (1979). *On thinking.* Totowa, NJ: Rowan & Littlefield.

Sagan, C. (1996). *The demon-haunted world: Science as a candle in the dark.* New York: Ballantine Books.

Skinner, B., & Porter, S. (2000). *The dynamic Earth: An introduction to physical geology* (4th ed.). New York: John Wiley & Sons.

Wade, N. (2001, February 12). Long-held beliefs are challenged by new human genome analysis. *The New York Times,* p. A20.

Walker, A. (1996). *The color purple.* New York: Pocket Books.

Chapter 3

CREATING SCHOOLS OF INQUIRY

Well, how do *they* know?

—ELIZABETH BARELL INQUIRING ABOUT THE EAGLE NEBULA, 2001

Students across the country confront Design Challenge No. 1 posed by "Spaceday 2002 Adventure to Mars" (www.spaceday. com): "Invent a device that will make living or working on Mars easier." This challenge results from the discovery that "unknown contaminants have polluted the water supply on the International Space Station."

Students on a Worldtrek (www.gsn.org) expedition question students living on Cyprus: "What are your schools like? What kinds of music do you like? What religions do you practice? What do you do for fun?"

As part of the "Teachers Experiencing Antarctica" (http://tea.rice.edu) program, students ask Marietta Clecky, a biology and chemistry teacher from Uniondale, New York, about her project to gather information from soil samples around McMurdo Station about the effects of human habitation in the area. As a former visitor to McMurdo, I ask if she has visited the Taylor Dry Valleys ("No") and if the icebreakers had completed clearing their channel into Hut Point ("No").

Students in Ralph Mazzio's classroom in Yorktown, New York, bombard him with questions during his introduction to the "Hands On Universe" course (hou.lbl.gov): "What's at the center of a black hole? What came before the Big Bang?"

These questions from students interacting with resource-rich Web sites (see Appendix A) thrive on a culture of inquisitiveness within the classroom. What can we do to foster and enhance students' inquisitiveness in our classrooms?

Reflective Pause

How do you go about creating a culture within a classroom, and within a whole school, that fosters inquiry? What have you done to enable students to feel comfortable posing questions?

Classroom Culture

When we think of "culture," many probably think of folks who live in faraway places, like the Pygmies in the Ituri forest, the Inuit of the Arctic regions, or the nomads in the Sahara Desert or in Outer Mongolia. But "culture" is a word that applies to all of us. There is a culture of city living and a culture of people living in the desert. The word "culture" usually refers to those patterns of living created by specific groups of people. These patterns answer such questions as "How do we survive? In what kinds of dwellings do we live? What do we eat? How do we relate to our fellow human beings? What, if anything, do we worship?" and so on.

And there is a culture of schools, as Seymour Sarason pointed out in his seminal work, *The Culture of School and the Problem of Change* (1982). He spoke about those behavioral and systemic regularities or patterns of behavior that one must be aware of in order to bring about changes. Sarason brought a problem-solving approach to such patterns of behavior by focusing, say, on teacher questioning and asking, "What are its intended outcomes?" and "What are the alternatives we might consider to reach the same or different desired results?" This approach can immediately be threatening to those of us who are comfortable with how we conduct ourselves in schools right now.

If there are patterns of adult and student behavior in the school as a whole, then, obviously, there are patterns within our separate classrooms. There are ways of going about our business, and there are also feelings and attitudes that we communicate to students. These patterns and attitudes or dispositions add up the central or core values or priorities of the classroom culture.

In a classroom where curiosity is valued most highly and where explorations of new territories like the World Wide Web will be commonplace, there need to be some changes in our behavior. We will need to communicate our valuing of curiosity through

- Setting high expectations,
- Using teacher modeling,
- Sharing our stories,
- Developing positive scripts,
- Creating questions and responses,
- Offering assignments and assessments, and
- Raising the quality of peer interaction.

By considering these elements and reinforcing what we already do, we can create within any classroom a culture of curiosity such that students will be expected to pose meaningful questions and search for good answers wherever they may be found.

Setting Expectations for Curiosity—Letters from the Past

One way of evaluating a class that I have borrowed from Barbara M'Gonigle of Dumont High in Dumont, New Jersey, is to have students write letters to students who will take the class next year. This is one way of assessing how well you have set expectations for the class. Do students reflect the priorities you had for them?

One such letter to future students in my college literature class started off inauspiciously: "GET OUT BEFORE IT'S TOO LATE! DROP THIS COURSE NOW!"

Others commented on all the elements of the class that I hoped they would: keeping up with the reading, maintaining journal responses, participating in class, and, most important, being prepared to offer one's own ideas and support conclusions with evidence from the text or personal experience.

One letter* summed up my expectations for these literature classes rather well:

Dear Fall of '98 Students,

Welcome to Intro to Literature, starring your host, Dr. John Barell. Don't let his good looks and witty charm fool you. He is a professor. As well as THE QUESTION MAN. . . . There is a method behind his madness. It's called thinking. Yes, you are paying for this class and you have to think. Isn't college great! Stay in this class and learn, damn it! It is the hottest new thing on the market. All the cool kidz are doing it. You too can utilize the rest of your 94% of gray matter. . . .

And if you feel like your life is a mystery that you just can't solve, you can feel at home and live with the Brothers Karamazov [by reading the novel and making a film]. . . . You are going to have a chance to express your opinion; in fact, it is the most important thing you can possibly do besides ASKING QUESTIONS. . . .

In closing, this class is one of the few places in this world where you really don't get a chance to be wrong, although you may not always be right. A professor is here to teach his students. A good professor is the one who also learns from his students. Remember: "The test of a good teacher is not how many questions he can ask his pupils that they can answer readily, but how many questions he inspires them to ask him which he finds it hard to answer" (Alice Wellington Rollins).

When beginning the unit on Dostoevsky's *Crime and Punishment*, I would pose questions about the book's opening chapter:

- "In what part of the world does Raskolnikov live?"
- "Why does he live in a garret?"
- "What is this plan he has in mind?"
- "Who is his landlady?"
- "Why would he be nervous about meeting her?"

By means of these questions, we explore the similarities and differences among the questions, noting which ones require some

---

*Reprinted with permission from Jeff Romstedt.

thought, and for which ones there would be no single "right answer." Students are always good at differentiating between what we would call questions calling for recall of information and those requiring some inferential thought process. We then create a simple framework for our questions: questions answered within the text, versus questions you need to think about, read between the lines, and make inferences about.

The first question—"Where does Raskolnikov live?"—can be answered by reading the text. He lives in a very small room in St. Petersburg, Russia. The second question, however, takes more consideration. Raskolnikov speaks of this apartment variously as a "closet like room . . . a cupboard . . . a garret . . . [and later] a coffin" (Dostoevsky, 1880/1968, pp. 13–14). Almost immediately, students want to know about this room and why Raskolnikov continues to live there. Yes, he's poor, but there's more to it.

I follow up this discussion by considering another passage— Raskolnikov's feared encounter with the landlady to whom he owes money—and asking students to generate both kinds of questions: ones requiring reading the lines of the text, and ones requiring making inferences. Then we work on answers and spend some time later reflecting on how we went about responding to our own questions. How did we figure it out? This places emphasis on another key element in our classroom: reflection and metacognitive awareness.

Over and over I ask the students, "What are you curious about? What do you want to know more about? What isn't clear? What do you wonder about?" With Raskolnikov, students become curious about his plan, the "new step, an authentic new word" he wants to proclaim. What is it? Can he carry it through as he steps out into the ferocious heat, the "closeness, crowds, scaffolding, with lime and brick and dust everywhere and that special summer stench familiar to every Petersburger who cannot afford a summer cottage" (Dostoevsky, 1880/1968, p. 15)? What is Raskolnikov up to?

These stem questions, in effect, become initial journal entries for the students' daily and weekly reading. Then I read their journals at least once a week and select several of their questions for discussion, or ask them to select ones from their own journals for discussion in small groups.

"Establishing a Climate Conducive to Learning"

Another way to set high expectations is to ask students, "What do you think constitutes a good learning environment? A good classroom? Good student behavior? Good teacher behavior?" Barbara Bald, a 6th grade teacher in Alton, New Hampshire, regularly engages her students in creating the classroom environment. At the beginning of one year, during the very first week when everybody was fresh, she and her students identified three major goals: "To become Skillful thinkers, Self-directed learners and Collaborative workers" (Barell, 1995, p. 78). Here is an excellent example of a teacher and her students asking, "What kind of classroom do we want? How do we want to grow this year?" Barbara Bald helped her students set personal goals; thus they had more at stake in their own learning.

Barbara helped her students clarify the nature of "good thinking." They found out that it involves data collection, problem solving, decision making, and prediction. Since she was focusing on science, Barbara might have easily helped students realize that good science starts with inquiry.

Direct Statements

Many teachers start the year with a declaration of what's expected in the classroom. Sometimes we hand out an outline of readings and assignments; other times we give an oral presentation outlining the rules and expectations.

This is an opportunity to tell students, "I expect that you will become experts at asking good questions about what we are studying. Don't ever fear asking a question. Please don't sit there puzzling over some idea thinking everybody else understands it! They don't."

It doesn't really matter how we communicate to students the expectation that curiosity and wonder are valued elements in this classroom. What's important is that we communicate it.

One final example: Another of my colleagues, Cheryl Hopper, was a social studies teacher in Paramus, New Jersey. (Now Cheryl is assistant director of the Center of Pedagogy at Montclair State

University in New Jersey.) When she opened her classroom in September, she told her students, "You know we have so little time together that I want us to use all of it wisely and well. We will develop a learning community where we all learn from each other. And," she said with a meaningful pause, "there are no rules!" Students leaned back and grinned broadly. "No rules, only high expectations!" And her students quickly learned the difference. We can break rules and receive a punishment, but expectations you live up to or not. Expectations say, "We know you can work to your fullest potential here, and that's what we expect of everybody" (Cheryl Hopper, personal communication, February 1999).

Teacher Modeling

Just about everything teachers do in the classroom sends a message about what we think and feel. As my colleague Michael Kaufman likes to point out, "Everything speaks." Everything we do, say, or act out speaks volumes about our priorities, beliefs, and values. This is how we model desired behaviors (Michael Kaufman, personal communication, July 2000).

If we think curiosity is important, we should model it for students. This means sharing our past and current thinking and feelings with them at appropriate times. For example, I share with my students my Internet explorations:

> Yesterday I came upon a new Web site called northernlight.com and decided to see if it could help me with something I've wondered about. So I asked the site master a question, "Who discovered Antarctica?" I didn't expect much in the way of response, because sometimes I try out these search engines that advertise that they are geared up to answer your questions and the response you get is, "We are unable to process your question."

But on this Web site not only did I find several relevant citations, but I even found one that referred to a seventh-century adventurer from Roatonga who "sailed south to a place of bitter cold where white rock-like forms grew out of a frozen sea." This was many centuries before Captain Cook crossed the Antarctic Circle in 1773 and even more years before the Englishman Sir James

Clark Ross and the Americans Nathaniel Palmer and John Wilkes concluded (in the mid-1800s) that there was probably a continent of land surrounding the geographical South Pole. (See http://terraquest.com/va/history/ages/discovery.html.)

I tell students about my excitement at this discovery and about my earlier explorations of pictures taken with the Hubble Space Telescope—brilliantly colored photographs of the Orion and Eagle nebulae, of supernovae explosions, of quasars 12 billion light-years away and powered by supermassive black holes radiating "as much energy per second as a thousand or more galaxies" (http://chandra.harvard.edu/xray_sources/quasars.html). All these phenomena are intense fuel for our imaginations!

What I want to do is convey my enthusiasm for exploring the cyberspace territories available on the Internet. At other times, I share with students questions I am fascinated by: "I wonder—just how big is our universe? How do black holes generate so much energy? How could this whole universe of stars, galaxies, and clusters of galaxies ever have been condensed down to the size of an atom at the Big Bang?" I still wrestle with these questions today.

When we model our enthusiastic pursuit of knowledge, it conveys several messages to our students, among which is the one that says above all, "I'm still learning, exploring, and having fun."

Sharing Our Stories—Leah's Questions

Another way to model enthusiasm about the pursuit of knowledge is to share stories of what has occurred to us when we ask questions (see Appendix B for contact information). The best story I've come across related to questioning comes from a Greensboro, North Carolina, business education teacher, Leah Kraus:

> From a very young age I can remember listening to my father and trying to understand and interpret what he was saying. He was talking about what it means to be a Jew. I can remember one of the most important qualities is that Jews question, ask, and learn as much as we can. . . . My mother and father have always encouraged my brother and me to ask questions. During this Passover season I have missed our family Passover Seder when we would ask not just the Four Questions

["Why is this night different: Why do we only eat matzoh? Why do we eat bitter herbs? Why do we dip our food twice? And why do we recline/lean on a pillow?"], but together as a family we would ask and answer many more. . . .

As I grew older, my questions began to address philosophical issues. I needed to find answers to questions that were about ideals and interpretations. I needed to find my own answers to universal questions. My parents and the Jewish interpretations were no longer satisfying my curiosities. Eventually I found myself in conflict with my parents. Unfortunately, as I found my answers, problems and conflicts and even more questions arose.

Finally, reflecting on her life's choices during a workshop I led in Greensboro, North Carolina, Leah saw that her parents "were great educators. They made me want to know myself, and they taught me to question and not always accept the easy way. . . . I have some answers, but I have so many more questions" (Kraus, 1993, p. 13).

Leah's story is one of the most powerful stories I have ever encountered in more than three decades as an educator! There is amazing power in what she learned from her parents and their educational philosophy. Leah has grown up to be a person with a strong disposition to wonder, to inquire, not to accept the easy answer or the most common solution. What better education could there be than that?

L. Ray Ferguson—"Did You Ever Wonder?"

My own story speaks of my grandfather, a scientist who invented D-Zerta, the United States' first dietetic dessert. He was enthralled with natural phenomena and would always ask me questions like "Did you ever wonder why the sun appears to be so much larger when it's setting on the horizon?" I had never thought of it, but L. Ray Ferguson had, and he wanted this grandson to awaken to the mysteries of nature. And he wouldn't just tell me the answers. No! He would lead me, in a kind of Socratic questioning, to consider the nature of the atmosphere and what might happen to light as it travels through a denser atmosphere when the sun sets upon the horizon, rather than when light is shining directly overhead. Subsequently, scientists seem to have demonstrated that the sun (or the moon) isn't really larger on the horizon; it just appears that way (Blakeslee, 2000, p. F2).

Peter the Great

Finally, there are many marvelous stories from history of men and women who exemplify the characteristics we wish to engender. For our purposes, the person who comes to mind is Peter the Great, tsar of Russia, who lived from 1674 to 1726. What was amazing to me in reading Robert K. Massie's wonderful biography (1980) is that Peter was an amazingly curious boy growing up, always investigating how things like guns and battlements and sailboats worked. Peter traveled west to Europe, to England, to France, and to the Netherlands in search of new technologies like navigation, sailboat building, and medicine that could help revolutionize his country, which at the turn of the 18th century was largely made up of peasant farmers and had an economy that had little or no industry or commerce with the west. Peter's curiosity changed the face and the landscape of Russia for good, resulting in the construction of the fascinating, often damp and mysterious city of St. Petersburg out of swamplands on the Gulf of Finland. Of course, Peter was a tsar, and as such, he was an autocrat and at times completely ruthless in dealing with dissent or with anyone who questioned his authority. But there were positive aspects of his amazing inquisitiveness (Massie, 1980).

Sharing stories like these shows us that history is full of people like us who wonder, question, and act on our curiosities, for better or worse. There are other books, of course, full of stories of marvelously inquisitive people. A few include:

- Richard Wright's autobiography, *Black Boy* (1966)
- Annie Dillard's memoir, *An American Childhood* (1998)
- Physicist Richard Feynman's compilation of autobiographical stories, *"Surely You're Joking, Mr. Feynman!" Adventures of a Curious Character* (1985)
- Robert Coles's reflection on his medical education, *The Call of Stories: Teaching and the Moral Imagination* (1989)
- Anne Morrow Lindbergh's *Gift from the Sea* (1955)

- Thomas Merton's *Seven Storey Mountain* (1948)
- Edmund Morris's *Theodore Rex* (2001)
- Chris Van Allsburg's *The Polar Express* (1985)

And, of course, there's the story I recounted in Chapter 1 and that I've admired for so many years—that of Isidore I. Rabi and his mother: "Did you ask a good question, today?"

Developing Positive Scripts

Leah Kraus and L. Ray Ferguson are two examples of the kinds of models we have in our families or among our circles of friends. Stories can be the most powerful kinds of educators (Coles, 1989). From these stories we can develop another element in our culture of curiosity, self-talk. Self-talk is what we say to ourselves while encountering life's situations. Self-talk can be unique to a particular problematic experience, or it can be a pattern, a habit of mind, a way of looking at these kinds of situations.

Have you ever heard someone say, "Oh, I'm not good at math!" That comment is a learned pattern reflecting a disposition to avoid mathematical problems, perhaps arising from remarks from parents or early experiences in school.

What we want to cultivate are more positive scripts related to inquisitiveness. I can still hear my grandfather asking, "Johnny, did you ever wonder . . . ?" Ever wonder about nature, about this or that personal situation, about how people are and why they do what they do?

I can hear my father saying, "There's no such word as CAN'T!" and "Never, *ever* give up." These statements, made to me in childhood, have left indelible marks on my psyche. They have become compass points guiding my journey through life.

If we wish to foster curiosity, wonder, and skepticism, there are questions we can ask ourselves aloud, in front of our students often enough that they can become mental habits for ourselves and for our students:

- What I am curious about is . . .
- What I do not yet understand is . . .
- I really want to find out . . .

- The mysteries and puzzles that really intrigue me are . . .

- If I could be somebody else . . . or visit another time period, this is what I'd want to discover . . .

- I really wonder why . . .

- What intrigues me is . . .

These kinds of question/statement stems, if modeled often enough and pointed out to students, might just become part of how we all do business in the classroom.

Such stems are the kinds I have used for journal entries for students who are reading and responding to the novels in an Introduction to Literature class. We would start each evening's assignment with one stem and then proceed to others. For example, "I wonder why Raskolnikov [*Crime and Punishment*] keeps giving away money . . . ." or "What I don't understand is how Celie [*The Color Purple*] could continue to live in that house with the man who kept beating her . . . ." I want students to become more comfortable with doubt, ambiguity, and uncertainty.

Another script I want students to internalize comes from my mother. She taught me this not with fanfare or stern looks, but by gently asking a question.

One day I showed her the picture of the Eagle Nebula (the "poster child of the Hubble Space Telescope," as some have called this star-forming region of our Milky Way Galaxy). "Look, here's where stars are born," I said, pointing to the image on my computer from the Hubble Web site.

"How do you know?" she asked quietly. I was slightly stunned by her response.

"Well," I said, "it says so right here." I pointed to the text where it said that astronomers believed that here was a star nursery.

She looked at me with that indomitable inquisitiveness and asked, "Well, how do *they* know?" In an instant I perceived her father's scientific mind, that penetrating wondering about the natural world and about the claims made by those in authority. *"How do they know?"*

With the frustration that comes from an unexpected, subtle, yet very powerful challenge, I attempted to explain to her what I knew of astrophysics and the formation of stars in places like the Eagle and Orion nebulae. She wasn't convinced.

Her lesson came much later in life than others, but it has transformed how I interact with visitors at the Museum of Natural History in that I try to inculcate within them this same kind of skepticism for learned authorities.

In the same way, I want to know how students arrived at their judgments. Teachers need to let students know early on in the year that we expect not just one- or two-word answers—we want their thinking. Eventually, students will respond to a question and then say, "I know, you want to know my reasons, don't you?" Yes!

Model Questions

Our questioning of students is a powerful mode of communicating what we think is important. I distinctly remember walking by a math teacher's classroom at Paramus High School in Paramus, New Jersey, and hearing her ask her students, "Now, what questions do we need to ask of this situation?" She was modeling for her students that whenever we encounter complex situations in mathematics (as in life), we pose certain crucial questions: "What do we know? What are the givens? What do we need to find out?"

In all our subjects there are model questions that professionals ask. For example, at the American Museum of Natural History in New York City, there is a video introducing visitors to the Hall of Vertebrate Paleontology. The film, *The Evolution of Vertebrates*, is narrated by Meryl Streep, and in the film's introduction we see beautiful images of wild and strange animals racing and cavorting across the plains. Then she asks, "Where did animals come from? When did they first appear? How are they related to each other? These are questions paleontologists ask" (Dingus, 1996).

Now, I find this fascinating, because I want to know what questions we pose in response to confronting complex, puzzling situations in our different subject areas. For example, what questions will historians ask about the terrorist attacks on the World Trade Center on September 11, 2001?

For example, they might ask:

- "What were the probable *causes* and the short- and long-term *effects*?"
- "Who were the perpetrators and how did they conceive and implement their plans?"
- "How were these attacks *similar to and different from* other terrorist activities, for example, the attack on the *USS Cole*, on the U.S. embassies in Kenya and Tanzania in 1999, on Pearl Harbor in 1941? How are they similar to terrorist activities in 19th-century Russia and Europe?"
- "How effective have been our various responses?"
- "How do these attacks *fit within the context* of other worldwide cultural, economic, political, military trends or forces?"
- "What, if anything, have these acts of terror accomplished? What have we learned?"

In math, students might also dig deeper and reveal their knowledge of problem solving by asking, "How does this problem relate to others I've solved already? Can I break it down into parts? How can I represent this problem?" These are excellent problem-solving script-type questions to embed within our normal approaches to problem solving in math, science, and humanities (Barell, 1995).

We can also refer to the Three-Story Intellect model (see Chapter 4) to devise questions that will challenge students to think critically and creatively. Some have advocated posing questions from each level during a lesson. This is a worthwhile experience if you are not familiar with asking "higher-order questions."

Others, including myself, would suggest that questions educators pose ought to confront students with an authentic problematic situation that will stimulate their curiosity. Remember from Chapter 2 Ms. Idoni's tour of the lake and Jane Rowe's presentation of all the clues regarding the "discovery" of America. In these cases, questions came in the form of "What do you observe?" and "What are you curious about?"

Teacher Responses

In responding to students' ideas, solutions, and questions, we perhaps communicate more clearly than at any other time our interest in how they think and feel in our classroom. Irv Sigel has noted that our responses are probably more important than the questions we pose (personal communication, April 1995). What kinds of responses have you given students that you find are most inviting to more in-depth thought?

I once probed someone's thinking in class so deeply and severely that after the interchange one student commented, "If you hadn't become a teacher, you'd have made a good dentist." Everybody laughed, but eventually I got the point. Asking probing questions was a good thing, but if you pressed too hard, you could back someone into a corner and make him or her feel very uncomfortable. In this case, I was questioning a nun.

Elsewhere I outlined the kinds of teacher responses that invite thoughtfulness (Barell, 1995):

- *"Please tell us more. We're interested in your thoughts."* (Elaborating on your thinking)
- *"Can you explain or expand on your thinking?"* (Clarifying, explaining)
- *"How can you relate this to what Jennifer has said?"* (Seeking relationships)
- *"Can you relate this to other concepts/ideas we have been studying?"* (Seeking relationships)
- *"How did/does this make you feel?"* (Sharing feelings)

We might also communicate our interest in students' reasoning:

- *"How do you know? What led you to that conclusion?"* (Seeking reasons for conclusions)
- *"Can you tell us how you figured that out?"* (Encouraging students to develop metacognitive awareness of thought processes)

What is most important here are the tone and attitude with which we deliver these responses. What we need to communicate is the genuineness of our interest, our deep curiosity about how students think, how they figure things out, and how they feel about a specific situation.

Once while teaching in New York City, I thought I was being humorous in my response to a student when I said, "Oh, so you have a good idea!" He took it another way and from there on did not want to participate in class. I learned a valuable lesson that day.

Assignments

We communicate our expectations for students by the daily tasks we give them to work through. Recently, for example, I observed Rose Cohen, a kindergarten teacher at PS 238 in Brooklyn, New York, preparing her students for a visit from the American Museum of Natural History's Moveable Museum, a large Winnebago-like bus filled with dinosaur fossil replicas. There were bone and trace (eggs and footprints) fossils for children K–4 to touch and wonder about.

Rose Cohen prepared her students by having them dig through sand looking for bones. Students were very excited by their discoveries:

> When Rose asked the children, "What did you find?" they all answered, "Bones and fossils!" One little boy added that he found a little dinosaur. Another boy argued, "You couldn't have; they're not alive." The other boy answered excitedly, "Of course. I saw him—he was so tiny. He was in my hand. Then he jumped out the window." This caused quite a debate among the children. The conclusion they came to was that the dinosaur lived in his imagination. We all had a great time being archaeologists. (Cohen, 2001)

Rose Cohen set her students upon a challenge and provided them with an opportunity to debate each other about the nature of dinosaurs as preparation for their visit to the dinosaur museum parked in front of PS 238. She created a meaningful, significant, and highly engaging experience for her young students to inquire about.

The Quality of Peer Interaction

One of the most powerful ways of fostering inquisitiveness among our students is to teach them to respond actively to the comments of their classmates. Too often we see students responding only to the teacher. I also observe this pattern in most of my classes with adults. After a question has been posed, many adults will respond primarily or only to me. I then gesture that I want them to share their ideas with everybody in the group. This works best when they are seated around a table or in some form of circular configuration so they can see each others' facial expressions.

A script that we can teach our students is the following: "When I respond to a comment or a question, I will speak to the whole class, not just the teacher." A more specific script will be the following: "When I hear something from one of my classmates that I doubt, or am curious about, I will ask her or him a question."

For example, when Tim says that he believes that President Truman was the greatest president of the 20th century, students can and should follow up with, "That's interesting, Tim. What makes you say that?" or "How did you arrive at that conclusion?"

We want our *students* to pose all of the questions above, not just the teachers.

It is peer interaction within the classroom that can not only foster and develop more inquiry, but it can also generate high-quality problem solving and decision making and, therefore, deeper understanding of complex issues (Johnson & Johnson, 1979).

School Culture

The teacher in her classroom needs to be supported in her push toward more speculation, questioning, and inquisitiveness by all personnel and practices in the school culture.

We should take note of these ways in which the culture of inquisitiveness permeates the whole school.

School Vision/Philosophy

The school develops a philosophy that clearly identifies curiosity and critical thinking as two student behaviors and intended outcomes. It further spells out how classrooms are to become environments for challenge, curiosity, choice, and personal or shared control.

Principal's Expectations

The principal speaks specifically to students about the need to awaken to the wonders of classroom experiences and to ask "good questions" as part of their day. Chapter 12 on leadership provides an example of a principal's modeling these expectations.

Principal's Memos Home

In his letters to parents, the principal presents the school's philosophy. These might involve such words as "Ask, Search, Find, Think, and Share." They might contain stories of students asking good questions during class and encourage parents to follow Mrs. Rabi's example.

Parents' Involvement

Parents visit the schools to help students with reading, math, and searching the Internet for answers to their questions. Parents regularly check in with their children's teachers and their assignments on such free Web sites as eboard.com and Schoolnotes.com.

School Displays

Throughout the corridors of this school, there are examples of students' questions and culminating projects. For example, they might have posted some of their findings from the following:

- Expeditions to Africa and Antarctica (www.gsn.org/expeditions)
- Spaceday 2002 Adventure to Mars—problem solving in outer space (www.spaceday.com)
- Virtual tours of the summit of Mt. Everest ("Virtual Field Trips" from http://www.oops.bizland.com)
- Astronomy projects from "Hands On Universe" (http://hou.lbl.gov)

- Webquests created by teachers and students (http://www.manteno.k12.il.us)

For additional Web sites that we can use as resources, see Appendix A.

Faculty Meetings

The culture of inquisitiveness permeates the whole building. Teacher meetings occasionally include students who sit in to ask their own questions about solving school problems. Teachers, in fact, are the ones who often invoke the questioning sequences learned in class: "What's the problem and how can we solve it?" or "What do we think we know about this situation?" and "What do we need to find out?" At first, students' attendance at meetings was threatening to some faculty members. But eventually, as more adults bought into the philosophy of inquisitiveness, faculty members realized that they could learn from one another, including from their students.

School Insignia

On some of the T-shirts and pencils sold by the school store is this quotation: "Izzy, did you ask a good question today?"

As Seymour Sarason notes, it is the culture of the school that we need to change, not just the ways of doing business in one or two classrooms (Sarason, 1988). Only when all members of the school community accept the philosophy of awakening to the mysteries of the world do we see significant change occurring.

Conclusion

There are so many ways to create or establish a culture that reflects our abiding commitment to children's questions and curiosities. One day I brought in a leaf to my class and started asking the students a bunch of questions that led one of them to inform me that all the fall colors of leaves are in there to begin with, in the spring. What occurs in the fall is that the chlorophyll dissipates its green color, leaving the reds, yellows, and browns of the remaining pigments. This was an amazing discovery, and typical of what occurs when we invite wonder into our classrooms.

On another occasion, the catalyst for discussion was a prairie flower from the hills of Wisconsin. I started posing questions until one of the workshop participants said I'd better not show that to a police officer since the flower was on the state's endangered species list!

The point is that we need to become highly conscious of what our priorities are in the classroom. If we want students to become inquisitive like Izzy and Leah, then we need parents and teachers like theirs to match!

References

Barell, J. (1995). *Teaching for thoughtfulness: Classroom strategies to enhance intellectual development* (2nd ed.). New York: Longman.

Blakeslee, S. (2000, January 11). Mind's trick revealed in case of fat and skinny moon. *New York Times*, p. F2.

Cohen, R. (2001, December). *PS 283 [New York City] parents' newsletter.*

Coles, R. (1989). *The call of stories: Teaching and the moral imagination.* Boston: Houghton Mifflin.

Dillard, A. (1998). *An American childhood.* New York: HarperCollins.

Dingus, L. (screenwriter) (1996). *The evolution of vertebrates.* Watertown, MA: Chedd-Angier Production Company.

Dostoevsky, F. (1880/1968). *Crime and punishment* (S. Monas, Trans.). New York: Signet Classics.

Feynman, R. (1985). *"Surely you're joking, Mr. Feynman!" Adventures of a curious character.* New York: W. W. Norton.

Johnson, R., & Johnson, D. (1979). Conflict in the classroom. *Review of Educational Research, 49*(1), 59–70.

Kraus, L. (1993, May). Leah's story. *Network,* 5(9). Greensboro, NC: Reasoning & Writing Center. pp. 12–13.

Lindbergh, A. (1955). *Gift from the sea.* New York: Pantheon Books.

Massie, R. (1980). *Peter the Great: His life and world.* New York: Ballantine Books.

Merton, T. (1948). *The seven storey mountain.* New York: Harcourt, Brace and Company.

Morris, E. (2001). *Theodore rex.* New York: Random House.

Sarason, S. (1982). *The culture of school and the problem of change.* Boston: Allyn & Bacon.

Van Allsburg, C. (1985). *The polar express.* Boston: Houghton Mifflin Company.

Walker, A. (1996). *The color purple.* New York: Pocket Books.

Wright, R. (1966). *Black boy.* New York: Harper & Row.

Chapter 4

The Nature of Good Questions

It's good for your body to be curious.

—A New Hampshire 5th grader in Cathy Brophy's class

We noted earlier that Isidor I. Rabi's mother asked him, when he returned home from school every day, "So, Izzy, did you ask a good question today?" That difference, asking good questions, changed the direction of his life toward becoming a nuclear physicist, and a Nobel Prize-winning one at that.

Reflective Pause

Now, we need to ask ourselves what makes a question "good"? Are there special characteristics about such questions? If we answer this question, we will have a good idea about how to plan instruction and assess our growth in posing questions.

Before writing this chapter I asked several teachers how they and their students would answer this question. Some of their responses follow.

Cathy Brophy asked her 5th grade students at Hampton Academy Junior High in Hampton, New Hampshire, what makes a "good" question:

- "A good question makes you feel good because you feel smarter. An example is 'What's a yucca plant's enemy?'"
- "If you want a simple answer, a yes or no question is a good question. If you want more than a yes or no, you need to ask a more complex question like: 'Would you classify *A Wrinkle in Time* as a science fiction book or a fantasy?' Since no one knows the real answer, it's a good question. A good question makes you think!"
- "It's good for your body to be curious and to wonder about things. [For example,] 'Why can't people fly?'"
- "I think good questions are questions that are important— questions that make sense—questions that are fun to talk about—questions that you need to know. [For example,] 'What would happen if all the trees died and there was no oxygen?' 'What is it like in the future?' Who on earth wants to talk about boring things?"

What I like about these definitions is that these 5th graders give us marvelous examples of good questions. As one of them said, "A good question makes you think!" Yes!

They also bring in matters that we do not often think of. For example, one student said, "It's good for your *body* [my emphasis] to be curious." I really wonder what this young person means by that! Perhaps that curiosity permeates our whole bodies, not just our minds? Maybe she is referring to the kind of behavior we witnessed with Nobel Prize-winning physicist Richard Feynman:

> Those who watched Feynman in moments of intense concentration came away with a strong, even disturbing sense of the physicality of the process, as though his brain did not stop with the gray matter but extended through every muscle in his body. A Cornell dormitory neighbor opened Feynman's door to find him rolling about on the floor beside his bed as he worked on a problem. (Gleick, 1992, p. 244)

And then there's the student who mentions that good questions affect how we feel! Here is a domain of education so vitally important, but too seldom dealt with—our feelings about intellectual operations.

Barbara M'Gonigle of Dumont High School in Dumont, New Jersey, shared with me some practical applications of a "good question" from her classroom observations in mathematics: "A good question is one that does not have an immediate answer, because it requires some thinking, feeling and application to previous knowledge . . .[it] extends and clarifies a concept . . . [and] leads to another good question . . ." (personal communication, April 2001).

M'Gonigle also added, "A good question develops out of genuine curiosity or confusion." You can see this genuineness in Cathy Brophy's students' queries.

And this is a good place to begin. Whenever we want to find out why or how something happened, or what the name of a certain tree is, or what would happen if a particular policy were instituted, then that's a good question. We genuinely want to know. What Nelson Goodman said about the reasons why we create symbols and representations in art is true here: "The drive is curiosity and the aim enlightenment" (1980, p. 317).

So here's our first criterion: A good question reflects a genuine desire to find out, a deep feeling for wanting to know more than we already do. This desire is at the root of inquisitiveness. And heaven help the teacher who does not warmly accept a child's eager inquisitiveness!

Questions That Help Us Think

Mary Wallace, of Thomas Jefferson Middle School in Fair Lawn, New Jersey, observed that a "good question opens doors. It demands more than a yes or no answer." This is a very interesting definition—opening doors to new ideas, novel ways of looking at a situation. Mary's definition suggests that a good question is one that is transcendent, one that helps us move beyond the immediate data or experience (personal communication, April 2001).

How can we plan for Mary's kinds of questions? How can we help students develop an ability to pose such questions? One way is to examine the kinds of questions that are designed to help us make experiences more meaningful than just reciting what occurred or describing what we have in front of us.

For years educators have used a framework of intellectual operations known as Bloom's Taxonomy. Benjamin Bloom, one of education's most influential thinkers, gathered a group of teachers together many years ago to determine the nature of intellectual operations that students engaged in while responding to teachers' questions. Figure 4.1 is the framework they developed. As used by most educators, this outline suggests levels of difficulty that become progressively more challenging as you move from Knowledge and Comprehension toward Synthesis and Evaluation. The final task, evaluating a piece of work, is supposedly the most complex and subsumes all the preceding operations within it.

Bloom never intended this list to become a rigid set of intentions for teachers to use in the classroom. But that's what it became over the years. Teachers were asked to teach to "higher-level thinking skills," and often that meant working your way up the ladder of Bloom's Taxonomy. Proceeding "up" Bloom's Taxonomy is useful at times; however, we can be more flexible. We might, for example, start a unit by asking students to solve the problem of poor voter participation in state and local elections

Figure 4.1
Bloom's Taxonomy of Educational Objectives

Knowledge (*Recall, Description . . .*)

Comprehension (*Understanding content . . .*)

Application (*Using knowledge in novel contexts . . .*)

Analysis (*Breaking complex issues into parts . . .*)

Synthesis (*Combining elements into novel designs . . .*)

Evaluation (*Using criteria to make judgments . . .*)

Source: Bloom, B. (Ed.) (1956). *Taxonomy of educational objectives: Handbook I, cognitive domain.* New York: David McKay.

or by challenging them to figure out where bacteria collect within a school building. These challenges require acquiring, analyzing, and then synthesizing knowledge in order to arrive at recommendations and solutions.

Bloom's Taxonomy, however, is a valuable guide for our purposes. We can see that questions that relate to different mental operations might be classified as "good," depending upon the context and purpose.

Reflective Pause

Generate a set of questions for a lesson you are teaching, using Bloom's framework. See if you can commence with questions that challenge students to think about complex phenomena like a problem in physical sciences, literature, or social studies. Then students will have to research, gather information, and analyze it to arrive at conclusions.

Another framework is, I think, derived from Bloom's, and I have worked more extensively with this one, especially in helping new and experienced teachers challenge their students to think critically, productively, and reflectively. Known as the Three-Story Intellect, it was developed by SkyLight Professional Development and was later adapted by Art Costa (Figure 4.2).

You can see how the three levels of the Three-Story Intellect relate to Bloom's levels of intellectual operations. What makes the Three-Story Intellect concept even better is that it serves as an information-processing model of how the mind works. At Level I we observe, describe, and gather information through all of our senses. This is called the Gathering or Input Phase. At Level II—the Processing Phase—we "process" this data in order to make it meaningful—to make sense out of it—by analyzing, comparing, contrasting, and explaining. At Level III—the Applying Phase—we "apply" what we have learned to authentic situations. We predict, judge, imagine, and evaluate.

These three levels, therefore, suggest a view into how we think—we gather information, process it for meaning, and then

Figure 4.2
Three-Story Intellect

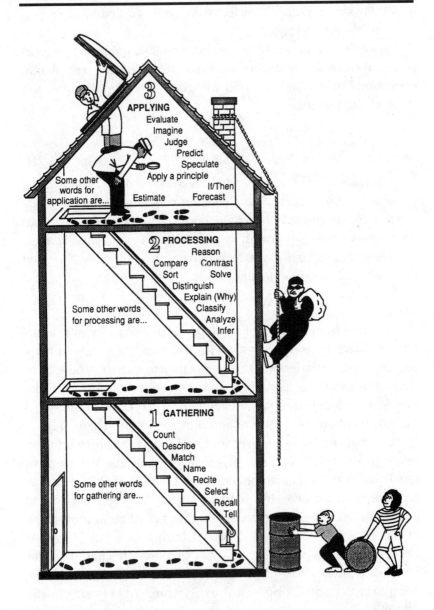

use it. At which levels do you spend most of your time in class? Why? What might you do to alter this situation?

Reflective Pause

Generate a set of questions for a lesson (or, better yet, a unit) you are teaching, using the Three-Story Intellect. See if you can commence with questions that challenge students to think about a problematic situation in your subject. Then students will have to research, gather information, and analyze it to arrive at conclusions.

What makes the Three-Story Intellect even more powerful for me is that it so neatly relates to another framework first proposed by David Perkins (1992). He has concluded that there are three main goals of education:

1. To acquire knowledge
2. To understand knowledge
3. Then to use or apply knowledge

These three goals align nicely with our three stories of the intellect: We gather information, process it in order to comprehend or understand it, and then find ways to make it practical by applying it in new and different contexts.

Another caveat with the Perkins framework—I don't think Perkins would disagree with the proposition that his three goals do not represent an ironclad progression from acquiring, through understanding, to applying knowledge. One of the certain ways of attaining deep understanding is by taking what we think we know and using it to solve a real problem or resolve an important issue. In other words, we comprehend concepts and ideas better after we have used them in a specific context. For example, we know more about the concept of democracy by seeing how it developed historically in our country and by applying this knowledge to emerging nations around the world today.

So what does all of this mean for what makes a question "good"?

We can teach each of these frameworks (Bloom, Three-Story Intellect, and Perkins) to our students so they can identify the kinds of questions they are posing. Teachers I have worked with have posted them around their room, and my colleague Ann Marie DiLorenzo, a geneticist at Montclair State University, posted the Three-Story Intellect on the lab refrigerator in her classroom in order to remind her to vary the intellectual demands of her questions. We can also use them to help us and our students assess progress toward asking better questions (Figure 4.3). If the only questions we currently pose require only a one- or two-word answer, then we can become better at asking questions that call for inference and prediction, for example.

We can see from Figure 4.3 how wide and varied are the kinds of questions we can encourage students to pose. We should make one important comment here about both taxonomies: We do not need to teach using a progression from Knowledge to Evaluation questions in Bloom's list, nor a progression from gathering to applying with the Three-Story Intellect framework. One of the best ways to capture students' imaginations and get them fired up about a topic is to begin with a problematic situation that raises lots of questions: For example, there's a pond behind the school. What do you observe in and around the pond? What do you think about this and what other kinds of questions do you have? Commencing with a problem means that we then must gather lots of information in order to find some answers. Ralph Tyler (1949), a noted curriculum theorist of the 20th century, observed that one of the best ways to acquire and retain knowledge is by solving a problem. I think he would agree that we don't need to master all the facts about pond water prior to beginning to wonder why such a body of water might be polluted.

Special Reflection Questions

Have you ever been in this situation: You get in your car, start driving toward a particular destination, and then suddenly realize you don't know where you're going? You don't know the territory well enough, because you failed to get out a map or chart to plot your course before starting out. Consequently, you spend

Figure 4.3
Examples of Using the Three-Story Intellect Method

Here are some questions using the Three-Story Intellect that help us "open doors."

Gathering Questions
- When did Thomas Jefferson become President?
- Where is Versailles?
- Who invented the microchip?
- What is a supernova explosion?
- How did we connect the East and West Coasts by rail?

Processing Questions
- Why do you think so many earthquakes occur in California and Japan?
- How were the presidencies of Theodore and Franklin Roosevelt similar and different? What conclusions would you draw from this comparison? (Too often we compare and contrast without doing the next logical thing: drawing reasonable conclusions.)
- How would you differentiate between dark matter and dark energy in the universe?
- Why have some countries in Africa, the Middle East, the Balkans, and Asia had such a difficult time gaining and maintaining political stability?
- If "all men are created equal," then why have women in this country struggled to break through the "glass ceiling"?
- How do we know that there was a "Big Bang" some 13 or 14 billion years ago? What's the evidence?
- What assumptions are you making when you say "Education in this country is in trouble?" or that "Children in this country are not achieving at the levels of those in other countries?"
- How can we explain why some people in any society engage in terrorism?

Application Questions
- What would the world be like without war?
- What would be the result if all history books had been written by women?
- What if everybody voted using a computer?
- If we continue to pump carbon dioxide into the atmosphere at current rates, then what are the logical consequences?
- How would you solve the problem of racial, ethnic, and gender inequality in this country? (*Note:* I put problem solving here in the application phase. It involves both processing and applying information.)
- How do Newton's three laws of motion apply to the planets, to an astronaut during a space walk, and to the same astronaut if her tether unfortunately snaps while she is walking in space?
- What advice would Macbeth, Holden Caulfield, Ivan Karamazov, Richard Wright, or William Wordsworth give the President of the United States, each other, or you? And why?

a lot of time asking for directions, and you arrive late, perhaps missing a very important function. I have and it's very frustrating. As a matter of fact, this has been a recurring dream—not quite a nightmare, but something that comes close—that involves failing to get to my class on time, getting all tangled up in mindless meanderings because I hadn't prepared well. It's a teacher's nightmare—in the dream I arrive and most of the class has left.

A triad of questions, if used judiciously, might help prevent such time wasting. These questions call for us to think about where we want to go ahead of time; then as we are under way, to closely watch our progress; and finally, upon arrival, urge us to take a moment to reflect: How well did I do in achieving my goal? Could I have done it differently, or better?

We should be asking ourselves three powerful questions as we work and go about our daily lives:

1. *Planning:* What's the problem and how will I go about solving it?
2. *Monitoring:* How well am I doing in working toward my goal?
3. *Evaluating:* How well did I do? What would I do differently next time? Why?

Similar metacognitive process questions include:

- "How did you figure that out?"
- "What made you think of that question/answer?"
- "Can you describe your thinking processes as you worked through this problem?"

These reflective questions give us awareness of our thought processes and, eventually, we hope, some control over how we think through complex issues (Swartz & Perkins, 1989). We are good at some things and not at others. If we display examples of students' thinking around the classroom periodically as they reflect on how they solved problems, all of us can learn a wider variety of ways of thinking through problems. We can all learn from each other.

Personal Questions

Have you ever been in a conversation with another person, and then, afterward, you suddenly realize, "She didn't ask anything about what I was doing!" or "He never paid attention to my feelings."

Too often have I come away from such encounters with family and others realizing that I've been the one to ask all the questions about what the other person has been doing with his or her life. I revealed nothing of my recent history.

It seems to me that personal questions are good ones, the kinds of questions that help create lasting relationships among people. Without these kinds of felt concerns there would be no friendships. Examples of such questions might be:

- "How are you doing?"
- "What have you been doing? What's going on in your life?"
- "What is it you want to do? What are you striving for?"

Questions like these are the ones we ask friends, people with whom we have good, strong, and lasting relationships. We ask these questions of loved ones. Or if we do not, we suffer the consequences!

Too often in listening in on conversations it seems to me that the talk is really one way. One person speaks about him- or herself and the other listens. Or, one person tells a story and another person tells a different story. Sometimes it seems to me that in adult conversations we have a mirror of what occurs in classrooms: One person speaks and the other responds with what is on her mind and there is no connection. It's like the Paul Simon song about a "dangling conversation."

Too often there is no real dialogue where people actually listen and respond to each other. The noted theologian Martin Buber observed, "All real living is meeting . . ." (Friedman, 1955, p. 58). This seems to me to sum up the nature of the human condition. All human endeavors involve making, sustaining, and nurturing good relationships, at home, in school, at work, and at play. Without thriving, trusting, and meaningful relationships, we are like isolated electrons bouncing around all alone in some cosmic plasma. We want to become attached, as Erich Fromm noticed, to larger organizations or groups in order to feel powerful and significant (1941).

These questions are just as appropriate in schools, and perhaps more so because we need to foster communities where people can work with and trust each other.

Without attentive listening and active responding to the person's feelings as well as his thoughts, such a goal is not possible. Too many of our children come to feel like that isolated electron, out in the void all by themselves. Sharing our personal concerns with our children brings them back into the family.

The Content of Our Questions—
The Greatest Ideas of All Time

Years ago, in the 1980s, when the critical thinking movement was blossoming, some schools became very interested in moving away from what they perceived to be the low levels of intellectual challenge presented in most classrooms. They began to work with the kinds of questions found at the higher levels of Bloom's Taxonomy and the Three-Story Intellect. They moved away from perceiving teachers as disseminators of information toward seeing students as young people capable of making important decisions, solving problems, and reflecting on their experiences.

During this time period some people argued that teaching people to think critically was something you couldn't do in isolation from subject matter. The argument was, "You're always thinking about *something!*" Subsequently, some have argued that thinking is contextual, meaning that critical thinking is different depending on the subject matter about which we are thinking.

More recently, observers have noted that "a fluency with the Great Books is no longer a prerequisite for professional or social success. Critical thinking skills arguably are" (Eakin, 2001, p. 41). In other words, you don't need to read Shakespeare, Milton, or Aristotle in order to learn to think. Nor, perhaps, to become literate.

Reflective Pause

Which side of this argument are you on and why?

It seems to me that there is something to these older arguments. We are always thinking about something and whether or not you believe reading Shakespeare is necessary, you would probably accept the notion that we can and do need to think about some very important ideas. Each of our subjects consists of fundamental concepts, ideas, and principles as well as ways of knowing.

Some of us think that Shakespeare did a marvelous job of opening our own personal doors to these wonderful ideas through the most amazing characters in literature. What better reason for reading these classics—to paraphrase Jacob Bronowski (1971)—than to expand our own inner worlds of experience by listening to Lady Macbeth and empathizing with Hamlet.

For example, here are what I would consider some good questions based on key concepts and ideas:

- "Exactly how much of nature can we trash and burn and get away with it?"—Natalie Angier, science writer, *The New York Times*

- "Is there enough information in the observable universe to identify the fundamental laws of Nature beyond all reasonable doubt?"—John D. Barrow, cosmologist

- "How do we make long-term thinking automatic and common instead of difficult and rare?"—Stewart Brand, founder of *The Whole Earth Catalog*

- "To what extent can we achieve a more just society through the use of better economic indicators, and to what extent is our choice of economic indicators just a reification of the wishes of those who are already economically powerful?"— Joan Baez, singer

These questions come from a wonderful Web site (www.edge. org) created by literary agent John Brockman (1997). Brockman "wants to arrive at the edge of the world's knowledge" by assembling "the most complex and sophisticated minds, put them in a room together and have them ask each other the questions they are asking themselves." Here are a few others from the same Web site:

- "What goes on inside the head of a baby?"—Freeman Dyson, physicist
- "Why is music such a pleasure?"—Nicholas Humphrey, psychologist
- "What do collapses of past societies teach us about our own future?"—Jared Diamond, biologist
- "Why are religions still vital?"—Elaine Pagels, professor of religion
- "Why are most individuals and all human societies grossly underachieving their potentials?"—Duncan Steel, author

Now, these sorts of questions get me to focus on subjects I'd never thought about. For example, consider Freeman Dyson's question, "What goes on inside the head of a baby?" Most of us have had experiences with babies in our families, and we read about scientists who study children's growing up, people like Piaget and others who have wondered about how children think. What's amazing about Dyson's question is, in part, that he's a renowned physicist who's done work on cosmology and the structure of the universe. Why is he wondering about life at its earliest stages? I don't know.

These questions provide us with a start on the journey to identify the nature of important inquiries by the subject they focus upon. Very often these are subjects we have neglected. So in looking for processes with respect to babies or explanations about religion's vitality, we are examining issues and subjects that perhaps we've taken for granted. That's one thing a good question does: It shines the light of inquiry on an area previously neglected.

Brockman's questions focus on these important areas:

- The nature of the universe—past, present, and future
- A just and equitable society for all citizens
- Life at its earliest and succeeding stages
- The nature of mind—how we do and do not think
- The history of societies—failed and successful
- Our human potential—physical, intellectual, spiritual, and emotional—and how we live up to it
- The nature and future of the arts

This is just a bare bones beginning to identify crucial subjects worth thinking about.

What are some other areas of human life and endeavor that you think are important to inquire about? As you and your students begin focusing more on your own questions, you might underline the subject of the questions to ensure that you are keeping track of what these questions are about.

The Big Ideas in Your Subject Areas

What are the major ideas worth thinking about in your subject areas? For example, because I have been an English teacher for so many years, I am used to challenging students to think about these concepts:

- The meaning and struggle for identity, sanctity, freedom, family, home
- The complexity and importance of human motivations, fears, hopes, dreams, and feelings
- The nature of heroism
- The effects of environment on human action
- The way we solve problems
- The nature of character—how it is formed and how it develops
- The nature of conflict—among people, between humans and nature, and how it gets resolved
- The nature of comedy and tragedy
- The elements of the writer's craft: themes, symbols, and figurative uses of language

What would you add to this list? What are the major concepts and ideas in your subject areas worth thinking about? The following lists some major ideas in various subject areas that teachers can use to challenge students to think about:

- **History and Social Studies**—The development, change, and decay of societies and political and economic systems; the struggle for freedom, self-determination, and equal rights; the acquisition, uses, and abuses of power; the role of religion in human affairs; the shaping of societies by their leaders; the search for patterns of behavior over time; search for causation in human affairs; relationships among political systems and economics, geography, and climate; the role of culture in shaping human experiences.

- **Mathematics**—Equalities; limits; patterns; geometry; symmetry; congruency; multidimensional space; volume; conic sections; the problem-solving processes of being able to logically analyze complex situations.

- **Life Sciences**—The nature of living things; ecosystems, the nature of organisms within their habitats; form and function in various species of animals; evolution and biodiversity; the cell, DNA, the human genome. As in all the sciences, our list should include being able to pose questions, establish hypotheses, then test them and derive logical results.

- **Physical Sciences**—Cause-and-effect relationships; pressure, force, and motion; heat, convection; magnetism, electrodynamics.

- **Earth Sciences**—Formation of the solar system; stars and galaxies; Earth and its history; Earth systems; plate tectonics and continent formation, vulcanism; the atmosphere and its effects on humans; carbon, rock, and water cycles.

- **The Arts**—Elements of composition: line, texture, light, balance, color, depth, rhythm, choreography, form, and perspective; the creation of symbols and representations of "reality"; the creative process of all art, including music, creative writing, dance, and more.

- **Foreign Languages**—Structure and syntax of language; culture and its influence on languages; alphabets; transliteration of ideographs; the nature of dialects.
- **Technology**—New technologies; how they affect our lives; problem solving in everyday life.
- **Physical Education**—Structure and function of the human body and its systems; physical fitness; wellness; games— their rules and structures—and the nature of play.

I have purposefully suggested a few concepts that come to mind without making an attempt to probe into each of your subject areas.

I hope it is evident that we not only speak here of big ideas and concepts but also of the intellectual processes that people in these disciplines use to acquire new knowledge—special kinds of problem solving and the creation of meaning. Too often we think only of the ideas and not the skills needed to work with those ideas. What's important in curriculum development is that "content" includes processes as well as knowledge about facts and ideas.

Reflective Pause

What concepts and intellectual processes especially important to your subject would you find it necessary for any student to understand fully? Or, as I have framed it for university professors on occasion, "If you had only one week to teach your course, what concepts, ideas, or ways of knowing would be absolutely essential for understanding your discipline?" The purpose of this question is to plumb the subject to its essential elements—its core concepts.

In all dimensions of human inquiry we have big and important concepts and ideas, and some of our "good questions" ought to focus on these. Some would then call these "essential questions." Others, like me, might refer to them as those questions that are "robust" because they transfer across subject areas; they are common across varied kinds of experiences (Barell,

1995). Robust questions penetrate the depths of the subject matter for the central, most significant concepts, the ones without which we cannot comprehend what the subject is all about. Robust questions are complex and multifaceted, yet accessible to students' inquiries. For example, "What caused the Second World War?" is a complex question, but a more fundamental, robust question would be: "What causes human conflict, and how successful have we been in avoiding conflict among humans?"

In each of these areas of human experience we have ways of knowing, methods of inquiry that lead to the acquisition of new knowledge. One good question to ask at this point is, "How does inquiry proceed in each of these subjects?" We might also ask, "How do we acquire new knowledge in the sciences and how is this different from what we do in the humanities?"

What Questions Do Professionals Ask?

In Chapter 3 I presented a set of three questions that drive the inquiries of paleontologists, those who study the origins of life on the planet, usually through examining fossil remains:

- "Where did animals come from?"
- "When did the first animals appear?"
- "How are they related to each other?"

We can see how fundamental these questions are, especially the last one. We all want to know how different species are related. The study of such relationships is called *systematics*. Without studying in precise detail how one specimen differs from another one, we would not know if they are from the same species or family. We need such knowledge to determine which animals may be becoming extinct and why; which plants resemble those we use for certain medicinal purposes; and how some species have been distributed all over the globe, today and more than 200 million years ago, when the continents were joined in the supercontinent known as Pangaea (which means "all lands").

We ought to know which kinds of questions other professionals ask as they seek to understand complex phenomena. What questions do they ask to help them analyze a situation and begin to draw tentative conclusions?

For example, when we view a work of art, we wonder about the following questions:

- "What is the work about? What are the major ideas and feelings expressed?"
- "What elements within it contribute to this idea? To these feelings?"
- "How has the artist used color, composition, line, point of view, perspective, and texture to create these impressions?"
- "In what ways has the artist broken rules or made a new statement?"
- "How is this work like others of the same artist (or works by different artists)? What are the developmental differences and how do we account for them?"
- "How does the work of art affect my perception of the major idea? Of other similar works of art? Of nature?"
- "How does the work of art affect me personally?"

We might ask these questions in an attempt to understand the work of art.

What questions does a geologist ask when he confronts a new rock formation? Ed Mathez is the curator of the Hall of Planet Earth at the American Museum of Natural History. He provides a wonderful example of the kinds of questions that would guide his inquiry into a new, strange set of rock outcroppings:

> Start by finding what you think to be bedrock, which is not always obvious, I should add, and then try to figure out what it is. Is it layered, does it look like it could have once been a sediment? Can you see individual grains? Are they individual minerals or grains of other rock? How does the rock break; how does it weather? If layered, are the layers flat, are they tilted? Take a sample. . . . Build up a series of observations and use them to develop an idea about what the rock is and how it formed. Afterward, compare to what you learn from a geologic map. (Mathez, 2000)

Ed Mathez presented these initial (or, as one geologist called them, "tool") questions to help a novice figure out the geology of her neighborhood. I find these beginning questions to be models for those of us just beginning to think as a geologist does. That's one thing we want to learn in any encounter with a professional: How does she think through complex, strange phenomena in her subject? What are her ways of inquiring?

How can we use Ed Mathez's model questions for our own purposes? What are the essential questions in your own subject area, ones you want students to be able to ask so that they can understand complex problematic situations?

Let me share a short diversion to a thinker I have long admired, the writer James Joyce. In his *A Portrait of the Artist as a Young Man* (1976), Joyce's hero, Stephen Dedalus, is reflecting with his chums about the nature of beauty. He has derived his thinking from St. Thomas Aquinas, the 13th-century theologian. "Three things are needed for beauty, wholeness, harmony and radiance" (p. 212). Dedalus interprets these three characteristics as follows:

> Determining how this object (for example) is different from what surrounds it. Separate the object/situation from its environment. What makes it whole? "*Integritas.*"
>
> Seeking out all the important elements and figuring out their relationships—"You apprehend it as complex, multiple, divisible, separable, made up of its parts, the result of its parts and their sum, harmonious. That is *consonantia.*"
>
> And, finally, the element that has always been most intriguing to me—"*Quidditas*, the *whatness* of a thing." (p. 213)

What makes the object unique?

These three elements help us frame a set of questions not only about the work of art, but also about all human and natural situations.

Reflective Pause

In a particular subject area, what do you want students to ask themselves and each other when they confront a new, complex, and difficult situation or problem? What questions do you want your students to pose?

In Chapter 6 there is a framework for analyzing any kind of complex, problematic situation. Before jumping ahead, try using your own framework on situations that arise in your own life—changing careers, meeting, and communicating with people—and in your areas of expertise.

"That Isn't Fair!"—Questions of Equity

When kids argue with adults about the fairness of having to be home by a certain time; when they compare gifts and find that a sibling or friend has received something bigger or better; and when, perhaps more seriously, we argue about our treatment in the workforce, we are raising questions of equity. How we are treated by others and how we treat our fellow human beings raise the most fundamental questions about life in society. Such questions go to the heart of what it means to live in a democracy. Millions of people today live within oppressive societies, treated not as human beings with rights to liberty and the pursuit of happiness, but as subjects, objects, and cattle.

These questions focus our minds and hearts on what we think of as right and wrong, about human values and the nature of the just society. Joan Baez, a singer known for sharing her perception of just causes through her music, raises perhaps one of the ultimate questions when she asks about the "just society." Such questions have been part of the human discussion since the ancient Greeks. Plato's *Republic* is a series of question-and-answer sessions between Socrates and Glaucon about the nature of the good in society, about who should govern and how, to ensure the full development of every human being.

When children say, "That isn't fair!" in response to how they are treated, when we ask why some men are paid more than some women for doing the same work, we are asking about equity and fairness. When we wonder why minority children do not perform as well on standardized tests as do children who are among the majority, we are asking fundamental questions about equal access to knowledge and the fruits of civilization.

And when we argue about civil rights and the access to the benefits of citizenship of persons of various ethnic, religious, and cultural backgrounds or sexual orientations, we are confronting the nature of what it means to live in a just society. No longer is it appropriate, we believe, for one person or persons to rule over others without their consent. We believe in government by the consent of the governed.

These questions of equity, justice, and the rights of all men, women, and children are, perhaps, the ultimate questions of political philosophy, ones we should be asking in our personal lives as well as in our schools.

How do we encourage our children to pose these kinds of questions, as well as the others mentioned here? By practicing one of the major strategies mentioned in Chapter 3—modeling. If we want our children to raise significant questions when they see social injustice in their classroom, school, home, or community, we must model these kinds of concerns for them, and with some depth of feeling or passion.

All we have to do is present students with a situation like the following to help them generate their own questions of equity and fairness: "Some children in this country and others grow up without adequate access to food, education, health care, and supportive, loving parents. Here are some of the details . . . . What do you think about this situation? What questions does it raise in your minds? What actions might we take?"

Social justice occurs when all of us are concerned.

Conclusion

"Good questions" are important because we have a strong desire to know. They are also good because they engage our minds in complex processes of analysis—posing problems and resolving them, uncovering unstated assumptions, and searching for evidence that will lead us to logical, reasonable conclusions. As Mary Wallace said, good questions help us "open doors" to new ways of thinking and feeling. They transcend our immediate sensations.

We have examined some of the questions posed by people who are on the frontiers of knowledge in their own fields. We have seen in their questions that there are concepts and ideas worth inquiring about, topics worth investigating now and in the future. We have begun to think about the kinds of analytic questions we want our students to become comfortable with so they can deal, independently and with confidence, with the complexities of human life.

Finally, we have noted the concerns we have about friendships, fairness, justice, and equity in our society. Until every person enjoys the rewards of full social partnership, we cannot refrain from posing hard questions about how we treat different people differently.

Let me conclude with an observation of one of Cathy Brophy's students: "A good question is if you're really curious. I like the kinds of questions that have a really good answer. An example is, 'Why is it good to ask 'Why?'"

References

Barell, J. (1995). *Teaching for thoughtfulness: Classroom strategies to enhance intellectual development.* (2nd ed.). New York: Longman.

Bloom, B. (Ed.) (1956). *Taxonomy of educational objectives: Handbook I, cognitive domain.* New York: David McKay.

Brockman, J. (1997 December). The World Question Center. www.edge.org. Accessed May 2002.

Bronowski, J. (1971). Knowledge of the self. In *The identity of man* (pp. 58–85). New York: American Museum Science Books.

Eakin, E. (2001, April 8). More ado (yawn) about great books. *New York Times, Education Life*, p. 41.

Friedman, M. (1955). *Martin Buber: The life of dialogue.* New York: HarperTorchbooks.

Fromm, E. (1941). *Escape from freedom.* New York: Avon Books.

Gleick, J. (1992). *Genius—the life and science of Richard Feynman.* New York: Pantheon Books.

Goodman, N. (1980). Art and inquiry. In M. Philipson & P. Gudel (Eds.), *Aesthetics today* (pp. 307–321). New York: New American Library.

Joyce, J. (1976). *A portrait of the artist as a young man.* New York: The Viking Press.

Mathez, E. (2000, October). Earth: Inside and out [Online course]. New York: American Museum of Natural History. Available: Classroom Connect and its Connected University courses at www.classroom.com.

Perkins, D. N. (1992). *Smart schools: From training memories to educating minds*. New York: Free Press.

Swartz, R., & Perkins, D. N. (1989). *Teaching thinking—Issues and approaches*. Pacific Grove, CA: Midwest Publications.

Tyler, R. (1949). *Basic principles of curriculum and instruction*. Chicago: University of Chicago Press.

Chapter 5

WRITING OUR CURIOSITIES

When you write, you lay out a line of words. The line of words is a miner's pick, a wood-carver's gouge, a surgeon's probe. You wield it, and it digs a path you follow. Soon you find yourself deep in new territory. Is it a dead end, or have you located the real subject? You will know tomorrow, or this time next year.

—ANNE DILLARD ON THE ART OF WRITING (1989, P. 3)

The writer's art and craft, as renowned author Anne Dillard describes it, is an adventure that we begin without knowing if we will strike gold or go bust. Writing is an expedition into the unknown that we embark on to develop our thoughts and feelings. We undertake such explorations in the hope of discovering new territories, new dimensions of ourselves and our worlds.

As William Zinsser (1988) notes, "Writing is how we think our way into a subject and make it our own" (p. 16). This makes sense to me.

I have used writing in classrooms for many years as a means for students to grapple with ideas and situations they are encountering for the first time. I ask students to write journals during and after class to give me an idea of what they are thinking about as they work their way into a novel or through a problematic situation. At first, some students are not comfortable jotting down their thoughts, perhaps because they are not used to it. But with practice and support, most become more comfortable with writing about their ideas and feelings.

Enriching Student Understanding—Research

It is important to note that some people have found a direct and positive correlation between writing journals related to specific content and success on assessments. Croxton and Berger (1999) found that "journal writing [about content concepts] enriches student understanding" of those concepts. They challenged students to relate course topics and ideas to their own personal experiences. The key word here is "relate." When we make connections among facts and ideas, we are creating our own mental web of relationships, thereby making them more meaningful to us. Croxton and Berger discovered that journal writing "resulted in deeper processing" of these ideas and, therefore, deeper understanding of what they were teaching. It stands to reason that if we ask students to work through concepts and ideas orally and in writing, they will have a greater chance of retaining these concepts and being able to use them.

Thinking Journals

A Thinking Journal is a place where a person can be alone with his or her thoughts, reflecting on what has occurred, making observations, attempting to figure out what happened and why, and generating some questions for the future (Figure 5.1).

Over the years, students have shared amazing insights and stories in their journals, some of which I have excerpted in this chapter. Let me share one of the most significant entries in a journal from a high school sophomore named Emily. She was asked to reflect on her abilities to pose and solve problems while in her mathematics class. Her teacher, Rosemarie Liebmann, shared Emily's journal with me several years ago:

> I guess I could call myself smart. I mean I can usually get good grades. Sometimes I worry, though, that I'm not equipped to achieve what I want, that I'm just a tape recorder repeating back what I've heard . . . .

Figure 5.1
Writing Stems for Thinking Journals

I wonder . . .

What fascinates me here is . . .

This is important because . . .

This reminds me of . . . I can relate this experience/topic/person to . . .

I do not see the relationship between_____and _____

What is the meaning of . . .

I do not understand _____

Why did/does . . .

I feel . . .

Key words/concepts/terms here are _____because . . .

The big idea here is . . .

My prediction is . . .

The themes that are emerging are . . .

The underlying assumptions/biases/interests here seem to be . . .

What puzzles me is . . .

I am changing my mind about . . .

*My goal for this week/month/semester is . . . . And here's how I intend to
    achieve it . . .*

What I am learning here about myself, my understandings, my feelings is . . .

I've done well on Iowa and PSAT tests, but they are always multiple choice. I worry that once I'm out of school and people don't keep handing me information with questions and Scantron sheets, I'll be lost. (Barell, 1995, p. 7)

Emily concludes by reflecting on how old she feels at 15 (!) and about how much she should be doing. Instead she watches TV and reads books. "As a matter of fact," she says, "I believe I will depart now and watch 'Star Trek' . . . An hour of bad TV programming will perk me up wonderfully. Beam me up, Scotty!" (Barell, 1995, p. 7).

Reflective Pause

What impresses you about Emily's journal? To what degree is Emily representative of students you see today? How is she similar? How is she different?

Emily's journal is an example of the power of reflections shared within the classroom community. It happens to reveal so much about what some have called "the hidden curriculum," what we teach by our modeling, and the way we present class material. I wonder: How often did Emily get to raise significant questions if she usually played the role of a "tape recorder"?

Before Writing

Before writing we need to help students become accustomed to what we are challenging them to do—share their ideas and feelings in writing. There are several things we can do, starting with thinking aloud to model our own thinking.

For example, before asking students to write, I would take the first line of a short story and think aloud about what it means. The opening lines of John Updike's short story "A & P" gave me an opportunity to think and inquire aloud in front of my students: "The opening line is, 'In walk three girls in nothing but bikinis.' Now, what I find interesting here is the syntax. Updike starts with a verb "In walks" and then we find out about the girls. Why didn't he just say, 'Three girls walked in'? I'm not sure. . . ."

I proceed to analyze this one sentence for all the things that are puzzling about it, and, pretty soon, the students are beginning to ask questions themselves as we read on: "Who's talking? Where is the narrator? Why is he [or she?] surprised at bikinis?"

We would list a set of questions on the board.

As I noted in Chapter 3, we could ask, "What differences do you see among these questions?" Students would quickly say that answers to some could be found in the text whereas others required thinking. "You have to figure it out . . . infer the meaning. . . ." We might refer to a model of how the intellect works, such as the Three-Story Intellect (see Figures 4.1 and 4.2).

We would continue with an analysis of one or more of their questions and, invariably, one question led to another and the inquisitive tone of the class was set. Students realized from the very first week that curiosity, recognizing and communicating your own puzzlements, were the important things here. The teacher was not the only one to ask questions in this class. Everybody had responsibility for this, and we all worked together on our uncertainties, doubts, and difficulties.

Modeling this attitude for students facilitated and invited their journal writing during and after class.

During and After Class

Vin Frick teaches high school science in Dumont, New Jersey, and from him I learned a simple but effective way to introduce journal writing during class. He would ask his students to take the last 5 or 10 minutes of a 60-minute biology class or lab to write about what they understood from the day's session. "Just write about what you've understood today and if you have questions about what we did, please jot those down."

Then Vin reserved a few minutes for students to share their understandings with each other and to raise a question or two about the content. This was a good way for him to check on their levels of understanding and, eventually, he communicated to them that whenever they were in doubt, they should note that and ask a question.

Some think that saying "I don't know" is a mark of ignorance and, perhaps, shame. Physicist Richard Feynman asserted that doubt is a hallmark of doing science: "Science is the belief in the ignorance of experts" (Feynman, 1999, p. 149).

Dorothy Lozauskas was a high school advanced placement (AP) biology teacher who followed the above processes to introduce her students to writing journals. One of her students, Michael, went home after a lab and wrote: "In lab, we are making models of molecules with different bonds, and have just made a butane molecule that has free-bond rotation. Even though they have the capability of doing so, why would they? Also, what makes them move? Kinetic energy? I wonder what the world would be like if there was no free-bond rotation—really cold?" (Barell, 1995, p. 89).

I wonder if Michael would have had these thoughts and curiosities had his teacher not presented him with an opportunity for reflecting on the day's laboratory project. Dorothy provided him with the assignment: modeling and a structure for his reflections. She took the time to make this assignment part of her curriculum.

On rereading this entry, I am amazed at the "what if" question that goes way beyond what Michael knows and leads him to speculate about an entirely alternate state of the world. Here is another example of what Mary Wallace meant (in Chapter 4) by a good question "opening doors." Michael speculates, poses a significant "what if?" question, and makes a stab at an answer. What a marvelous discussion question for the next day's class! Here, Michael is following Albert Einstein's model of posing "thought questions," engaging in what he called "combinatory play" with "more or less clear images" by asking "what if . . . ?" (Ghiselin, 1964, p. 171).

Einstein gave speculation, wondering, questioning, wistful playing with concepts, and daydreaming a very good name!

Reflective Pause

Are such hypothetical, contrary to reality questions important? What do you think?

Some would say that these "what if?" questions are good assessments of understanding. It is like asking, "If Thomas

Jefferson had been the 16th U.S. president instead of Abraham Lincoln, would he have acted as Lincoln did?" To draw a reasonable conclusion, we need to be thoroughly familiar with the personality, priorities, and philosophy of Jefferson and Lincoln as well as being well grounded in the historical circumstances in both eras.

What kind of "what if?" question might you ask students about a topic or concept or experience now that would test the limits of their understanding?

Problem Solving

Several years ago I had the pleasure of working with several elementary school educators who were determined to help their students become better thinkers. More specifically, they were focusing on what they considered to be an area needing development: problem solving. We tried to find ways to help students become better at thinking through problematic situations. We knew that Benjamin Bloom had asked students to think through math problems aloud at the University of Chicago and that this had helped them become better problem solvers.

As an English teacher, I had been accustomed to asking students to write about the novels and plays they read and we put two strategies together and developed several structures for students to write about how they solved problems.

Here is one straightforward approach:

- "What is my problem?
- "How will I go about solving it?" (identify strategies, not solutions)
- "How well am I doing?"
- "How well did I do [after reaching a solution]? Would I do anything differently, and why or why not?"

Here is one 1st grader's journal entry using this format: "We were solving how our friends were different to [sic] each other . . . I made a list . . . I think I had good iders and a lot of queshens [sic]."

A classmate evaluated his thinking and problem solving this way: "I did bad becs I bid not open my mind [sic]" (Mary Mulcahy, personal communication, May 1988).

My thought has always been that if we continually use such questions, and if they are powerful enough, then we help students approach complex situations in an organized way that helps them take control of the situation. These questions become like internal "scripts" they can follow for the rest of their lives (Barell, 1995, p. 103).

After-School Problem Solving

Teachers have experimented with another problem-solving format, one that explicitly calls for students to identify a problem and then pose questions in their journals. Here is Sarah's journal entry, written at home after she returned from school:

> *Problem:* My sister and I share a room and we also do our homework in this room. The problem is my sister listens to the radio while doing her homework and I am totally opposite. I have to do my homework in a quite [sic] atmosphere, or else I seem to get distracted. She won't shut the radio off because she claims she can't do her homework without it.
>
> *Questioning:* What if I found a quiet spot where I wouldn't be disturbed by the radio or my family? What if my sister and I compromised, making a system where the radio would be on for a specific amount of time and the rest was spent in quiet? What if my sister wore her headset so that she could listen to music while the same time I could do my homework with a quiet atmosphere? (Quoted from student's original journals, Rosemarie Liebmann, personal communication, May 1988.)

Our belief was that problems create good opportunities for questioning ourselves, what our feelings are, what our strategies might be, and what kinds of resolutions we were expecting.

Research by Cranton (1994) suggests that keeping a double-entry journal is an effective way to think through complex issues. Here is Rich's double-entry mathematics journal entry:*

---

*Reprinted with permission by the publisher from John Barell, *Teaching for Thoughtfulness: Classroom Strategies To Enhance Intellectual Development*, 2/e. Published by Allyn and Bacon, Boston, MA. Copyright © 1995 by Pearson Education.

This problem scared me while reading it. It got better after I read it six or seven times. I just took it step by step. First assign variables. This took time to figure out, but I remembered doing a similar problem in class.

Success in the last problem builds my confidence for this one. This is the same format, just slightly altered.

When reading the problem I almost got thrown with the word *area*, thinking of the idea to square y—but it's wrong.

So far we can see Rich using very important thinking processes:

- Reading and rereading for understanding
- Breaking the problem into smaller steps
- Relating it to ones he's done in the past
- Checking and monitoring his progress, followed by self-correcting

Rich continued:

Again the problem is very similar to the last one. The hardest part is organizing the variables.

They are trying to trick us by using square roots.
The best thing to do is to square both sides. Simplicity.
This part is tricky!
I thought I ran into a problem when I calculated the left side to be one.
It's Cake! (Barell, 1995, p. 261)

The self-reflective problem solver is ever mindful of what he or she is doing and in this case Rich would not let himself be drawn into an ineffective strategy. He kept his eyes wide open and his pen moving.

These problem-solving strategies have a major goal of helping us to become aware of and in control of our thinking. "Inking our thinking" is what Robin Fogarty used to call this kind of metacognitive reflection (Fogarty, personal communication, February 1994). We need to know what we are doing, if it is effective, how to change it if it isn't productive, and when to use the kinds of strategies we are learning.

Inquiry begins in some kind of doubt, "a situation that is ambiguous, that presents a dilemma, that proposes alternatives," as John Dewey notes in *How We Think* (1933, p. 14). That's what problems are—states of doubt or difficulty—and we naturally begin to ask questions like, "What *is* the problem, and how can I solve it?"

Field Notes

There are kinds of writings we engage in, not focused upon the traditional classroom. Many scientific investigations take place out in the field, often in wild and uncivilized terrains. While in the field, we need to record our observations with objectivity and accuracy so we can make sense of what we see. When we go out to do "fieldwork," we have a purpose, something we are searching for or a question we want to answer.

While I was in the U.S. Navy, I sailed to Antarctica, where I then flew to the Russian base, called Vostok. Devoted in part to glaciological investigations, the base is located on the polar plateau where the ice is over two miles thick. I took a small notepad, and on the flight back to McMurdo Sound where my ship, *USS Glacier* (AGB-4), was berthed, I jotted down what I had seen and heard while standing on the polar plateau. Because it wasn't known at that time, I was not able to record that a freshwater lake the size of Lake Ontario, never seen or touched by humans, is located two and a half miles below the buildings of the Vostok base. Years later, in a new millennium, researchers are figuring out how to sample these waters without contaminating them with their instruments. They too are making notations in their notebooks about a lake that has been sealed off from our atmosphere for between 500,000 and more than 1,000,000 years (www.resa.net/nasa/antarctica.htm#lakevos_main).

When teaching in an alternative school in New York City, my colleagues and I took our students on mini-expeditions to the mountains of upstate New York to explore the geology and fauna there. We all took notes.

And now when I go to work at the American Museum of Natural History, I always bring my spiral notebook because I want to record what happens and when, and what my responses to that work are. Sometimes I work in one of the exhibit halls at the museum, like the Hall of Planet Earth or the new Hayden Planetarium, and I usually have a notepad along with me.

Field notes are for the purpose of recording one's impressions during an expedition and analyzing them later on, when back at home base. In terms of inquiry, field notes are indispensable. They become our record-keeping devices. Today we can keep notes in a traditional form of journal as I did years ago, or we can use a laptop computer, as *New York Times* correspondent Tom Friedman did while researching *The Lexus and the Olive Branch* (1999).

Barbara Bald teaches 6th grade science students from Alton, New Hampshire, and shares with her students her thoughts on the nature of observing: "When observing an object, watching a movie, reading a book, or listening to a lecture, our minds are seldom quiet. Usually they are asking questions, making judgments, or comparing new material with what's already known" (Barell, 1995, p. 258).

When one of Barbara's students, Portia, examined a wasp's nest, she had plenty of questions: "What's it made out of? How old is it? Why so many holes? Why is straw sticking out? Where did it come from?"

Portia will use these questions and they will lead her to various different lines of investigation.

When Stephen Reynolds goes out to do geology fieldwork, he always takes a field journal with him, as all good scientists do. It is essential to make precise observations of what he has encountered—the locations of objects and the surrounding territory and immediate environment, including upper and lower stratigraphic layers. Figure 5.2 is a copy of one of his journals posted in the Hall of Plant Earth at the American Museum of Natural History. It is part of an exhibit on the structure and history of the Grand Canyon. What impressed me most about Dr. Reynolds's journal are the questions he poses and his attempts at answers. What he saw puzzled him, and he recorded his questions along with some possible explanations.

You will recall from Chapter 2 that every spring Ms. Idoni takes her biology class to an environment that she is certain will pique their interest. "The field trip will help you decide what question you want to pursue," she tells her students.

Figure 5.2
Dr. Stephen Reynolds's Field Journal

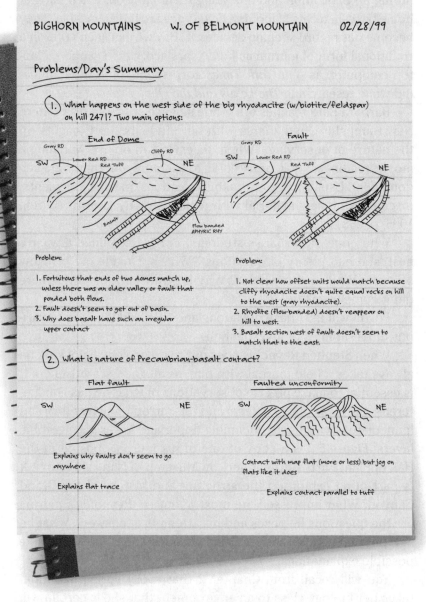

When students arrive at the lake in the city park, she "asks the students to simply walk around the lake, to observe the lake, and to think about questions that they may be interested in answering." She asks them to record the observations and questions in their journals (National Research Council, 2000, pp. 66, 67).

Mrs. Idoni's students are at the beginning of a long-term inquiry project, and keeping a journal is important for them, both to record recent field observations and to structure their reflections on these notes when they are back home. In planning our field expeditions, we might at home structure our notes as follows:

- Questions to research
- Plan of investigation
- Technology we will use in the field (for example, audio, video, notebooks, still photography, rock hammers)
- Kinds of evidence we will search for and gather information about
- Hypotheses we are testing
- Alternative conclusions ruled out because . . .
- Conclusions and explanations

Such a format could be used not only for fieldwork in science, but also for field work in social studies and in language arts with some modifications. If we are researching local social and political structures, we will surely have a set of questions we are investigating as well as hypotheses we are testing. Should we see a Shakespeare play, we can also venture out with curiosities about how different actors might interpret various scenes, how the director's interpretations might differ from others, or how the set designer influenced the performances.

Research is not just for sciences and field notes are not just for investigating the possible pollution of nearby lakes.

Having engaged in this kind of long-term investigation where their own questions guided their research, students should expect that a culminating assessment would take advantage of these inquiry and critical thinking skills: "For the final assessment, Ms. Idoni presents a new problem and asks each student to prepare a report describing how he or she would investigate the problem" (National Research Council, 2000, p. 72).

Reflection

When we are close to being finished with our investigations, there is a most important piece of writing and discussing we must not forget: reflecting on our learning, our progress, using questions to guide us:

- What did I learn about the subject that was important?
- What surprised me? What contradicted my expectations, my hypotheses?
- What did I learn about inquiry, with or without groups of others?
- What did I learn about myself?

After attending an inquiry-based graduate course in biology taught by Christine Muth and me at the American Museum of Natural History, elementary school teachers had these reflections on their inquiry processes:

Susan: "I've experienced how much more fun science is when there is something you are trying to find out, and that one question always sparks other questions, so that the possibilities are endless . . ."

Jane: "We need to organize our questions. That's why scientists work in teams so that colleagues can help each other clarify and identify ideas and [other] questions."

Beverly: "Inquiry in science can lead to a lot of discoveries as new questions are always being formulated based on unexpected results . . ."

Kevin: "I need to experience it [inquiry] myself *and* be more knowledgeable than I am now."

Reflection on past practice is what Socrates meant when he said, "The life without examination is no life for a human being" (Plato, 2000, p. 315).

Too often in schools we have marvelously intense and potentially meaningful experiences without the opportunity to reflect on them, analyze their meanings, and learn from them. That is surely one of our purposes in taking notes on our thoughts and feelings: to give us an effective context for our thoughts.

Notes from the Polar Plateau

The best set of field notes I have ever read were written almost a century ago under extremely trying conditions on a journey from McMurdo Sound in 1911 to the South Pole and back. They were composed in the dark-green four-man tent that British explorer Captain Robert Falcon Scott used while man-hauling his sledges through deep snows of the Ross Ice Shelf in an attempt to be the first human to set foot at the South Pole. We all know the tragic story by now. Scott arrived at the Pole on January 16, 1912, a month behind the Norwegian explorer Roald Amundsen (December 17, 1911). There were many reasons why Scott came in second: he used Siberian ponies instead of dogs, as Amundsen had; his planning for food rations did not provide enough fat to supply the necessary 5,000 calories a day needed for such an arduous journey; and, among other things, at the last minute he chose to include a fifth person in a trip planned for four.

But his journals captivated me as statements of amazing courage and determination when I read them at age 14. Here are just a few excerpts:

> *January 17, 1912.* The Norwegians have forestalled us and are first at the Pole. It is a terrible disappointment, and I am very sorry for my loyal companions . . . . Tomorrow we must march on to the Pole and then hasten home with all the speed we can compass. All the day-dreams must go; it will be a wearisome return . . . . Great God this is an awful place. (Scott, 1913, p. 374)

Edward A. Wilson was the physician, scientist, and artist on the trip. On the return journey from the polar plateau, on February 8, the party stopped for lunch near Buckley Cliffs at the head of the Beardmore Glacier, an ice highway to the Pole. Wilson wrote:

> After lunch we all geologized on till supper, and I was very late turning in, examining the moraine after supper . . . . Magnificent Beacon sandstone

cliffs. Masses of limestone in the moraine, and dolerite crags in various places. Coal seams at all heights in the sandstone cliffs, and lumps of weathered coal with fossil vegetable. Had a regular field day and got some splendid things in the short time. (King, 1982, p. 156)

Scott continued his entries:

Friday March 16 or Saturday 17. Lost track of dates . . . . Tragedy all along the line. At lunch . . . poor Titus Oates said he couldn't go on; he proposed we should leave him in his sleeping-bag. That we could not do, and we induced him to come on the afternoon march . . . . Should this be found I want these facts recorded. Oates' last thoughts were of his mother, but immediately before he took pride in thinking that his regiment [the Inniskilling Dragoons] would be pleased with the bold way in which he met his death. We can testify to his bravery. He has borne intense suffering for weeks without complaint . . . . It was blowing blizzard. He said, 'I am just going outside and may be some time.' He went out into the blizzard and we have not seen him since . . . . We leave here our theodolite, a camera and Oates' sleeping-bags. Diaries, etc., and geological specimens carried at Wilson's special request, will be found with us or on our sledge.

Thursday March 29. Since the 21st we have had a continuous gale from W.S.W. and W.W. We had fuel to make two cups of tea apiece and bare food for two days on the 20th. Every day we have been ready to start for our depot 11 miles away, but outside the door of the tent it remains a scene of whirling drift. I do not think we can hope for any better things now. We shall stick it out to the end, but we are getting weaker, of course, and the end cannot be far.
   It seems a pity, but I do not think I can write more. R. Scott
   [last entry] For God's sake look after our people.

Reflective Pause

What responses do you have to these journal entries? Have you ever encountered writing such as this? By whom and under what circumstances?

I have introduced several of the best-known pages in all the literature of south polar exploration for a number of reasons.

First, I want to note how scientists and their leaders were determined *to record their journey*. They did this, sometimes in the face of the most horrific conditions imaginable. Scott and his party of four, including Wilson, Bowers, Evans, and Oates, suffered temperatures of 30 degrees below zero Fahrenheit and lower, blizzard-force winds, and low food rations, and traveled over sandy granular surfaces and through extremely deep snows, all for the sake of their quest to reach the Pole. Even in their supreme disappointment, they did not stop writing and acting as if science were one of the main objectives of the trip. It was Wilson who said that Amundsen "has beaten us in so far as he made a race of it," whereas the British had been out for loftier goals: "We have done what we came for all the same and as our programme was made out" (Huntford, 1985, p. 480).

Second, what we see here is the *importance of precise observations*. Wilson knew where he was, and where the rock and plant specimens came from, and both he and Scott were determined to haul a lot of extra weight all for the sake of science—about 40 extra pounds! Scott didn't even dump the rock specimens along with the surveying equipment and the camera! What does this tell us? That here were scientists determined to preserve a record and to make a contribution. Examining Wilson's sketches of the Transantarctic Mountains, it is amazing that under conditions of snow blindness, Wilson captured the geological stratifications and evidences of former life with amazing clarity:

> Wilson with his sharp eyes, has picked several plant impressions, the last a piece of coal with beautifully traced leaves in layers, also some excellently preserved impressions of thick stems, showing cellular structure. In one place we saw the cast of small waves in the sand. Tonight Bill has got a specimen of limestone with archeo-cyathus—the trouble is one cannot imagine where the stone comes from . . . . (Scott, 1913, p. 389)

Finally, I am always deeply impressed by the dedication of Scott and other explorers to writing and recording their observations. They are not full of explicit inquiries. Rather they are a record, and also contain some reflections on the nature of an expedition that one expedition member, writing in 1922, called "The Worst

Journey in the World" (Cherry-Garrard, 1937).These journals are, however, the stuff of inquiry. They record a quest devoted to knowing more about our planet and its forbidding environments.

These excerpts lead us to formulate many questions of our own: What did the rock specimens tell Wilson about the geological history of this area, and of the continent itself? Did he speculate on Antarctica's temperate climate several million years earlier? Did he think in terms of that range of time?

One of the specimens Wilson dragged homeward was of a fossil plant, *Glossopteris*, evidence that Antarctica once experienced a temperate climate. Subsequent discoveries by scientists from the American Museum of Natural History uncovered the bones of a swamp-dwelling dinosaur (*Lystrosaurus*), thus confirming the hypothesis that Antarctica was once joined to Australia, Africa, and South America as part of a land mass called Gondwanaland (Colbert, 1973) over 200 million years ago.

And, above all else, why did Scott and his party fail to return to Hut Point at McMurdo Sound safely?

Some conclusions about Scott are not, however, as favorable as my young impressions (Huntford, 1985). They speak of Scott's poor judgment, of how he pushed his men in ways that Amundsen was able to avoid through methodical planning and excellent preparation, of the squeamishness of the British explorers about killing their dogs for food, of their desire to "man-haul" their sledges rather than use the more efficient dogs as a means of over-the-ice transportation. It seemed as if Scott wanted to prove something about British manhood and courage by using human foot power rather than animal power.

When their companions found them the following Antarctic spring (in the autumn of 1912), they suspected that Scott and his companions had succumbed to scurvy, the dreaded disease of sailors caused by lack of vitamin C.

Susan Solomon (2001), however, offered a more recent hypothesis—that unusually severe weather conditions were responsible for Scott's demise. "Nature dealt them a crushing blow in the form of conditions that can now be shown to be far colder than normal . . .[they] did everything right regarding the weather but were exceedingly unlucky" (p. xvii).

Conclusion

Of the moment he laid claim to the South Pole, Roald Amundsen wrote:

> I had decided that we would all take part in the historic event; the act itself of planting the flag. It was not the privilege of *one* man, it was the privilege of *all* those who had risked their lives in the fight and stood together through thick and thin . . . . Five roughened, frostbitten fists it was that gripped the post, lifted the fluttering flag on high and planted it together as the very first at the Geographic South Pole. (Huntford, 1985, p. 455)

These journals still stand in my mind as some of the most amazing writings in human history—a testament to our need to share with our families and like-minded men and women the discoveries spurred on by the deepest of curiosities about our world. Reading these journals throughout childhood has left deep impressions on me, impressions as marked as those of the fossil *Glossopteris.* Writing about what we see and feel, about our whereabouts and wonderings, and about our progress toward goals gives us a sense of orientation, navigation, and striving toward visions of new territories. Writing is a fine way to struggle through life toward our own South Poles.

References

Barell, J. (1995). *Teaching for thoughtfulness: Classroom strategies to enhance intellectual development.* (2nd ed.). New York: Longman.

Cherry-Garrard, A. (1937). *The worst journey in the world—the story of Scott's last expedition to the South Pole.* London: Penguin Books Limited.

Colbert, E. (1973). *Wandering lands and animals: The story of continental drift and animal populations.* New York: Dover Publications.

Cranton, P. (1994). *Understanding and promoting transformative learning: A guide for educators of adults.* San Francisco: Jossey-Bass.

Croxton, C., & Berger, R. (1999, August). Journal writing: Does it promote long term retention of course concepts? [Online course] National Teaching and Learning Forum. Available: www.ntlf.com. Accessed June 2000.

Dewey, J. (1933). *How we think.* Boston: D. C. Heath.

Dillard, A. (1989). *The writing life.* New York: Harper & Row.

Feynman, R. (1999). The value of science. In J. Robbins (Ed.), *The pleasure of finding things out* (pp. 141–149). Cambridge, MA: Perseus Books.

Friedman, T. (1999). *The Lexus and the olive branch: Understanding globalization.* New York: Ferrar Straus Giroux.

Ghiselin, B. (1964). *The creative process.* New York: Dell Publishing Co.

Huntford, R. (1985). *The last place on Earth.* New York: Atheneum.

King, H. (Ed.). (1982). *South Pole odyssey—Selections from the Antarctic diaries of Edward Wilson.* Cambridge, England: Scott Polar Research Institute.

National Research Council. (2000). *Inquiry and the National Science Education Standards: A guide for teaching and learning.* Washington, DC: National Academy Press.

Plato (2000). *Selected dialogues of Plato. The apology.* (B. Jowett, Trans.). New York: Modern Library.

Scott, R. F. (1913). *Scott's last expedition.* Toronto: McClelland, Goodchild & Stewart.

Solomon, S. (2001). *The coldest march: Scott's fatal Antarctic expedition.* New Haven, CT: Yale University Press.

Zinsser, W. (1988). *Writing to learn.* New York: Harper & Row.

Chapter 6

QUESTIONING TEXTS

The mind-forged manacles I hear.

—WILLIAM BLAKE, "LONDON," 1794

When I was in high school, my marvelous English teacher, Claire Slattery Heffernan, introduced us to the mystic and romantic English poets. One of my favorites was William Blake. I liked his poetry probably because I was going through a phase where I had visions of growing up to be a Trappist monk. But my other passion, Antarctic exploration, became dominant. Eventually, I sailed off to college and joined the Navy, deciding not to be the silent Trappist standing at the South Pole.

One of Blake's poems that always raised questions in my mind was "London." Here the poet speaks of wandering through the "charter'd" streets of London "Near where the charter'd Thames" did flow, seeing "marks of weakness, marks of woe."

In every cry of every Man,

In every Infant's cry of fear,

In every voice, in every ban,

The mind-forg'd manacles I hear. (Blake, 1946, p. 112)

I'm sure Mrs. Heffernan had us interpret these lines, providing us with clues and cues to look at in order to arrive at our conclusions about Blake's meanings. She urged us to figure out what the poet intended by "mind-forg'd manacles." What were they? "Manacles" are like shackles, things that hold us down and restrain our freedom of movement. We become manacled in prisons of our own creation. I wondered what that meant for my own life. Where had I created barriers to my own successes? How had I squelched my own personal and professional development with these "mind-forg'd" imprisonments?

These were questions that have been part of the deep geology of my psyche ever since I took her high school class in Wellesley, Massachusetts. I generated them from reading literature at the prompting of an outstanding teacher. It has taken me the better part of a lifetime to realize their truth and to begin to deal with some of the self-inflicted "manacles" I have created.

Perhaps for masterpieces of literature we do not need specific strategies. If we are intrinsically interested in the subject, we will allow our minds to playfully generate questions about the text. We might not need teachers to probe and prod us toward wondering about how the poet speaks to us.

But for others like me, we need help in figuring things out. We can benefit from structures and strategies that help us focus on the most important concepts in a poem like Blake's "London."

The KWL Strategy

The KWL strategy has had one of the most positive effects in influencing students' ability to read effectively (Ogle, 1986, pp. 564–571). The letters "KWL" stand for the questions:

K "What do we think we **know** about whales?"
W "What do we **want** to find out about whales?"
L And, after reading, "What have we **learned** about whales?"

Known as a prereading strategy, this approach is effective in tapping into readers' prior knowledge, thereby preparing them for learning (Marzano, Pickering, & McTighe, 1992, p. 39).

Reflective Pause

Why are the preceding questions important ones to ask students before they read any text or begin any study unit?

I'm sure you've thought of a number of reasons. Here are some others:

- We can determine the extent of students' prior knowledge of facts, skills, and concepts.
- Their now-activated prior knowledge provides students with a structure within which to assimilate new knowledge.
- Students learn that they, collectively, as an entire class, know quite a lot about a certain subject (for example, whales), and this is likely to make them more interested.
- The process of tapping into what students think they know often results in identifying misunderstandings, which other students will immediately challenge. For example, I once used the KWL strategy when teaching a 5th grade class about Christopher Columbus and the Age of Exploration, and one student said Columbus was born in Spain and was related to Queen Isabella. Another 5th grader quickly corrected him.

The second question, "What do we want to find out?" or "What do we need to determine?" has many benefits as well. What are some of them?

- When students generate their own questions, this provides them with a sense of ownership.
- This process also enhances students' motivation: We are trying to answer students' questions, not only have students answer teachers' questions.
- Challenging students to identify what aspects of a subject they are curious about is bound to bring to light some contradictory information, some puzzles, and raise students' doubts about their own and classmates' understanding

about the subject—for example, whales. One student may say, "Whales are becoming extinct." This may surprise a classmate, who then wants to know "Why?" and another student will certainly ask a question most important to critical thinking—"How do you know?"

The final question "What have we learned?" is an obvious opportunity to compare what we "thought" we knew with what we in fact did find out. It is also a wonderful occasion for students to keep apprised of the full extent of what they have learned and compare it with their prior lack of knowledge. Actually comparing the before and after concept maps and preserving them as parts of students' portfolios can be a very worthwhile endeavor.

So engaging students' curiosities before they set out to read about any topic is a proven-by-research strategy that enhances the meaningfulness of the learning experience. In Chapter 8 we will discuss an expansion of this prereading strategy as a way of thinking about longer-term curricular units.

Modeling *Othello*

As we mentioned in Chapter 3, it is a good and proven strategy to model the behavior we want others to emulate (Bandura, 1986). In this case I found myself asking the three KWL questions about Shakespeare's *Othello* before teaching it to college freshmen and sophomores. Most of what I found out was that some people knew the plots of various Shakespearean plays; others knew a little about the Globe Theatre and how it was constructed. Some other students were voluble in expressing their displeasure with how studying Shakespeare had been approached in the past.

The questions students developed came less from our initial considerations of what they did not know about Shakespeare than from puzzling situations in the play that arose as we read and acted it out.

Philosophy for Children

Perhaps the most comprehensive and model thinking program that I have had firsthand experience with is Matthew Lipman's

Philosophy for Children. This program is based on the notion that very young children are good thinkers who teachers can involve in good discussions about philosophical topics if the students are meaningfully engaged in reading interesting stories.

Lipman, who was a faculty member at Montclair State University, in Montclair, New Jersey, during my own tenure there, wrote his own stories. One, called *Harry Stottlemeier's Discovery* (1982), was written for upper elementary school students, and is perhaps the most famous of all of Lipman's stories.

I was fortunate enough to attend much of a two-week training session on many of the program's novels and the strategies used to encourage thinking among young people. The strategy often consisted of children reading the story in segments, with each child taking a different portion. Then students stated what they found interesting or challenging and the teacher wrote these observations on the board. Next, students identified which comment they wanted to discuss. As you can see, the strategy is very student driven, giving students opportunities to analyze and pose questions on that which they find meaningful.

Asking students to identify what they find interesting in their reading, then having students generate questions for discussion is the strategy that I most often use in working with literature. Some practice stems for eliciting meaning from text include:

- What I find most interesting here is . . .
- The big ideas here are . . .
- I wonder why . . .
- What confuses me is . . .
- I can relate this episode/segment/story to . . .
- This makes me feel . . .

One of the most fascinating books I've ever read and taught is Dostoevsky's *The Brothers Karamazov*, first printed in 1880. This is a complex, often violent tale full of sin, debauchery, patricide, epilepsy, and courtroom drama. But throughout the story we find Dostoevsky's search for meaning in life and for the nature of God's presence in the world. One of his characters, an intellectual named Ivan, writes a poem called "The Grand Inquisitor," which he presents to his brother Alyosha, who at age 20 entered a monastery to escape the "darkness of the wicked world."

In the following passage, Ivan presents his poem to Alyosha, describing what happens when Jesus Christ returns to earth during the Spanish Inquisition of the 16th century. Christ enables the blind to see and the dead to live again, but then is accosted by the Grand Inquisitor: "Why did You come here, to interfere and make things difficult for us? You wanted people to be free, to think for themselves. You have seen free men. Yes, that business cost us a great deal . . . but at last, in Your name, we saw it through. For fifteen centuries we have been wrestling with Your freedom, but now it is ended and over for good." Then the Grand Inquisitor gives Christ his reasons for denying men their freedom:

> Man was created a rebel and how can a rebel be happy? . . . men can never be free because they are weak, vicious, worthless, and rebellious. . . . So long as man remains free he strives for nothing so incessantly and so painfully as to find someone to worship . . . . I tell You that man is tormented by no greater anxiety than to find someone quickly to whom he can hand over that gift of freedom with which the ill-fated creature is born . . . . Men rejoice at being led like cattle again, with the terrible gift of freedom that brought them so much suffering removed from them . . . . We will convince them that they will only be free when they have surrendered their freedom and submitted to us . . . . Freedom, free thought, and science will lead them into such straits and will bring them face to face with such marvels and insoluble mysteries, that some of them, the fierce and rebellious, will destroy themselves, others, rebellious but weak, will destroy one another, while the rest, weak and unhappy, will crawl fawning to our feet and whine to us: "Yes, you were right, you alone possess His mystery, and we come back to you, save us from ourselves!"

As the Grand Inquisitor awaits an answer, Christ approaches him and kisses him "on his bloodless, aged lips."

Reflective Pause

Using the text from this story, we can model for our students a variety of observations and questions. Read the text, think about the scene, creating an image in your mind, and then jot down a few observations and/or questions.

Here are some questions others have asked:

- Who is the Grand Inquisitor and what did he do during the Inquisition?
- What was the Inquisition?
- Why does the Grand Inquisitor think human beings cannot live freely or cannot tolerate the "terrible gift of freedom"?
- Most of us seem to value our freedom. Why would anybody surrender it as a form of worship?
- How can knowledge and thinking ever be detrimental to us?
- How would you respond to the Grand Inquisitor?

If we use the Three-Story Intellect from Figure 4.2 to analyze our initial questions, we can see that some of these questions are asking for information. They are what reading teachers would call "reading the lines." There are also processing, or "reading between the lines," questions here. Perhaps the last one is what we might call "reading beyond the lines."

What would be an example of a Level II processing question? Perhaps asking students to compare/contrast, analyze, and draw conclusions? For example: "Compare the message of the Grand Inquisitor with another person's (or your own) on the nature of being human (rebellion, corruption, and the need to worship) and on the value of freedom." And "If the Grand Inquisitor is accurate in his observations about the masses of humanity, what would you predict about the status of civilization tomorrow, and years into the future?" (Level III, or application question).

Questioning Frames

Over the years I have attempted to analyze situations to determine the kinds of questions we might pose about them. One result has been the development of what I call Questioning Frames, modeled after work of David Perkins of Harvard on frames for thinking (David Perkins, personal communication, July 1990). Figure 6.1 is a frame I have used over the years to analyze a variety of complex situations and issues.

Figure 6.1
General Questioning Frame

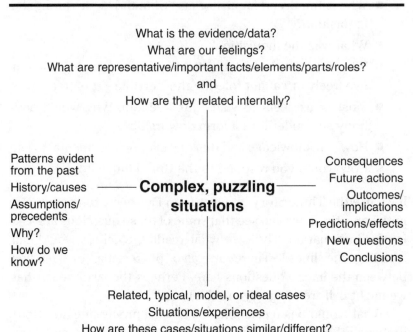

What is the evidence/data?
What are our feelings?
What are representative/important facts/elements/parts/roles?
and
How are they related internally?

Patterns evident from the past
History/causes
Assumptions/precedents
Why?
How do we know?

Complex, puzzling situations

Consequences
Future actions
Outcomes/implications
Predictions/effects
New questions
Conclusions

Related, typical, model, or ideal cases
Situations/experiences
How are these cases/situations similar/different?
What conclusions can we draw from the comparisons?

Try using the Questioning Frame in the figure with the following news item.*

CAPE CANAVERAL, Fla., Feb. 11 (2001) AP—Two space commanders opened the door today to Destiny, the American-made science laboratory that is the newest and most expensive addition to the International Space Station.

The moment the hatch was raised by the astronauts, William M. Shepherd and Kenneth D. Cockrell, space station Alpha became the largest orbiting outpost ever in terms of habitable volume.

"It looks awesome," Mission Control told Mr. Cockrell. "We hope you guys enjoy your new room on your house . . . ."

In a brief ceremony, Mr. Shepherd signed for the delivery of the $1.4 billion laboratory, which had been installed by the visiting shuttle

---

*Reprinted with permission of the Associated Press.

astronauts on Saturday. The laboratory is intended to give the orbiting outpost the ability to do cutting-edge science over the next 10 to 15 years.

The Destiny laboratory, 28 feet long and 14 feet wide, was a brilliant white inside. Its shelves and wall compartments were covered with strips of protective cloth that the crew members promptly removed. On one of the wall covers were a couple hundred signatures of those who had prepared Destiny for flight, along with these words: "Dreams are like stars; you choose them as your guides, and following them, you reach your Destiny . . . ." (Associated Press, 2001, p. A16)

Reflective Pause

By now, the Space Lab may be fully functioning. What sparks your curiosity from this story about the Destiny *space laboratory? Use the written-out version of the Questioning Frame.*

Here are some of my own questions, generated from using the Questioning Frame:

- How long did it take to create *Destiny*? Who built it? What difficulties, if any, did they have? (History)
- What are the key elements within this very large structure and what are their purposes? What roles will scientists play in the lab? (Representative elements)
- How does *Destiny* differ from SkyLab projects? From the Russian space station, *Mir*, launched in 1986, that burned up plunging to Earth in 2001? How is it similar to or different from an "ideal" space station? (Relate to others)
- What are the implications for science? For interplanetary space travel? (Conclusions, consequences)
- What do we need to do to ensure success for this experiment?
- What would happen if we abandon the space station as, for example, too costly?

Reciprocal Teaching

Reciprocal teaching is a strategy that brings teacher and students into dialogue about the essential ideas within a text.

Figure 6.2
General Questioning Frame—Text Form

Historical Perspective

What are the causes of the situation? What led to the events observed? What assumptions are we operating under? Are there historical precedents or patterns that might be evident or instructive?

Key Elements

- What is the evidence before us?
- What are the important facts, elements, or parts?
- What feelings do we have about this situation?
- What are the significant roles people are playing?
- What relationships exist among the various elements? (*"consonantia"*)
- Which elements or facts are most important and why?

Significant Relationships

- How is this situation related to others? How is it separate and distinct? (*"integritas"*)
- Are there model cases of this situation that exemplify "typical" elements?
- How would you compare this situation with others? What are the similarities and differences?
- What conclusions do you draw from these comparisons? What alternative conclusions are possible?
- What is the essence (*"quidditas"*) of this situation? What makes it meaningful or unique?

Projections into the Future

- What do you predict might occur in the future?
- If we modified one or more of the variables, what might then occur?
- What are the implications, now and in the future, of this situation?
- What do we predict would be the consequences of action we might take?

Developed by Palincsar and Brown (1985), it consists of teaching students four different comprehension strategies:

1 Summarizing the most important information in the text
2. Generating questions
3. Clarifying for meaning
4. Predicting what the author will say in the following text

As you can see from these questions, they are student centered and proactive, and at least two of them require that students be able to identify important or confusing information and pose questions.

Research indicates that students taught with this method have improved in both their comprehension scores and the quality of their dialogue that occurred daily in class. "Experimental students functioned more independently of the teachers and improved the quality of their summaries over time. In addition, students' ability to write summaries, predict the kinds of questions teachers and tests ask, and detect incongruities in text improved" (Palincsar, 1986, pp. 19–20).

Reciprocal teaching is, in microcosm, an excellent example of what classrooms can become—opportunities for students to share more control in their own learning. By encouraging students to pose meaningful questions about what they know or don't understand, teachers become more responsive to students' needs and to the directions in which they are growing.

The World Wide Web—Another Form of Text

We have considered traditional books as our primary texts in this chapter. But Web sites and related information available on the World Wide Web also can be considered as texts worth reading and evaluating. This is an area where we as educators must be ever diligent. For example, when researching this chapter I searched www.google.com for the term "reciprocal teaching." One of the sites was the North Central Regional Educational Laboratory (NCREL), a federally funded research laboratory in suburban Chicago that I have worked with in the past (http://www.ncrel.org/sdrs/areas/issues/students/atrisk/at6lk.38

.htm); another site I did not recognize at all (http://ed-web3.educ. msu.edu/literacy/stuwork/recip.htm).

Now, what questions should I be asking about these two sites? What do you think?

Of course, the first question is, "What is the important information on this site and can I believe their representation of it?" The first site, NCREL, consisted of one long quotation from one of the program's creators, Ann Marie Palincsar. NCREL's function is to conduct research on educational matters; therefore, I found this Web site devoted to reciprocal teaching to be believable.

But I did not recognize the other site. There was no name prominently displayed anywhere. No credentials were given. But the Web site's Internet address (http://ed-web3.educ.msu.edu/ literacy/stuwork/recip.htm) has some key words in it. For example, we recognize "edu" as the signifier of an educational institution, often one involved with higher education.

There were other positive factors. The citations were mostly recognizable and the text contained information on the program that replicated what I'd found at the preceding site where the author of the program was cited. So the information was verifiable.

Now, one of the things we need to do with our students is to develop our own set of criteria for a good Web site. These criteria can consist of questions we might ask in order to determine its believability, usefulness, timeliness, and comprehensiveness. You might undertake this valuable task before reading Chapter 9, where we investigate Web-based information thoroughly. Challenge your students to develop their own set of criteria for assessing whether a Web site is valuable.

Conclusion

Raising questions from reading a text is a process of interpretation and of acquiring meaning. But there is more to it than that. When we question an author's words (or a painter's images) we are beginning a process of dialogue with the artist. We are starting to project ourselves into the work of art and beginning to think along with its creator. As John Dewey (1934) suggests, we are "recreating" the work in our own mind, searching out what is significant and how the work of art is organized.

In James Joyce's *A Portrait of the Artist as a Young Man*, Stephen Dedalus creates amazing images of his aspirations for being an artist that have served as a source of inspiration for me. His thoughts are ones that I have mulled over in my mind ever since I first read this book in Wilbury Crockett's senior English class at Wellesley High School, trying to imagine myself as Joyce and as Stephen. At the sound of someone calling his name (Dedalus) by the sea, Stephen reflects:

> Was it a quaint device opening a page of some medieval book of prophecies and symbols, a hawklike man flying sunward above the sea . . . a symbol of the artist forging anew in his workshop out of the sluggish matter of the earth a new soaring impalpable imperishable being?

And at the novel's end, he proclaims, "Welcome, O Life! I go to encounter for the millionth time the reality of experience and to forge in the smithy of my soul the uncreated conscience of my race" (Joyce, 1916/1956, pp. 169, 253).

What are the lives that we are forging in the smithies of our own souls?

References

Associated Press. (2001, February 11). Crew tears the wrapping off space lab. *New York Times*, p. A16.

Bandura, A. (1986). *Social foundations of thought and action: A cognitive theory*. Englewood Cliffs, NJ: Prentice Hall.

Blake, W. (1946). *The portable Blake*. (A. Kazin, Ed.). New York: Viking Press.

Dewey, J. (1934). *Art as experience*. New York: Capricorn Books.

Joyce, J. (1916/1956). *A portrait of the artist as a young man*. New York: Viking Press.

Lipman, M. (1982). *Harry Stottlemeier's discovery*. Upper Montclair, NJ: Institute for the Advancement of Philosophy for Children.

Marzano, R., Pickering, D., & McTighe, J. (1992). *A different kind of classroom: Teaching with dimensions of thinking*. Alexandria, VA: ASCD.

Ogle, D. (1986). K-W-L: A teaching model that develops active reading of expository text. *The Reading Teacher, 39*: 564–571.

Palincsar, A. S. (1986). Reciprocal teaching. In *Teaching reading as thinking*. Oak Brook, IL: North Central Regional Educational Laboratory.

Palincsar, A. S., & Brown, A .L. (1985). Reciprocal teaching: Activities to promote read[ing] with your mind. In T. L. Harris & E. J. Cooper (Eds.), *Reading, thinking and concept development: Strategies for the classroom*. New York: College Board.

Chapter 7

An Intelligent Revolution

I learned what happens when people in public life fail to ask questions.

—Senator John Kerry, reflecting on his service in Vietnam and his time as an antiwar organizer (July 31, 2002)

Living in our democracy brings many priceless benefits—among them the freedoms guaranteed to us within the Bill of Rights. Concurrent with these rights as citizens is our responsibility to be thoughtfully engaged in the democratic process. This means that we become informed about the nature of democracy, about issues and problems that confront our society, and, most significantly, that we learn how to ask intelligent questions about policies, practices, and uses of power. If we educate students to become more active in the process of self-government, if we help them ask the kinds of questions that challenge authorities (in person, in books, and on the Internet), we would initiate an intelligent revolution within this country. Such a revolution would be respectful (unlike the American, French, and Russian revolutions!), but it would eventually change the balance of power in our society. Students would no longer be the dependent, passive citizens we so often see. They would be up, asking tough questions, searching for information, and drawing their own conclusions about subject matter issues, social equity, and the just uses of power.

Being a participant in this revolution requires that we know how to think analytically and critically about ideas and problems, and that we be proactive with our curiosities.

Critical Thinking

There may still be many folks who are angry about the way the 2000 presidential election turned out. In the aftermath of the election itself, any person who read the newspapers and watched the news on television was treated to one of the best civics lessons since the impeachment of President William Clinton two years before.

What transpired during the more than 30 days after the election was an excellent example of how democracy works and how we as citizens were challenged to be good "critical thinkers." One of the definitions of critical thinking that I have long thought was both practical and enlightening came from Matthew Lipman of Montclair State University, in Montclair, New Jersey: "Critical thinking is skillful, fully responsible thinking that facilitates [making] judgments, because it (1) relies upon criteria, (2) is self-correcting, and (3) is sensitive to context . . ." (Lipman, 1988, p. 1).

What I like about Lipman's definition is that he focuses on our arriving at judgments, at conclusions in accordance with criteria. For example, when a student says, "This book is terrific!" (or "It's terrible!"), we have a wonderful opportunity to follow up with questions, such as "Why do you think it is terrific or terrible? What are your reasons [criteria]? What, specifically, are you using as evidence, data, information to arrive at your judgment?"

We are always making judgments about things: the weather, our classes, our food, the state of the economy, our health, our friends and business associates, our state and national politics. Figure 7.1 points out questions we can raise about using Lipman's definition of critical thinking to judge various things, from friends to the quality of Web sites.

Figure 7.1
Using Criteria To Make Judgments

Using Lipman's definition of critical thinking, consider the kinds of criteria you might use when making judgments about the quality of the following:

- Newspaper article or editorial
- Television program or movie
- Mathematical solution
- Computer software
- Friend
- Politician's position on issue
- Scientific experiment
- Web site
- Work of art
- Other categories people might make judgments about

Additional Exercise: When students draw conclusions about any of these materials or individuals, what questions can we pose to engage their reasoning processes?

Election 2000

The results of the Florida ballot caused a lot of people much consternation. First, the networks declared a winner too soon. Second, local community election boards in Florida were seen attempting to figure who voted for whom by holding the paper ballots up to the light, twisting them around, trying to detect "the intent of the voter." And finally, there were judges attempting to make fair assessments of how to proceed given the confluence of federal and state laws.

Reflective Pause

What do you remember about the presidential election of 2000, and what is now important about it to you? Why?

What was fascinating to me was that at so many turns a question that held our focus during most of this time was "What constitutes a legal vote?" In other words, what criteria or standards are we using to determine if what we have in our hands are "legal" ballots?

When dealing with paper punch card ballots that required the voter to press a stylus through the paper, thereby leaving a definite mark that could be read by a machine, we found that Lipman's definition of critical thinking came into play. We needed to ask very pointed and direct questions. "At the moment, the question of who wins the presidential election comes down to what criteria you use to identify a hole," said professor Achille Varzi of Columbia University (Stille, 2000, p. B11).

Here's where we got into "dimpled, swinging, and pregnant chads" (Tapper, 2000). The situation was confusing to most of us, simply because election officials were asked to make judgments and determine their own criteria for decision making.

In the end, the U.S. Supreme Court ruled by a vote of 7 to 2 that the manual recount ordered by the Florida Supreme Court was unconstitutional and could not be completed by a state-imposed deadline of December 12, 2000. By another, closer vote of 5 to 4, the justices ruled that no manual recount at all could proceed, allowing George W. Bush to win the election. One of the determining factors in the higher court's rulings was that the state of Florida had no uniform system—no commonly accepted criteria—for determining what constituted a legal ballot.

Here was civics in action! Here was a situation where inquisitive minds posed the most important questions: "What were the standards that fairly, accurately and reliably could be used to determine the wisdom of the voter?" We constantly heard about inferring the "intent of the voter." This was, indeed, difficult to do, and the U.S. Supreme Court's decision confirmed this observation.

Critical Thinking as "A Certain Skepticism"

Another person who has provided us with a definition of critical thinking is John McPeck. His rendering of critical thinking focuses on what he calls "a certain skepticism, or suspension of assent, towards a given statement, established norm or mode of doing things" (McPeck, 1981, p. 6).

This definition is powerful, because it challenges us to stop and think before we accede to someone's claim or conclusion about anything. We ought to think about some judgments rather carefully.

For example, suppose you read or hear the following statements. What would you want to know about them? What questions might you pose of the person who made the judgment, claim, or conclusion?

- "They are attacking us for who we are."
- "Our most hard fought freedom is the right to bear arms."
- "I went to Europe once. I don't need to go again."
- "Our educational system is the best devised by a free people."
- "The market will continue in its current trend for the foreseeable future."
- "All human beings are 99.9 percent alike."
- "The Internet has not been a boon to all people on Earth."
- "If it were possible to see the universe as a whole, from afar, it would appear pale green, between aquamarine and turquoise" (Wilford, 2002, p. A18).

Reflective Pause

When someone makes a claim such as the statements above, we, as active and engaged citizens and consumers, ought to ask a few good questions. List some questions you would pose about any one of these statements. What would you be curious about? What would you want to know more about before deciding what to believe?

Perhaps you have thought of questions that relate to an acronym I find useful (SEADS). It comprises a number of questions we need to think about when considering whether or not to accept somebody else's conclusions:

S What is the **source**? Who said it? In what setting or context? Is it believable?

E What **evidence** is presented to support the claim? Is it objective, accurate, reliable, and representative?

A What **assumptions** are being made or implied? Are they realistic and valid?

D What **definitions** of key terms are being used? Is the language clear, unambiguous, and specific?

S What is the **slant**, bias, or special interest reflected in the statement? What might be the motivation of the people who made the statement?

Each of these sets of questions represents a major area of concern that we need to be concerned with. For example, the source needs to be considered because we rightly need to know who he or she is and what that person's special interest or motivation might be. Every September for 25 years, I listened to one university president after another tell my colleagues and me what a wonderful, talented, intelligent, and industrious group of faculty we were. Of course, it was true! But you had to consider what the president's motivation might have been at the opening of the new academic year.

We always need to clarify our terms when speaking and writing. What we mean by something might be similar to or different from what others mean by the same term. For example, when we assert, "life does not exist beyond our planet," what terms immediately call out for definition?

Similarly, when we claim that "the U.S. economy will continue to grow well into this century at a steady pace" or "we will continue to accrue significant surpluses over the next two decades," what words require clarification? Now there are some questions that need to be asked of these assertions. For example, what economic assumptions are they based on? What are we taking for granted when we claim that our economy will continue to grow and build up surpluses? Too often, we simply aren't even aware of what we take for granted in our daily thinking. Use the exercise in Figure 7.2 to rethink some common statements.

Figure 7.2
Challenging Everyday Assertions

Using the SEADS suggestions, what questions would you ask about these claims?

- "Earth is sure to be struck by an asteroid within the next 200 years or so."
- "Genetically modified foods are better for you."
- "Conflict is good in a democracy."
- "Washington and Lincoln were our two greatest American presidents."
- "Violence on TV and in movies has a bad effect on children."
- "Children without good self-esteem may not succeed."

Additional Exercise: Write your own claims for students to challenge.

"Where's the Data?"

During the 1960s, some of us in education became immersed in the child-centered educational model. We firmly believed that the curriculum needed to be made "relevant" to students' interests and needs. We further believed that students should have some choice over what they do in school. It seemed logical that if you wanted students to be interested in what they were doing, they should have some stake in their young educational careers.

Well, this might be true, but where was the evidence? Where does it come from? Who produced it, and is it representative of large groups of students? I remember my doctoral advisor, Gary Griffin, then at Teachers College at Columbia University, who continually asked these kinds of questions many years ago about all the so-called "romantic critics" of education who espoused a more child-centered curriculum and who demanded, "Give students choice. Make the curriculum relevant!" and so forth. Gary Griffin was speaking about writers like Herb Kohl and A. H. Neal, who based curriculum on students' interests and who advocated teaching reading when students were ready, respectively.

"Where's the data?" Gary would ask. "What does it say?" Often there was only anecdotal data from one classroom, and many of us, myself certainly included, were rushing to judgment about what kinds of learning experiences were best for our children. We saw students were bored and disengaged from the subject-centered curriculum and found that when you gave kids choices, some decisions to make on their own, they became more actively engaged in their own learning. Today, evidence from brain development confirms some of our approaches based on a more student-centered curriculum (Jensen, 1998).

Consider these kinds of claims and the evidence you may or may not need to be able to accept them:

- Children learn best when the content is related to their personal experiences, needs, and/or interests.

- Inquiry is the beginning of meaningful learning.

- Teaming of teachers is the best arrangement for middle schools.

- Interdisciplinary teaching makes learning more significant.

- Every child should have equal hours per week of math, science, history, and language arts.

- "As students work through different problems that a teacher presents, they develop their understanding into principles that govern the topic" (Bransford, Brown, & Cocking, 2000, p. 239).

In weighing in on any one of these more or less accepted ways of thinking, we need to ask about what evidence and data support these conclusions.

Questioning the Status Quo

As I mentioned previously, Seymour Sarason is a social psychologist who, in his seminal book *The Culture of the School and the Problem of Change* (1982), acted as a gadfly in terms of questioning the common "behavioral regularities" or patterns of behavior we accept as necessary within schools. I remember teaching this book for so many years to teachers who were working toward their supervisor certificates and how enraged some of them became at the questions he raised.

For example, he enjoyed asking, "Why should we teach physical education in schools?" or "Why teach math five times a week?" He asked the same questions of teachers of math and other subjects for a specific reason: to plumb the depths of their understanding of the rationale for such practices. His goal, or at least one of them, was to call into question what we take for granted as accepted realities in order to ask if there aren't better alternatives. Sarason wanted to help us identify problems by asking us to examine what we do every day in our workaday worlds without question—accepting the status quo, accepting blindly the authorities under which we labor.

Here is a sequence of questions derived from his seminal work:

■ What is the pattern we are concerned with?

■ What was its original purpose?

■ Are we achieving our goals using this pattern?

■ If not, what are some alternative means toward achieving the same goal?

■ Which would you select now and why?

Try examining the status quo as reflected in the school patterns shown in Figure 7.3 to see if questioning any one of them will cause you to wonder whether or not this is the best practice.

My colleagues and I used a questioning pattern like this when working in an alternative school in Brooklyn, New York (located in the basement of Thomas Jefferson High School). We were charged with providing different ways for high school students in Brooklyn to learn, so we had to challenge every pattern. Over the course of two years we tried various new approaches:

■ Establishing the school of 100 students in a basement without any interior walls.

■ Recruiting students with average grades and not just those who were failing.

■ Turning off the bells from the main building to create our own time frames.

Figure 7.3
Questioning the Status Quo

Select one or more items. Describe the patters of behavior you observe.
Analyze why we engage in it: What was our original purpose? Are we achieving our goal? If not, what alternatives might better serve our needs today?

	Pattern	Rationale	Alternatives
Raising hands			
Lining up			
Everybody relying on a common textbook			
Students sitting in rows during most of the class time			
Students listening primarily to the teacher			
Teachers asking most of the questions in class			
Many questions requiring only short answers			
Students posing few content questions			
Teachers creating the curriculum			
Grades based on tests (short answer, Scantron, essay, multiple choice)			
Teachers as the primary or sole evaluators			
Access to the Internet			
School five days a week, 8 a.m. to 3 p.m.			
Math/English/social studies/science every day			
Faculty meetings			
Others			

- Developing our own philosophy of how students learn best.
- Creating what we called "experiential learning units"—in outdoor education, internships in business and the arts, retail store management, and carpentry (where faculty member David Hamlin built a house indoors).
- Taking students on long weekend camping trips to develop leadership and team-building skills.

Through these methods and in other ways, we challenged the status quo of the "traditional" ways of learning—all students using the same book, sitting in a classroom with four walls during a 45-minute period. We experimented with block scheduling long before it became fashionable during the 1990s.

How can we use this critical questioning strategy with our students?

1. Challenge them to document and then question the "regularities" or patterns of their lives in and out of school (for example, attending school every day, learning in a "classroom," being home by a given hour). Here we need to be ready to be flexible in some areas where they definitely will have questions and concerns.

2. Challenge them to find the patterns and regularities within the subjects they are studying—things we take for granted in literature, math, history, and science. (See the list of questions derived from Sarason's work, above.) We might undertake this approach when they are having some difficulties learning content in the "traditional" fashion. Or we might follow the lead of Kathy Martinson of Dumont High School in Dumont, New Jersey, who asked her students to outline (using a concept map) the roles of "good" teachers and students. This kind of display could then lead students to answer the question, "How do we learn best? What helps us learn this subject in this classroom?"

3. Challenge them to document and then question patterns in the lives of different groups of people—teenagers, teachers, parents, civic leaders, politicians, artists, characters in history and in fiction, and so forth.

4. Study the lives of famous questioners and challengers of the status quo: Rosa Parks, Nelson Mandela, Bob Dylan, Betty Friedan, Amelia Earhart, Marie Curie, William Safire, and many more. Investigate the lives of these people to see what elements of the status quo they were questioning, why, and what their alternative solutions were.

Such exercises will be helpful in bringing about both awareness and control over how we lead our lives. We learn patterns of behavior for seemingly good reasons at certain times of our lives—for example, raising our hands to speak—that in time maybe we may want to question as to their appropriateness. I know that asking students to critique how they are learning their subjects will be perceived by some as threatening. This is not an exercise we could undertake lightly, because once we open such a Pandora's box for students' input, *we must see it through*. We need to determine, for ourselves, which patterns are open to question and which are not. By using Kathy's example, above, we can find constructive ways of challenging students to find those patterns that may no longer serve a useful purpose and to engage them in some hard thinking about who are the authorities in the classroom and at home, why order is very important to reasoned discussion, and why we want them to listen to the thinking of their classmates and not just the teacher's.

It is possible that some students may use such questions to reject adult authority, partially or entirely. What do we do then? We can reason with them about their goals and how best to achieve them. Any one of us who embarks on this reflection on the status quo will have the courage and empathy to develop a viable plan with such students.

"Obliteration by Incorporation"

Sociologist Robert K. Merton of Columbia University was responsible for introducing significant concepts into the way we looked at society, among them such concepts as "role model," "deviant behavior," and "self-fulfilling prophecy." Another one is applicable here—"obliteration by incorporation." That is, certain patterns and ways of thinking become so ingrained in our daily lives that we forget why we engage in them. We obliterate the reasons for engaging in them by blindly incorporating them into our lives (Cohen, 1999, p. 5).

There certainly are patterns of thinking in schools that have become incorporated by "obliteration" and, consequently, need to be continually challenged, at least by adults, and, preferably, by teachers and their students as well.

"Why Do You Have Such Crazy Ideas?"

One of the most fascinating books I ever read was written by June Goodfield and was entitled *An Imagined World* (1981). This is the story of the daily life of a scientist at Rockefeller University here in New York City, one who was engaged in cancer research. Goodfield, a science writer of exceptional ability, followed the unnamed scientist around for a long time chronicling her scientific investigations of lymphocytes, white blood cells that are disease-fighting immune cells.

At the end of the long time they spent together while the book was being researched, the scientist said to Goodfield in some exasperation, "They never asked me where I got my ideas from. They never asked me, 'What made you think that way?'"

The scientist, a young woman, said to Goodfield, "You never asked me why I had such crazy ideas . . . nobody actually says, 'Why on earth do you say such a crazy thing?'" (p. 220).

This might be a question about searching for evidence and data. But it might also be a reflective, metacognitive question, such as, "How did you figure that out? Please share with me your thinking processes. How did you arrive at that conclusion?"

This may be one of these most important questions for us as citizens of our democracy. We ought to know how people have arrived at the policies and practices they espouse, the conclusions they have arrived at.

Figure 7.4 deals with circumstances when the question "What made you think that way?" may be appropriate.

Figure 7.4
"What Made You Think That Way?"

Asking this question may be appropriate under these circumstances:

1. When modeling our own thinking.
2. When students respond with an answer or statement that differs from our expectations.
3. When students pose an unusual question, such as, "If there were no plate tectonics, would there be volcanoes?"
4. When students make an error in calculation, application, or comprehension. We need to honor children's thinking processes, perhaps especially when they are in error.
5. Other situations that you can think of . . .

The Most Important Question—"How Do You Know?"

When my mother was growing up in LeRoy, New York, a small town near Rochester, she had a memorable encounter with her father. They were standing in their living room watching the snowflakes flutter down to cover their lawn and the street on which they lived. My grandfather was a chemist who worked for General Foods. Through his own inquisitiveness and persistence, he created the first dietetic dessert, D-Zerta, for people who had diabetes. He used a sugar substitute still common today, and his was arguably the first dessert for weight-watchers as well.

"Look at all those snowflakes, Betty. Aren't they wonderful? You know they're all unique!"

"How do you know?" she asked immediately.

I'm sure my grandfather launched into a thorough explanation of the proof of his assertion, being the scientist he was.

But after listening intently and still looking out at the snow falling on LeRoy, my mother concluded that not all those flakes, nor all those that had fallen to date on earth, could be "unique" or truly one of a kind.

"Well," she said, "I don't believe it!" My grandfather gave up on his too-independent daughter on this question.

What I've admired about my mother's conversation with her dad is her healthy skepticism about a claim that just seemed too extravagant. She asked the most important question we can ask when confronted with judgments that just seem unrealistic or untrue, "How do you know?"

This is the question we need to pose when anybody makes claims about the correctness of a policy or procedure, whether political, scientific, or personal. Sometimes as I talk back to the television and ask pointed questions, my wife Nancy will ask, "Who are you talking to?"

"I'm asking these folks why they think theirs is the best solution or best idea. What proof do they have? They never say what they're basing it on nor whether or not they've considered any alternatives." My hunch always is that many politicians are presenting a position primarily from a particular set of assumptions or ideological framework, not a solution based on reasoned analysis of a problem and associated evidence. I hope I'm wrong.

Recently, as I took my mother on a tour of the Rose Center for Earth and Space at the American Museum of Natural History in New York City, she declared emphatically, "And I don't believe that all grains of sand are unique either." They have to be, I said.

"How do you know?" she again asked and I tried to explain my understanding of the geologic processes that create sand, but I don't think she believed me. "How could they be?" she said quietly.

My mother has always reminded me just how important it is to listen carefully and to question what people say.

Conclusion

The nature of our lives in a democracy is predicated, at least in the abstract and the ideal, on a questioning citizenry. This is why the fourth estate, the press, is guaranteed its freedom, as is our expression of freedom of speech within certain specific limitations.

The well-being and future development of our civilization are also predicated on a questioning peer review process. It is not just in science that we need solid peer review that raises questions about other peoples' claims. This is true in business, philosophy, and the arts as well. Recall the comments from Chapter 1 about what may inhibit certain cultures from scientific advancements: "mutual admiration societies" that do not engage in hard critique of the kind Carl Sagan advocated.

We need to help students ask the "rude questions" that Lewis Lapham claimed our students do not ask because we educate them to "know their place" in society, to sit quietly and accept what they're told (Lapham, 2000, p. 7). We learn to be passive and dependent. We need to work toward challenging this status quo, wherever it might exist.

If and when we consider that our rights as citizens (or those of others) are being challenged and in danger, we need to speak up loudly and clearly. Our "intelligent revolution" may, at times, become a "rude revolution." It was Thomas Jefferson who wrote that, "The government of the United States is the result of a *revolution in thought*. It was founded on the principle that all persons have equal rights, and that government is responsible to, and derives its powers from, a free people" (my emphasis) (Jefferson, 2002; http://etext.virginia.edu/jefferson/quotations/jeffcont.htm).

We cannot afford to be passive and succumb to the charge of disloyalty because we dissent. Dissent is what turned a group of British colonies into this great nation we now inhabit. Dissent and a healthy skepticism are what keep our searching for truth alive and appropriately focused. An active self-monitoring of our own thoughts and actions that is full of doubt and questioning is what can keep us alive to our own best intentions.

We cannot afford to maintain the kind of passive acceptance that has so characterized education in this country. Our students here in the 21st century deserve far better!

A young teacher I knew had an instructor who wrote on the board every day, "Question Authority." In the aftermath of September 11, 2001, we as citizens need to continually wonder about the world we live in and what we are being told by those in authority. As Senator John Kerry of Massachusetts observed about his service in Vietnam as a gunboat commander and as an antiwar organizer: "I learned what happens when people in public office fail to ask questions" (Dao, 2002, p. A1).

We saw in Chapter 1 how accountants, managers, and journalists did not question how some companies like Enron were making money. We also saw how some in President George W. Bush's administration viewed any questions of their foreign policy as aiding and abetting the enemy. The same kinds of observations were made during the Vietnam era when antiwar protesters raised their voices. John Kerry's kind of patriotism includes both military service and questioning authorities when appropriate. In a democracy our challenge is to be ever vigilant.

We need to question the status quo—in schools, families, relationships, government, business, and society in general. General passivity, lack of interest, and unconcern are no longer viable options for those who call themselves citizens of democracy. This will be the nature of the intelligent revolution that inquiring students can initiate in our society.

References

Bransford, J., Brown, A., & Cocking, R. (Eds.). (2000). *How people learn: Brain, mind, experience, and school.* Washington, DC: National Academy Press.

Cohen, P. (1999, Spring). What's the (next) big idea? In *Inside The New York Times* [special insert], 3, 1. p. 5.

Dao, J. (2002, July 31). In attacks on Bush, Kerry sets himself apart. *The New York Times,* p. A1, A5.

Goodfield, J. (1981). *An imagined world.* New York: Harper & Row.

Jefferson, T. (January, 2002). Thomas Jefferson on government and politics. Available: http://etext.virginia.edu/jefferson/quotations/jeffcont.htm.

Jensen, E. (1998). *Teaching with the brain in mind.* Alexandria, VA: ASCD.

Lapham, L. (2000, August). School bells. *Harper's Magazine, 301*(1803), pp. 7–9.

Lipman, M. (1988). Critical thinking: What it can be. *Cogitare, 2*(4): 1–2.

McPeck, J. (1981). *Critical thinking and education.* Oxford, England: Martin Robertson.

Sarason, S. (1982). *The culture of the school and the problem of change.* Boston: Allyn & Bacon.

Stille, A. (2000, November 18). Staring into the navel of ballots. *The New York Times,* p. B11.

Tapper, J. (2000, November 19). Reading the chads. Available: www.salon.com/politics/feature/2000/11/19/chad/. Accessed May 15, 2001.

Wilford, J. N. (2002, January 11). Scientists paint universe as a vast sea of green. *The New York Times,* p. A18.

Chapter 8

INQUIRY- AND PROBLEM-BASED LEARNING

Are there rocks in outer space?

If continents didn't move, would we have volcanoes?

How are rocks formed?

—FOURTH GRADE STUDENTS OF TEACHER ANN WHITE
AT THE JACKSON ACADEMY, EAST ORANGE, NEW JERSEY

As Ann White's students studied the nature of rocks, the questions poured forth from them so much that the 4th grade teacher called them "Rock Hounds." Their questions provided a guide for a unit focused on the mysteries and wonderment of nature's building blocks. Ann structured their inquiries as a problem-based learning unit that used a wide variety of resources, including the Internet and a local geologist.

Problem-based learning seeks to engage students in thinking through ill-structured realistic problematic situations found within the curriculum. A "problem" is anything that involves doubt, uncertainty, or difficulty. We encounter problems of all kinds, from personal to professional, from spiritual to practical. What these situations have in common is that they often cause us to question, to wonder how to solve them, and how to resolve the issue. We might also call structured learning experiences based on such problematic situations "inquiry-based" learning, because they challenge students to identify their own questions and undertake a rigorous investigation to find answers.

Reflective Pause

Now, why do we want to challenge students to engage whole-heartedly in identifying and resolving problematic situations? Why do you think these are, potentially, good learning experiences? What does your own personal experience tell you about the relationship between problem solving and learning?

The reasons for challenging students are many. First, our minds are capable of thinking through complex experiences. We as a species have been confronting all kinds of challenges during our time on Earth: surviving on the savannas of East Africa, navigating vessels around the globe, and reaching and walking on the moon.

Second, research (Caine & Caine, 1997; Diamond & Hopson, 1998) indicates that engagement with such high levels of challenge is what fosters intellectual development and, hence, our ability to think productively. "Kids need complex, challenging problems to solve" (Jensen, 1998, p. 35).

Third, these kinds of challenges engage our minds and bodies in thinking through complex, multifaceted situations where there are no easy, one-word, Scantron-like answers. What to do about pollution in a local stream or how to get more citizens involved in local politics requires what some call "higher-order thinking." If we want our students engaged in productive thought, problem-based learning is one approach. There is no single solution just one mouse click away.

Fourth, engaging a group of students in thinking through situations like these requires problem identification, one of the most important aspects of problem solving. Being able to identify what the problem is without referring to a textbook is a life skill (Barell, 1995).

Fifth, working through these kinds of ill-structured problems requires teamwork and collaboration, skills required in most workplace environments. We have to be able to listen, analyze, compromise, and synthesize ideas and draw our own and group conclusions in order to solve most difficult problems today. Imagine the cool-headed collaboration involved in solving the problem of *Apollo 13* as it hurtled toward Earth in its terribly crippled state! On April 13, 1970, at 200,000 miles from Earth, their oxygen tank exploded, necessitating the crew's moving into the lunar module as a lifeboat. Only good thinking and close teamwork on the part of mission control personnel on the ground in Houston enabled Jim Lovell and his shipmates to return to Earth safely.

Sixth, most state standards in the various disciplines are calling for inquiry—thinking through science and history as scientists and historians do. For example, in New Jersey: "All students will develop problem-solving, decision-making and inquiry skills reflected by formulating usable questions and hypotheses, planning experiments, conducting systematic observations, interpreting and analyzing data and drawing conclusions and communicating results." (See the New Jersey State Educational Standards—Science at www.state.nj.us/njded/cccs/02/s5_02.html.) Such processes, of course, apply not only in science, but in language arts and social studies as well. In New York, students in social studies classes are expected to "write a series of questions using stems which indicate increasing levels of complexity for use as a guide for problem solving" and then to develop plans for solving these problems. (See the New York State Educational Standards—Social Studies at www.nybeacons.org/standards.html#state.)

A search of many state educational Web sites reveals that most problem solving and inquiry are associated in the minds of curriculum developers with science and the so-called "scientific method." I had to search through many states' language arts and social studies sites to find *anything* related to inquiry! Evidently, these planners do not regard inquiry as a seminal process in the humanities. We seem to identify asking good questions with learning that "method" found in Chapter 1 of so many science textbooks and then seldom heard about again during the school year—pose a problem or question, develop an hypothesis, create an experiment or investigation, gather data, and analyze and draw conclusions.

Good readers ask themselves questions about the conflicts in stories. Good historians pose hard questions about the often conflicting reports of complex events. Good artists question their creative interpretations—imagine how many questions and self-reprobations Beethoven engaged in as he scrapped so many versions of the opening movement of his Fifth Symphony (Bernstein, 1954; www.leonardbernstein.com)!

Seventh, research from cross-cultural studies by Stigler and Hiebert (1999) indicates that this problem-based approach is used in countries like Japan, where teachers sometimes start a math lesson with a challenging problem for the students to analyze and determine how many ways to approach it. These teachers are not, on these occasions, interested in solutions or plugging values into an algorithm. They see such problem analysis as a way of helping students analyze problems, one of the most important aspects of problem solving.

Some teachers in the United States, by contrast, seem more interested in helping students perform a procedure or practice a set of discrete skills. Thus, a problem-based approach may be one of the best ways to come to a deeper understanding of the subject's fundamental concepts and problem-solving processes.

Eighth, the effort expended on posing and resolving such problems more than likely develops our capacity to do so in the future and helps us apply what we have learned from one problem to another (Bransford, Franks, & Sherwood, 1986; Mayer, 1989). Years ago, Ralph Tyler (1949) asserted that one of the best ways to acquire information is within a problem-solving context. This, of course, still applies today.

And, lastly, the World Wide Web serves as an example of an "enriched environment" full of complexity and challenge with rich opportunities for students to choose some of their own curiosities and to gain some creative control over their own learning (Diamond & Hopson, 1998, p. 108). Problem-based learning provides us with excellent opportunities to take advantage of the Web as a major resource.

What I have been interested in is the inquiry aspect of problem-based learning. It seems to me that one of the challenges of such learning is for students to pose their own problems; one way to do this is for us to give prominence to their own questions. We know from the classroom observations of Dillon (1988) that *students ask very few questions about content during the course of a class session.* Our curricula are driven, by and large, by teacher-initiated questions and objectives. What I am describing here is a reorientation of our curricular priorities such that students share some of the control of our objectives, strategies, and assessments. Here is where we break the silence of student passivity (see Figure 2.2).

I want to see students grow toward independent thinking, taking more control of and responsibility for their own learning. Barbara McCombs (1991) asserts that such development results in part from students' own metacognitive reflections and inquiries.

The Rock Hounds

Ann White's students began their studies with careful observations of various kinds of rocks, some from science kits and others they had brought from home ("What do you observe? What does it suggest or make you think of?"). They then used the KWHLAQ strategy (see Figure 8.1) (Barell, 1998).

Reflective Pause

Examine all elements of the KWHLAQ strategy and determine for yourself why it might be important to use each question in this long-term inquiry strategy.

Starting any unit with what students already know acknowledges and honors their personal knowledge, taps into their prior knowledge about rocks, and provides an opportunity for them to express any misconceptions they might have.

All students' prior knowledge of facts, as well as their ideas and their misconceptions about rock formations and locations, are webbed out for all to see. In this concept map we have a pre-assessment of students' prior knowledge and we should keep a

Figure 8.1
KWHLAQ Strategy

K   "What do we think we know about the subject?"
W   "What do we want or need to know?"
H   "How will we go about finding answers to our questions?"
L   "What are we learning on a daily basis and what have we learned after
       our culminating projects?"
A   "How can we apply the major concepts, ideas, principles, and skills to
       the same subject, to other subjects, and to our lives beyond the class-
       room?"
Q   "What new questions do we have now?"

Source: From *Problem Based Learning: An Inquiry Approach,* by John Barell. © 1998
SkyLight Training and Publishing. Reprinted by permission by SkyLight Professional
Development. www.skylight.edu or 800-348-4474.

record to serve as a baseline. We will be adding to this webbed
map as we explore and gather information during the unit. If each
student keeps a personal copy of her first web, the initial class
web, and adds to it (perhaps in a different color) as she proceeds,
she has a running record of what she is learning.

Students then posed their own questions, identified ways to
gather answers, and conducted research using the Internet,
books, and local geologists. Students' identifying their own
curiosities gives the unit focus and provides them with their own
personal reasons for engaging in the unit's learning experiences.

Some of their questions included the following: "Can you eat
other rocks besides halite? Do rocks have energy? What's the
most popular rock?"

These were initial questions and as Ann conducted her lessons introducing students to various kinds of rocks, their origins,
and Earth's history, students generated more and more questions.

High School Social Studies

Not too far away in Paramus, New Jersey, Cheryl Hopper has
been guiding her 9th graders through a unit on Africa using the
same KWHLAQ strategy. Her students first webbed out what they
thought they knew about Africa (see Figure 8.2).

Figure 8.2
Concept Map of Africa

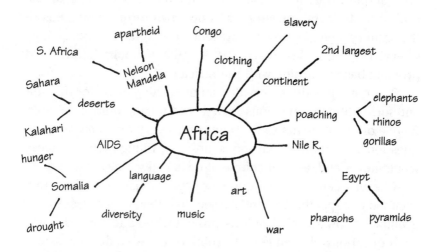

Source: Reprinted from *Developing More Curious Minds,* ed. Arthur L. Costa. © 2001 ASCD.

Then she asked them what they wanted and needed to know about Africa. The "need" to know is important because we want our students to think like historians and scientists and not all 4th or 9th graders are fascinated by rocks and Africa. The "need to know" provides us with frameworks for thinking within the subject matter about complex problems and issues. It should help us generate the kinds of questions good mathematicians, historians, and art critics would pose.

Here are some of their curiosities:

- "How and why did powerful kingdoms emerge in Africa, especially West Africa?"
- "How do geographical features account for the cultural diversity of the continent?"
- "What were the effects of European rule? Of apartheid?"

Cheryl's students then combined these curiosities into "core questions" that reflected her students' personal interests as well as all of her own curricular priorities. Cheryl said, "They gave me all the topics and ideas I wanted to think about!" When students are not as comprehensive in their inquiries, we need to supplement their curiosities with our own curricular objectives in the form of questions. We are, after all, still in charge of the process. Both our students' questions and our own form the nucleus of the inquiry unit. Figure 8.3 presents a diagram showing how Cheryl Hopper's class used the KWHLAQ inquiry model and problem-based learning with the Africa unit.

The core questions provided an organizing focus for the unit and for additional questions raised by students during the unit. As one of her students said, "How come every time I answer one question . . . another one pops up?" He thought this process would never end, and, of course, if he is lucky it never will!

Cheryl's central questions were the robust ones that transcended her specific unit and subject to reflect deeper issues, for example, "How do civilizations grow, thrive, and then decay?" Such questions challenge us to think of broader, deeper issues, ones that go beyond immediate concerns (Barell, 1995).

"How will we find answers?" is the next question, and as in Ann's class, Cheryl's students teamed up to research different questions. Her 9th graders also assumed roles of experts in different areas, such as geography, Atlantic slave trade, and art. They made assignments for the whole class. For example, the geography experts gave this homework assignment:

> Read about the geography of the continent of Africa in your textbook. Now, imagine you are taking a hot air balloon trip across the continent. In your journal describe what you see. Include geographic features, changes in climate, and so forth.

Students, in effect, planned out the entire unit, not only giving assignments, but also planning trips to a local African art exhibit and determining how they would share their information with classmates. We shall have more to say about the fascinating learning experiences students planned for the museum in that chapter.

Sharing Control with Students

Both Ann and Cheryl have engaged their students in one form of problem-based learning, an approach that focuses on the KWHLAQ inquiry strategy (Barell, 1998).

Figure 8.3
Students' Questions Radiate From the Teachers' Core Questions

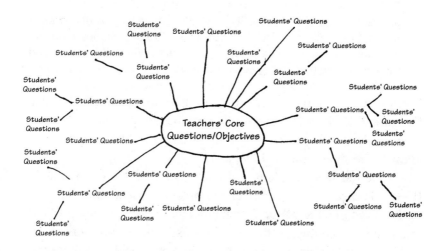

In 4th and 9th grades the students are investigating topics found within the curriculum, but doing it in ways that challenge them to identify their own curiosities. Dewey (1933) said reflective thought begins with a perplexity, and their questions reflect these kinds of personal doubts and put them right at the center of constructing the unit.

Both teachers are also engaged in a personal learning approach that consists of their sharing control with their students. Students become more personally invested in their own learning when there are choices involved. Giving students opportunities to make choices taps into their "inherent motivation to learn," says Barbara McCombs (1991, p. 6). If we help students perceive that they are in control of their own educational destinies by the choices they make, they can then learn the "benefits of their agency and the value of self-regulated learning strategies" (p. 10). No longer will we receive, as I used to as a young teacher, a "thank you" for an A grade and a severe complaint for anything less! We are saying to students, "You made the decision and this is one of the results."

And Jensen (1998) notes how brain research supports educators offering students opportunities to make choices:

> We've come to understand the two critical ingredients in enrichment are challenge and feedback. Since what's challenging for one student may not be challenging for another, this makes a tremendous argument for choice in the learning process, including self-paced learning, and more variety in the strategies used to engage learners better. (p. 39)

Brain research also supports our tapping into students' inquisitiveness. "The brain is essentially curious, and it must be to survive. It constantly seeks connections between the new and the known" (Wolfe & Brandt, 1998, p. 11).

Students make choices not only in the kinds of questions they will research in a personalized problem-based unit, but also in the ways in which they gather information, how they process and make it meaningful through their assessment projects.

Personal problem posing and problem resolving give students opportunities to become more meaningfully involved because educators trust their students, to different degrees, to organize their learning and fashion meaningful culminating experiences, such as projects that will reflect the depth and quality of their understanding (see Chapter 11).

Searching the Web

When Cheryl's students posted all their questions, they had an excellent set of destinations with which to chart their navigation of the World Wide Web. Searching, in general, on online directories such as Yahoo, InfoSeek, Lycos, and AltaVista, and on megasearch engines like Google.com, Profusion.com, and Northernlight.com, they used keywords like "Africa," "economic development," "United Nations," "Sahara," and the names of specific countries like "South Africa," "Zimbabwe," "Namibia," "Congo," "Egypt," and "Kenya."

They discovered sites for each country, comparative development statistics at sites related to the United Nations, the Agency for International Development, the World Bank, and the U.S. Congress.

Students would come in to class full of excitement about the new sites they had found, wanting to share them with the rest of the class. At one point they created a chart of hot Web sites and posted it on the bulletin board.

Much of the searching went on during students' own time, at home, during free periods in the library, as well as during class time. Cheryl did not need to urge her students to explore the vast resources of the Internet. Most of these 9th graders were experienced explorers and as soon as they engaged in figuring out how to find answers (recall the **H** of the KWHLAQ inquiry strategy: "How will we go about finding answers to our questions?"), they were heard to rattle off a number of different search engines and potential Web sites to explore.

During times of sharing information back in class, students brought in printouts of multiple pages from the Web. Many of these, unfortunately, showed no affiliation with a home page; many showed no authorship or any kind of reference to sources of information. The printed pages read as if they were abstracted from lengthy master's degree theses.

Teachers like Cheryl, therefore, have to spend considerable time helping everybody analyze their information using some of the criteria developed in Chapter 7: reliability of sources, relevance, objectivity, representativeness, and believability. Students at first believed everything they printed off the Net. Some students were seen to press the "Print" button as soon as something with a relevant title came on the screen. These patterns had developed earlier in elementary and middle school, even though their teachers had similarly stressed critical literacy skills in the form of questions to ask yourself during Net investigations: "Who is the author? What are his or her qualifications? Can I believe what I'm reading? Why or why not? Is the information accurate? Relevant? Representative? Objective?"

Cheryl had to stress that students should be like reporters, checking their sources of information against other sources, trying to obtain at least one other reference that would confirm or disconfirm their findings, just like newspaper reporters.

For some students this was their first extensive experience searching the World Wide Web for information in a school project.

They had come from schools with limited access to the Internet and did not have computers at home. Some students with learning difficulties found their time on the Internet fascinating because they could point and click more or less at will, using their own power of control. They were not comfortable just sitting in class listening to somebody else talk. "I like doing what I want to do," one of them said. "It's more fun when I can like do it myself, you know?"

Yes. Learning is often more engaging and fun when we are making important choices, and searching the Internet affords these kinds of decision points for students.

One of our goals for the future is for both the 4th and 9th grade students to engage in online question and answer sessions with researchers embarked on such expeditions as those found on GlobalSchoolNetwork (www.gsn.org). Here we could join global trek expeditions in East Africa (or the Middle East or China) or Quest journeys to Australia (AustraliaQuest). Students post questions to the trekkers on location and search out answers.

Another excellent resource for reference materials and for students' posing their own questions is www.refdesk.com. Here you can select from hundreds of experts in all major professions: astronomy, botany, history, literature, mathematics, science, and much, much more! (See Appendix A.)

And the potential for collaborating with other 4th and 9th grade classrooms anywhere in the world is a territory yet to be explored.

Authentic Assessment

In both classes teachers used the principles of authentic assessment to create a scenario that would challenge students to use the information they have learned in practical and real-world appropriate fashions. Cheryl and Ann presented these culminating projects to their students at the beginning of their units so students would have real goals toward which to work.

Ann's Rock Hounds took what they had discovered about sedimentary, igneous, and metamorphic rocks around their school building to create an exhibit on local geology for their school and a partner school several miles away. A visit from geologist Dr. Jonathan Lincoln of Montclair State University helped them answer some of their questions and generated the intriguing discovery that those indentations in a purple rock were the fossilized footprints of dinosaurs running around New Jersey, back when it was part of Africa around 200 million years ago.

Cheryl presented her 9th graders with her core concepts and skills in the form of a scenario:

> You are an African nation that desires a substantial loan from the World Bank. Your goal is to convince the World Bank that your country's needs are great and you deserve a loan. The World Bank has a limited amount to lend and many other countries are asking for loans. Therefore, you must prepare a strong case for receiving a loan and be able to defend your need for the money.

Reflective Pause

What do you think of Cheryl's assessment? What are the advantages and some of the difficulties with engaging in this kind of learning experience at the end of her unit? How might you undertake such an assessment?

I have always loved this challenge for students. It seems to me that this is what we do in the world: we use information to solve problems. How well do you think Cheryl's very high expectations meet Wiggins's (1998) criteria for authentic assessment?

1. Students make judgments involving critical thinking and problem solving.
2. They are "realistic" in that they "replicate contexts in which a person's knowledge and abilities are 'tested' in real-world situations."
3. They "do" the subject as historians or economists would.
4. They present their findings in such settings where they can rehearse and receive immediate, direct feedback, thereby being able to modify their conclusions. (p. 22)

This scenario is the kind of learning experience we should strive to incorporate into as many of our units of instruction as possible.

Cheryl designed this one, but do you think it's possible for us to sit down with our students and ask them, "Now, what do you think you can do with the information you are learning to demonstrate that you can really use it? What kinds of problems will it help us solve?" I'm sure we can do this with most of our students if we couch the challenge in language they understand!

"You Can't Build a Hospital!"

The scenarios Ann and Cheryl created are designed to incorporate the major content they want students to demonstrate understanding of. As Perkins (1992) has noted, three of our primary goals in education are to ensure that students can retain, understand, and use knowledge. We want our students to be able, through a variety of strategies, to demonstrate their understanding of concepts, ideas, principles, and information (Barell, 1995).

The Rock Hounds had to figure out what kinds of rocks were to be found around Jackson Academy, determine how they were formed, and then design an exhibit to communicate these findings to their classmates and to students in their partner school. In the process they were, of course, engaged in collaborative problem solving.

The final three steps in the process—L, A, and Q—provide us with additional opportunities for students to demonstrate understanding. The applicants to the World Bank had to become very familiar with one African nation, assess its economic status, and engage in problem solving to determine the nation's priority needs and how to fulfill them. In responding to this problem they had to understand and use the knowledge they had acquired. Cheryl describes how when representatives of one nation presented their case to the World Bank (represented by Cheryl), the students, because they had done so much research, could challenge the applicants, "You can't build a hospital for that amount of money!" and "Have you thought of the long-range implications of such a road through the rain forest/jungle?" Her students confirm recent findings that "to develop competence in an area of inquiry, students must (a) have a deep foundation of factual knowledge; (b) understand facts and ideas in the context of a conceptual framework; and (c) organize knowledge in ways that facilitate retrieval and application" (Bransford, Brown, & Cocking, 2000, p. 16).

Daily, Ann asked students what they had learned as she did at the end of the unit. So there were always new things learned and, of course, new questions for students to add to their list of curiosities posted on the bulletin board.

"How can we apply what we have learned?" is a question designed to help students transfer new knowledge and skills into the same and other subjects as well as into their personal lives. "If I compared my country to a state in the U.S. or another developed country about the same size, it was easier for the World Bank to understand our problems," noted one of Cheryl's students.

Pictures and video simulations of the moving continents, plate tectonics, and how one plate subducted beneath another caused volcanoes to spew molten magma intrigued a student in Ann's class. During the visit of the geologist, Dr. Jonathan Lincoln, she posed this question, "If the continents didn't move, would there still be volcanoes?"

"No," he said. "It's the moving of the plates that causes volcanoes to erupt." And he demonstrated subduction with both hands, one hand sliding beneath the other as if it were a moving continental plate with the resulting volcano spewing forth ash and molten lava. This question was an excellent example of one student's using previously learned information to generate an insightful application question. I continue to be amazed by the depth of understanding this question reflects, a question from an average 4th grade girl who became very intrigued as she sat in Ann's class analyzing rocks firsthand and struggling to understand the concept of plate tectonics, and the movements of large continental and ocean plates across the planet.

And, finally, we bring the strategy full circle by asking for new questions. Where do we go from here?

"I ended with the question of why people continue to reproduce if their lives are so hard," observed one 9th grader.

And Ann's class wondered, "Where will the continents be in a million years?"

What Students Say

McCombs (1991) has noted that students who set goals for their own learning and reflect on their progress are well on their way toward becoming self-directed individuals. Students in Ann's 4th grade classes found this inquiry approach, "fun, because you asked your own questions. . . . I never knew that you could eat some minerals. . . . I found out that the biggest rocks in the world are not as important as the oldest. . . . The oldest rocks are millions of years old. . . ."

Cheryl's students had these reflections:

- "The information was easy to get, but we had to focus on the problems and that was hard."
- "I enjoyed taking my friends to the museum and creating all the artwork. We were the teachers for a day."

In general, I find that when we tap into students' interest in having some control over their own learning, we energize them, the learning process, and the whole class experience. Indeed, as so many have pointed out, having a choice among selected alternatives is a very powerful way of transforming the classroom. All we have to do is ask ourselves what kinds of experiences we enjoy and benefit from the most: those we do under some kind of pressure or duress, or those wherein we have some degree of choice among alternatives we generate?

Posting Reports on the Web

One of the exciting possibilities offered by the World Wide Web is the opportunity for students to become authors. In many schools students are posting their research questions and findings on the Web for peers to comment on. It's really very easy. Students in many schools post their research findings on their home page. Others use sites like www.angelfire.com to share their findings with the world.

It's also possible that Ann and Cheryl's students could have joined up with other students conducting similar kinds of research in a joint WebQuest. (See Appendix A for suitable Web sites, for example, www.manteno.k12.il.us.) Sharing products then becomes a process of gathering feedback from students around the world, not just in your local community. This is an opportunity to experience one of the important aspects of what Wiggins (1998) calls "authentic assessment."

Conclusion

Problem-based learning provides us with excellent opportunities for students to engage in inquiry that takes advantage of sources in school, in local centers of culture like museums, in the community, and on the World Wide Web. By offering them opportunities to pose their own meaningful questions, to research them in ways that are fun and involve transferable skills, and to wrap all their knowledge up in an authentic task as a culminating experience, we offer students experiences that can help them learn content and transfer the results into other areas of study as well as their personal life. Furthermore, we provide them with knowledge and skills that are, potentially, transferable to other life situations (Bransford, Franks, & Sherwood, 1986; Mayer, 1989; Stepien, Gallagher, & Workman, 1992).

Once again, let us recall Anatole France's educational vision: "The whole art of teaching is only the art of awakening the natural curiosity of young minds for the purpose of satisfying it afterwards" (1881/1932, p. 248).

Yes! And in problem-based learning with a focus on group and individual inquiry we have a vehicle to do just that.

References

Barell, J. (1995). *Teaching for thoughtfulness: Classroom strategies to enhance intellectual development* (2nd ed.). New York: Longman.

Barell, J. (1998). *Problem based learning: An inquiry approach.* Arlington Heights, IL: SkyLight Training and Publishing.

Bernstein, L. (November 14, 1954). Omnibus Television Program. Available: www.leonardbernstein.com. Accessed July 2001.

Bransford, J., Brown, A., & Cocking, R. (2000). *How people learn: Brain, mind experience and school.* Washington, DC: National Academy Press.

Bransford, J., Franks, N., & Sherwood, R. (1986, June). *New approaches to instruction: Because wisdom can't be taught.* Paper presented at the

Conference on Similarity and Analogy, University of Illinois, Champaign-Urbana.

Caine, R., & Caine, G. (1997). *Education on the edge of possibility*. Alexandria, VA: Association for Supervision and Curriculum Development.

Dewey, J. (1933). *How we think*. Lexington, MA: D.C. Heath.

Diamond, M., & Hopson, J. (1998). *Magic trees of the mind: How to nurture your child's intelligence, creativity, and healthy emotions from birth through adolescence*. New York: Penguin/Plume.

Dillon, J. T. (1988). *Questioning and teaching: A manual of practice*. New York: Teachers College Press.

France, A. (1881/1932). *The crime of Sylvestre Bonnard*. New York: Walter J. Black, Inc.

Jensen, E. (1998). *Teaching with the brain in mind*. Alexandria, VA: Association for Supervision and Curriculum Development.

Mayer, R. (1989). Models for understanding. *Review of Educational Research*, 59, 43–64.

McCombs, B. (1991). *Metacognition and motivation for higher level thinking*. Paper presented at the annual meeting of the American Educational Research Association, Chicago.

Perkins, D. (1992). *Smart schools: From training memories to educating minds*. New York: Free Press.

Stepien, W., Gallagher, S., & Workman, D. (1992). *Problem-based learning for traditional and interdisciplinary classrooms*. Aurora, IL: Center for Problem-Based Learning, Illinois Mathematics and Science Academy.

Stigler, J., & Hiebert, J. (1999). *The teaching gap: Best ideas from the world's teachers for improving education in the classroom*. New York: Free Press.

Tyler, R. (1949). *Basic principles of curriculum and instruction*. Chicago: University of Chicago Press.

Wiggins, G. (1998). *Educative assessment*. San Francisco: Jossey-Bass.

Wolfe, P., & Brandt, R. (1998, November). What do we know from brain research? *Educational Leadership, 56*(3), 8–13.

Chapter 9

WISELY USING THE WORLD WIDE WEB

I ask myself, is this what I want? Is there enough info? Is it about my topic? I read it to see . . . if it has anything important.

—FIFTH-GRADE STUDENT KIM,
REFLECTING ON HOW SHE USES WEB SITES

How do we use the Web when "nobody's in charge"?

Whenever we enter schools, we are likely to see and hear about students, young and old, using computers to access the resources of the World Wide Web, as we saw them doing in Cheryl Hopper's and Ann White's classes in the previous chapter. We hear of kindergarten children doing research on starfish and creating PowerPoint presentations (Guernsey, 2001). There are 5th graders in Cathy Brophy's class in Hampton, New Hampshire, who are comfortable weaving their way in and out of the Web. Students in Ralph Mazzio's 9th grade astronomy classes in Yorktown, New York, are searching for asteroids and supernovae (exploding stars) using a program called "Hands On Universe" (http://hou.lbl.gov) and requesting images from specific telescopes that they will then download from the Web and process.

Reflective Pause

Given the access to virtually unlimited amounts and kinds of information on the World Wide Web, what concerns do you have about how our children and students use these resources?

This chapter is not a presentation of fascinating Web sites (see Appendix A). Rather, it is an attempt to deal with some of the questions you have just posed. In preparing to write this chapter, I asked Cathy Brophy of Hampton, New Hampshire, if she would ask her students how they used the Internet.

Katie said, "Some of the things I look up are for projects, my favorite bands, and pictures. I always use it for science projects . . . except at home I don't have the Internet, so at school I always use my free time to go on the Internet."

Amanda wrote, "Go to Yahoo!, type in what [you] need and click search. Find what [you] need and print it. Then read it. If it has a lot of facts, keep it." Sounds simple enough (Cathy Brophy, personal communication, April 2001).

Perhaps Mrs. Brophy's students are like some of those Don Tapscott writes about in *Growing Up Digital: The Rise of the Net Generation* (1998). Eight-year-old Claire reported: "I can't remember not using the computer. We had a lot of computers in the house and everybody played with them all the time" (Tapscott, 1998, p. 41). And 16-year-old Kim said, "I think that technology has changed the way adults treat me. They seem to take my opinions more seriously because they realize I just may know something they don't" (Tapscott, 1998, p. 37).

When I've worked with teachers who are interested in learning how to take advantage of the information on the Web, they tell stories of the alacrity with which students use technology. Their students and children would say to them when the teachers get confused about accessing information, "Let me do it for you. It's easier than trying to teach you."

Many of our children and students are as comfortable with computers as they are with pencils, and that's the way some educators think of this technology. "Why have a Computer Room?"

they ask. "We don't have a Pencil or a Ruler Room. Computers ought to be just like any other resource."

But there are, of course, significant differences. We can completely control where our pencils go and what they do. But we cannot control what our students search on the Internet, nor can we control the content of the messages we find during our searches.

I recently learned of two 4-year-olds whose parents have quite different approaches to their children's learning. John is already comfortable using the mouse to click around the screen, said his mother. Molly's mother, on the other hand, hasn't taught her anything about the computer, the mouse, or the World Wide Web. "I don't want her getting into all that stuff," she said. John's mother is an oceanographer. Molly's mother is a music educator, both highly educated people with widely divergent views on their children's use of the World Wide Web.

This little comparison comes to mind in thinking about inquiry and using the Internet, because with the increasing access we have to information and to flashy Web sites, and with the immediate availability of such communications worldwide, it seems appropriate to raise a few questions about how we want our children to use this most amazing resource:

- How does using the Internet enhance presentation of our curriculum? Of learning significant concepts found therein?
- What does the Web do best?
- What skills do we need to empower students with in order to maximize their use of this wonderful resource?
- How can it foster inquiry and investigations, both for personal and curricular purposes?
- What are our roles as stewards of best practice when it comes to educating our children and ourselves in using the technology that has already revolutionized business affairs and has the potential for doing the same in education? If Thomas Friedman of The New York Times is correct when he asserts that "Nobody is in charge!" of the Web, then what responsibilities do we have to ensure that our students wisely use the Web? (Friedman, 1999, p. 93).

- And, most significantly, how might our early use of the Internet and access to the World Wide Web be affecting how we think about ourselves, solving problems, learning, and the world we inhabit?

Enhancing the Curriculum

When Cheryl Hopper's 9th grade students researched African countries, and when Ann White's 4th grade students sought information about rocks (see Chapter 8), they were all using the resources of the World Wide Web to enhance the major concepts and ideas within the curriculum. Cheryl and Ann were able to elicit from their students questions that tapped in to their own curiosities, but these questions also reflected what was important in the curriculum. "I got it all from my students," Cheryl said. "Their questions dealt with everything I wanted and needed to deal with in the curriculum."

What we have to keep in mind is that any resource, a visiting geologist, a trip to a museum, or accessing www.askjeeves.com needs to be in service to the content of our curriculum. The content of the curriculum is those concepts, ideas, skills, and attitudes that we want to introduce our students to. The content is the stuff of the curriculum we want to teach. (Of course, students can and will access sites with information that appeals to their own interests, and we can nurture their investigations as we deem appropriate.)

Now, what questions ought we to ask of any search our students want to undertake on the Web? What might be some of our concerns? Here are some things we might want to think about as students click from one site to another:

- How are their Web browsings related to curricular content—the concepts, ideas, principles, skills, and attitudes we wish to teach?
- To what degree is their work enhancing their understanding of the major curricular problems—those issues or conflicts that are at the heart of our investigations?

- To what degree will their searches result in abilities that are transferable to other subjects and to their personal lives—for example, critical thinking, inquiry, and problem solving?

- To what extent are their excursions around the Web in pursuit of their own curiosities and interests? How will their lives be enriched by what they are learning?

Questions such as these might help us determine just how we want our students to access the World Wide Web. For example, when Ann's students searched through Encarta for images of various rock formations, were they acquiring and refining skills usable within our subjects? Were they enhancing their understanding of a major content concept—rock formations and origins? Were they gaining deeper knowledge about how the Earth changes over time—one of their essential questions? Were they developing lifelong interests, perhaps, in earth sciences that we might encourage? Were they having fun?

So, why use the Web? I suggest that we use these virtually unlimited resources to enhance our curricular objectives. This does not mean, however, that we short-circuit students' pursuits of their own interests! Far from it. When students become excited about a rock/soul/rap group, when they investigate formation of the Rocky Mountains, or when they become deeply involved in Spanish or French culture, we have the beginnings of meaningful learning. All of these queries might not directly relate to the curriculum we teach in school. They might, however, help students set directions for their own lives and we can help them structure these investigations in appropriate directions that lead to responsible investigations and decisions.

What Does the Web Do Best?

Let us hear from one of Cathy Brophy's 5th graders, Brendan, on how he uses the Internet:

> I use the Internet to find information, correct spelling, games, cheat codes, and to buy things. I use www.ask.com for a search engine. The

> Internet is a fast, easy tool to get things or information. Instead of looking for a book, reading the book, writing down notes, you can type a few words, click, print, and then read the page or two of information on your subject. The Internet is so unlimited you can find exactly what you want, but it just might take you a little bit longer. Say I wanted to know how James Marshall found gold, I would type in "How did James Marshall find gold," click Ask, and find my results (Brophy, personal communication, May 2001).

Brendan has summarized, from his point of view, some of the benefits of using the Internet—speed, ease, efficiency, and the virtually unlimited access to information presented.

What do you think of his approach? What would you add to Brendan's list?

You might think of the choices that the Internet presents us with—so many sources from which to select. You might also consider that with so many options comes the responsibility to act wisely and not automatically—that is, just click, print, read, and present. This is not the wisest use of the resources found on the World Wide Web.

"A Cut and Paste Mentality"

Let me make a cautionary comment here. When I first began to teach literature, I was quite surprised to find some of my more recalcitrant and reluctant students handing in exceptional papers. I didn't know what to do, until I conferred with the department chair, Jim Nash. He told me that it was common practice for students to go on the Internet, find papers already written on the subject, pay a fee, download them, and submit them as original works (Nash, personal communication, October 1996). Jamie McKenzie calls the source of the problem the "cut and paste mentality," where students think that more information is better. They don't think of it as plagiarism. "They are simply collecting information and don't understand the whole concept of intellectual property," he said (Hafner, 2001, p. G6).

More recently a young colleague of mine taught a course in genetics and became concerned that the language in the students' final projects did not appear to be original. We discussed what to do and I shared Jim Nash's advice. He then proceeded to type sets of significant words into www.google.com and, sure enough, he found the sources of his students' papers in a variety of Web sites!

This is a sad commentary on what students are learning—point, click, print, and hand in. What's even more unfortunate is if teachers and college professors are accepting this kind of work because they are apprehensive about upholding the highest standards for intellectual work. We cheat our students if we condone this kind of behavior. Every student needs to be responsible for his or her own conclusions reasoned thoughtfully from evidence.

I learned how to cope with such challenges by asking students to show me and discuss face to face the sources they've cited within their papers. At the time I hadn't heard of a Web site called turnitin.com, where you can submit lines of written text to see if there is a match somewhere on the Web—one way of determining if a work is plagiarized.

How Should We Read the Web?

I recently gave a report to a group of adults on how educators use the resources of the Internet. One of the findings concerned how many adults merely copy what we see on a Web site and pass it along as useful information.

Another one of Cathy Brophy's students, Kim, gives us a good way to begin thinking about what we discover on the Web:

> You type in where you want to go . . . . You read and find out what you're looking for and if it's there. If I have a topic, I see if it is about the topic. What comes up I hope it is what I want. *I ask myself, is this what I want? Is there enough info? Is it about my topic? I read it to see if it is about my topic to see if it has anything important* . . . [emphasis added].

Notice how different Kim's response is from others who want to point, click, print, *then* read. Look at the kind of questions Kim is asking herself:

- Is this what I am searching for? Many times we get on to fascinating Web sites, but they are not exactly what we're looking for. This question demands that we assess the site for *relevance*. For a site to be relevant, it must relate to our subject, to us personally, or to issues we consider vital or significant.

- Is there enough information? Maybe there is some information, but not sufficient to make a significant contribution. Perhaps there are gaps and omissions that are misleading.
- Is there anything important? This is an important critical thinking decision. Does it meet my criteria for significance?

"Is It Important?"

Kim's last question is essential. We need to establish for ourselves what we consider important or significant. This is an important analytic question that calls to mind a set of criteria, what the observer considers worthy of notice. Just how do we determine the importance of a Web site, an article, or a piece of information?

To determine the importance or significance of anything, we can use several lenses or sets of relationships. How does the writing relate to ourselves, the subjects we are studying, our social group or community, and the nation, or to issues or problems we face as inhabitants of Earth?

First, we can determine if the information relates to us personally. For example, I pick up an issue of *The New York Times,* and there in column one is an article with the headline, "Lyme Disease is Hard to Catch and Easy to Halt, Study Finds." I am immediately drawn to read this article, because, living out on the eastern end of Long Island on weekends, where the deer roam with increasing frequency, I once noticed that I had the telltale rashes associated with this disease. As the article states, if detected and treated with an appropriate antibiotic (as in my case), you can stem the development of this disease. So this article is highly relevant and important to me.

On another level, it is certainly important to the community within which I live, because many people have suffered from Lyme disease.

The editors of the *Times* obviously consider it of national importance, because the deer that are responsible for carrying the tick and transferring it to smaller animals can roam all over the country.

And I would add that another element of significance is in the substance of the article, which reports on studies to prevent the spread of the disease. The studies affect how health professionals treat those of us who may show symptoms of Lyme disease.

Thus, importance can be determined by comparing a story to our personal, social, and national needs and interests. Perhaps Kim is now thinking primarily of her report and whether or not a Web site relates to her topic and provides sufficient information to help her finish her assignment successfully. Eventually, she may consider parameters beyond her own needs.

Reflective Pause

Kim has presented us with a most important beginning for analyzing information on the Web. You may recall that in Chapter 6 I suggested you develop with students your own set of criteria to use in evaluating Web sites and Web pages. Take a moment to recall what your original thoughts were on critiquing Web sites.

Using the SEADS strategy from Chapter 7, here are a few suggested questions that may help you analyze any Web site:

S What is the source? Is it believable, credible, relevant?

E What evidence is presented to support claims or generalizations? Is it presented logically, reasonably, clearly, and without ambiguity? Is it easy to navigate?

A How accurate is the information? And is it presented in an aesthetically pleasing and informative format? Does it provide access to other useful sites?

D What is the date of the last revision? How timely and relevant is it?

S Does it present two or more sides to any issue? Is it biased, or does it present a specific slant to its presentation?

Recently, I spoke with a colleague who had applied for a job at a local museum of art as a consultant for the Web site they were developing. I asked him what criteria he would have used in analyzing the site that presented art works for educators to use in their classrooms. Mike spoke of the following:

- *Usability*—How easy is it to use and navigate?
- *Aesthetic value*—Is it organized like a Leonardo or a Rembrandt? Is it clearly focused on the subject with colors and shapes that appeal to the eye? Is there enough white space or is it cluttered with too much text?
- *Comprehensive*—To what degree does it present not just a snapshot of an artist, but a more in-depth presentation of the artist or of an era?
- *Connectivity*—How well does it connect to other sites that present related and more in-depth information about an artist or a movement in art?

What other criteria might you develop with students, some of whom have spent more time visiting Web sites than you or me?

Adding Up the Costs of Cyber-efficiency

Whenever I asked my students in English Literature 106 to write a paper, I gave them specific instructions about the kinds of reasoning I expected—above all, that their arguments would present clear evidence from whatever texts they were using. I also expected them to avoid what we used to call "glittering generalities" without examples. I did not want to write "examples?" or "e.g." in the margins too often. We sometimes used sample essays to clarify these expectations.

Another point I made was, "Please proofread your manuscript. Spell Check will not catch the differences between *the* and *he*, and *too* or *two*." As you can imagine, this admonition worked to some degree, but I still received papers where students had used the Spell Check command on their word processing program and assumed that this would catch all of the errors.

Spell Check is just one way in which computer usage has affected the way we write, conduct research, and, most important of all, think. I recall 4-year-old Molly and her mother, a colleague of mine, who does not want to influence her daughter's approach to life with computer technology too soon.

What are the questions we ought to consider as our students grow up digitally, as Don Tapscott says? A few examples follow.

Linking to Opposing Points of View

The World Wide Web is constructed democratically—anybody can post anything on it (remember Thomas Friedman's admonition, "Nobody is in charge!"). Therefore, we find lots of sites that represent one point of view. So we must concern ourselves with this question: Are we exposing our students and ourselves to diverse points of view? Cass Sunstein, a law professor at the University of Chicago, has raised this concern in a book entitled *Republic.com* (Stille, 2001). Sunstein believes that a "shared culture" is a vital element within a democracy, a culture wherein different points of view can be entertained, discussed, and debated. What he sees in cyberspace, however, is mostly one-sided presentations of specific points of view. Most political Web sites, he says, only present links to other sites with similar points of view. "We might want to consider the possibility of ways of requiring or encouraging sites to link to opposing viewpoints" (Stille, 2001, p. B11). Sunstein would like to see a cyberspace equivalent of the popular television show *CrossFire*, where you have the views of the political left contrasted with those of the right, leaving viewers to make up their own minds.

Sunstein and his like-minded colleagues fear that democracy will suffer if access to the Web leads to students and others acquiring information that only presents one side of an issue.

Do you think that Web designers of political persuasions are likely to create links to opposing or different points of view? What would be their incentives to do so?

What can we do as stewards of our students' growing up in a democracy to ensure that students actively search out other points of view? Other political persuasions? Other ways of looking at the problem?

How can we enculturate our students to be on the lookout for one-sidedness? To make it a part of their ways of thinking always to consider other points of view?

I once sat with Doreen Guzo, a New Jersey English teacher, in a luncheonette as she posed that question. We took out a pencil and drew a concept map on the placemat. From the central issue, topic, or problem, we webbed out different ways of examining any issue: from the point of view of philosophy, religion, art, law, economics, science, ethics, history, and so on. Whenever I saw Doreen thereafter, she showed me this folded-up piece of paper that she carried around with her for years to remind her how easy it was to help her students look at the complexities of any issue from multiple perspectives. What we want is for our students to automatically search for the complexities in human situations by asking themselves, "What are the issues here? From how many different points of view can we examine this issue?" Figure 9.1 presents this concept in graphic form.

A Click Away

Will instant access to millions of Web sites create in our students the impression that truth is easily attainable? That solutions to problems are just a mouse click away? That all we have to do is type, click, print, read, and present? It seems to me that the "Net generation" is growing up with the ability and *perhaps* the predisposition to click their way toward gathering information and then pasting it together in reports or PowerPoint presentations without thinking too deeply about what they are doing. Technology makes gathering information so easy that we may create a perception that that's all there is to figuring out life's complex issues and problems. In the process, are we avoiding the all-important process of intellectual analysis that leads to understanding and intelligent use and application?

As Princeton historian Robert Darnton notes, "Digitizers often dump texts onto the Internet without considering their quality as sources, and students often fail to read those texts critically. Instead, they scan them with search engines, locate key words, jump in at any point and cobble passages together by computerized cutting and pasting." Darnton provides these words of caution: "Instead of turning our backs on cyberspace, we need to take control of it—to set standards, develop quality

Figure 9.1
Considering Many Points of View

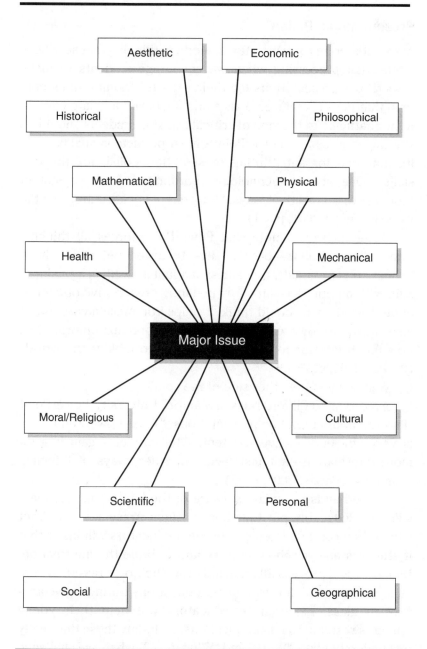

controls and direct traffic" (Darnton, 1999, p. A15). In other words, we need to think critically and establish our own criteria.

Presentational Polish

Are we fostering a presentational mode of thinking that sacrifices intellectual processing when we encourage students to make PowerPoint presentations for their reports? "Some critics contend that PowerPoint's emphasis on bullets and animated graphics is anathema to the kind of critical thinking students should be learning in class . . . . PowerPoint's most pernicious quality . . . is its potential for substituting presentation polish for thinking skills." One school technology coordinator, Jerry Crystal of Bloomfield, Connecticut, says, "It fosters a cookie-cutter mentality" (Guernsey, 2001, p. G1).

Other naysayers note that PowerPoint forces all thinking into bulleted points—perhaps five to seven per slide. "It is, almost surreptitiously, a business manual as well as a business suit, with an opinion—an oddly pedantic prescriptive opinion— about the way we should think. It helps you make a case, but it also makes its own case: about how to organize information, how much information to organize, how to look at the world" (Parker, 2001, p. 76).

Well, what is the other side of the coin?

According to Clifford Nass of Stanford University, PowerPoint "lifts the floor" of public presentations. "What PowerPoint does is very efficiently deliver content. What students gain is a lot more information—not just facts but rules, ways of thinking, examples" (Parker, 2001, p. 87).

In the hands of teachers aware of the limitations, students will knowledgeably put together excellent presentations about which they can talk intelligently. Such educators will insist that if students analyze their sources and critique the information, then they will process all data and draw their own reasoned conclusions from which they can field questions during a give-and-take in class. Experienced educators will help their young students respond to lots of questions, including those that really test understanding, "Why?" and "What if . . . ?" where we challenge them to manipulate the various factors and elements within their topics.

We need to focus upon the students' understanding of the content and not merely the flash and dash of bulleted points and sensational graphics about the Victorian age or about Emperor penguins. We need to ensure that students can speak intelligently about the processes of thinking by which they arrived at their conclusions. Students need to be able to mentally leave a PowerPoint presentation to tell a related and interesting story about their investigation and not be merely tied to the number of bullets allowed on each slide (Parker, 2001, p. 87).

What Are the Connections?

Will students grow up being able to see and determine complex relationships, given the speed with which they can link from one site to another? Are we challenging them to answer the question, "How is this site related to the previous one? How does the information within each compare and contrast? What are the relationships?" Without such processing questions, we may foster the attitude that if one set of information is connected through hypertext links to another, then these sites must have a common theme or thread and there must be logical connections readily evident between them. We expect so, but we should challenge students to ask themselves, "What are the connections here?" and "How are these relationships related to what I'm trying to find out?" It is through establishing these kinds of relationships and connections that we create our own personal meanings. We cannot leave the creation of meaningful connection up to webmasters!

A Sense of Community

Are we fostering a sense of community when we send students off to search on the Internet? When I enter a computer lab, especially the ones at the high school level, I often see individual students sitting before one screen. But sometimes at both high school and elementary levels there are groups of students hovering around the screen, searching out information.

To what extent are we encouraging students to work together to pose and resolve problems? To investigate collaboratively complex issues? If students are working to put together a PowerPoint presentation, I assume they are arguing and debating about what their conclusions are, what texts make the most sense to support their conclusions, and how to arrange these in an aesthetically pleasing fashion.

We return to Kim's excellent questions, "Is this what I want?" Is this related logically, historically, and personally to what I'm searching for? And is it important? The latter question requires judgment, a set of criteria, and decision making. These operations can be undertaken individually and/or collaboratively. I would not like to see students growing up feeling comfortable with the World Wide Web but uncomfortable working toward compromises in problem resolution and presentation of findings.

Reflective Pause

What new questions do you have about your students' use of the Internet? What concerns you about their hours of surfing and clicking?

One major concern is that students might wander onto inappropriate sites. Currently, there are reports in the media about young people who spend lots of time in chat rooms being taken advantage of by others. This is a danger that we must guard against daily! It is most unfortunate when students find more solace and comfort in electronic communications than with their families and friends. This may be another reason for our working strenuously to create communities of inquiry within our classrooms where students collaborate and learn to rely on one another.

And we might be concerned that they might find or even create inappropriate sites that are offensive to certain people or groups. You may have heard stories of students creating sexually explicit sites or ones that demean or degrade individuals or groups. The presence of hate messages is of great concern to all of us.

Beyond these kinds of concerns, how do you think so many hours of active pursuit of knowledge on the Web is affecting the way kids think? Their attitudes toward problem solving, for example? How is it affecting how they relate to others in the world?

Conclusion

Don Tapscott sees the Net generation as characterized by entrepreneurship, curiosity to investigate and invent, a fierce independence, a sense of openness, and willingness to collaborate and communicate with others (1998, p. 72). These words probably describe many of our students. Perhaps what concerns me now is how we nurture our students toward these admirable qualities. We cannot assume that all our children are growing up with equal access to the Web and with the kinds of dispositions to critique and think logically as we are suggesting in this chapter.

As Katie told Cathy Brophy: "I determine if it's useful by reading it and seeing if it is *really* useful" (Brophy, personal communication, April 2001, emphasis added). Katie has the inquiring spirit required for successfully navigating and learning from the World Wide Web.

References

Darnton, R. (1999, June 12). No computer can hold the past. *The New York Times*, p. A15.

Friedman, T. (1999). *The Lexus and the olive tree: Understanding globalization*. New York: Ferrar Straus Giroux.

Guernsey, L. (2001, May 31). Learning, one bullet point at a time. *The New York Times*, p. G1.

Hafner, K. (2001, June 28). Lessons in the school of cut and paste: E-mail and the Web make plagiarism a plague; will computers be the cure, too? *The New York Times*, p. G6.

Parker, I. (2001, May 28). Absolute PowerPoint: Can a software package edit our thoughts? *New Yorker*, pp. 76–86.

Stille, A. (2001, June 2). Adding up the costs of cyberdemocracy; experts worry that the Web encourages extremism. *The New York Times*, p. B9.

Tapscott, D. (1998). *Growing up digital: The rise of the Net generation*. New York: McGraw-Hill.

Chapter 10

OF MUSEUMS AND FIELD NOTES

Why doesn't the T-Rex fossil have eyes?

—FOURTH-GRADE STUDENT SOPHIA, ON THE *TYRANNOSAURUS REX*
FOSSIL AT THE AMERICAN MUSEUM OF NATURAL HISTORY,
NEW YORK CITY, 2002

When my grandfather and I used to take long walks along the Post Road in Connecticut, he would ask me all sorts of questions. One day, when I was about seven or eight, he posed a particularly challenging question: "Do you know why the sun rises in the east?" He was interested to see if I knew that the Earth rotated on its axis and that the sun, indeed, stood still in the center of the solar system, as somebody named Copernicus had first proclaimed. I knew nothing of Copernicus, but I did know that the Earth rotated every 24 hours.

"How do we know that?" he asked in his ever-so-invitational way.

"I don't know," I said, eager to find an answer.

Then he said he would show me a demonstration of the Earth's rotation if I would accompany him to the Stamford Museum.

So we were off on another journey, another adventure in learning.

There in a huge hall, as I recall, swung a huge pendulum, back and forth and forth and back across what I remember as a huge compass rose embedded in the floor, identifying the four cardinal points, North, East, South, and West. It was only recently that I learned that this demonstration is named Foucault's pendulum, after the scientist who first used it to illustrate Earth's rotation. This 19th-century physicist suspended his pendulum in the Pantheon in Paris, and to observers it seemed to rotate across the Pantheon floor. What was actually happening, however, was that the pendulum stayed in the same plane as the Earth rotated beneath it (Pasachoff, 1983, p. 20).

Most children have such stories of parents and grandparents taking them to one museum or another and their being amazed at the strange and wondrous exhibits within. Here we see animals from strange lands, and ones from millions of years ago—dinosaurs; we have exhibits on Earth and space; and halls full of the culture of peoples near and far.

At museums we can witness through films, models, and remnant lavas the amazing power of volcanoes and the incremental power of plate tectonics to move continents. At planetariums, we can witness the night sky in all seasons, and, if you visit the American Museum of Natural History and the Hayden Planetarium in New York City, you can take a simulated spaceship out 1,500 light-years to the Orion Nebula in the Milky Way Galaxy to observe the birthplaces of stars.

Museums are informal settings where we can seek out some answers. Because of their rich collections of artifacts and finely crafted exhibits, they are wonderful accompaniments to what we do in the classroom. Because most of their materials are authentic, students have an opportunity to see and, often, to touch, the real thing, be it a meteorite or the fossilized impression of a dinosaur skin. Whenever I am in the Hall of Planet Earth at the American Museum of Natural History, I run my hands over a 3.96-billion-year-old specimen of a type of metamorphic rock called gneiss from the Acasta Shield in northwestern Canada. It feels like other rocks, but I know it dates to close to the formation of the Earth itself!

But all museums are more than accompaniments to our class-rooms. They are informal learning centers where we can freely explore and create our own learning experiences. Some days I wander down the halls of Asian peoples and am enthralled by the artworks of Taoist painters that depict human beings as very small characters within the immense and towering creations of Nature. At moments of such enchantment I am reminded of the immensity of our observable universe, stretching out 13 billion light-years, and reflect on my own diminutive stature within the galaxy and the universe. In both the work of art and the nature of the universe, however, human beings are the ones who have cre-ated visions of our places in time and space.

Reflective Pause

Based on your experiences, what are some helpful ways of thinking about visits to museums and other informal learning settings? What do you like to do when you embark on such a journey?

Embarking on Expeditions

Have you ever wanted to embark on an expedition to lands far away where you could explore unknown terrains and discover new geographies and people different from yourself? Well, that's what a trip to a good museum can be: an expedition to explore and learn. When you visit a museum you come with the hope of encountering something so strange, fascinating, and awe-inspiring that you leave full of wonder, full of curiosities about *Tyrannosaurus rex* teeth ("Did they regenerate?"), about the Great Wall of China ("How long is it and when was it built?"), and about the migration habits of monarch butterflies ("How can they survive and navigate such a journey from North America to Mexico and back?").

Very often you'll touch and see the "real thing" within its nat-ural context or habitat. How different from viewing an object, animal, specimen, or event within the confines of a very small photograph in a textbook! When I see visitors at the American Museum of Natural History gazing in awe at the African elephants or the explosions from Hawaiian volcanoes I wonder what they're thinking and feeling. And I am delighted that they do not have worksheets in their hands to fill out with the correct answers to somebody else's questions. Yes, answers are important, but we need to take time to view, to allow our eyes and hands to explore the objects and gather in as much information as we can and leave full of curiosities to satisfy in our own ways.

As Myles Gordon, Vice President for Education of the American Museum of Natural History, notes, we are undergoing a "paradigm shift"—from students primarily coming to the museum for answers on worksheets to students coming to explore, make exciting discoveries, and leave with even deeper and richer curiosities about the world (personal communication, June 2001).

Getting Started

Before we visit a museum we might want to have a purpose. We determine what our subject matter content is, what our essential questions are that we are trying to answer. We can use the KWHLAQ format described in Chapter 8 (*What do we think we know? What do we need to find out? How will we go about it? What are we learning? How does new learning apply? And what are our new questions?*), but regardless of how we proceed, we need to engage our students in determining what we want to find out. No great expedition into Antarctica or Africa or to the bottom of the ocean or the planets proceeds without an objective that we want to pursue.

Figure 10.1 provides a structure for our journey. We will need not only questions, but also resources and a plan for how to find answers to our questions. These plans should include observations of artifacts and the accompanying signage. They may also include discussions with tour guides or scientists who work at the museum.

Figure 10.1
Expedition Planning

Before Your Visit

Territory to be explored (country, animal group, etc.)

Goal/objective (What are you curious about and why?)

What do we already know?

Plan (What will you do at the museum to acquire answers?)

Resources (What you need to bring, including food, notebooks, money)

During Visit

What are you discovering? What surprises, intrigues, and delights you?

What are you observing that fascinates you?

Are you answering your own questions?

Do you have new curiosities?

Back at Home/In the Classroom

Reflection: What did you learn? Why is it important? What new questions do
  you have?

Continued investigation: How will you find answers to your new questions?

"Is This Fun?"

Lots of students walk through the American Museum of Natural History, and I have had many occasions to observe them in the halls. Too often I have witnessed them with their fill-in-the-blank kinds of worksheets, lazily copying descriptions of the oldest known rock specimen in the museum (a zircon crystal dated at 4.2 billion years old) or the definitions of a supernova explosion. These students look bored and quite disengaged.

"Is this fun?" I ask, pointing to the worksheets.

"No."

"What would make it fun?"

"Not doing it."

"What's the project you will be working on with the information on these worksheets?" (assuming that raw information needs to be processed and acted on to become meaningful—see the Three-Story Intellect model in Chapter 4). "This is the project," the high school student replied without any enthusiasm whatsoever.

Unfortunately, too many students are "working" their way through the museum and many others in this fashion. Students are busily copying information from the exhibits or asking their teachers where they can find the appropriate information. I wonder if they are taking any time to observe closely the marvelous wavy distortions in the large metamorphic rock formations? How much time are they spending just looking to attempt to understand?

When one student poses the question about metamorphic rocks, "How did they get that way?" the answer is quickly given, "Heat and . . . yes, pressure."

But there are alternatives.

During Cheryl Hopper's unit (see Chapter 8) on Africa, students planned an expedition to a local museum of African art. They assumed all responsibilities, including arranging for transportation, a tour, and other activities at the museum.

Before the group visit, students in charge researched the museum, and each one of four students took an area to become expert in. Back in the classroom, these students presented an overview of the kinds of African art they would be experiencing. They discussed historical, geographical, and cultural background information. At the museum the investigators became the tour guides for the entire trip.

After initial tours in small groups, the leaders brought their groups together for a discussion on what they found fascinating about the art. Students posed their own questions about the masks and other cultural artifacts of Yoruban art.

Finally, the tour guides asked each person to draw her or his own work of art. Why? They wanted to see how their friends would represent what they had seen, and they wanted each to take home a remembrance of the museum that really meant something to them.

"The discussion and the drawings," recalled Cheryl, "generated a lot of questions. This got them to focus in on part of the process—[the creative process, theirs and the artists'] .... Art lends itself to this [kind of reflection]. It's down to earth and kids could say why they liked it or didn't." In other words, being amid the artwork elicited students' critical thinking, especially because they were able to get close to it and handle it in some cases.

"This mask is important, because. . . ." This simple statement requires making judgments and, remembering Matthew Lipman's definition of critical thinking (making judgments in accordance with criteria [1988, p. 1]), we can challenge students to give reasons that relate this mask to what they know about other masks in the culture and about the aesthetics of the creative process itself.

The drawings elicited from the students what *they* felt was important, not just answers to prepared questions.

Trips to a museum can be just escapes from the routines of school or, as in Cheryl's case and so many more I have witnessed, they can become integral explorations within the curriculum.

Figure 10.2 gives us a format for field notes. On the left we note our observations, attempting to be as precise and accurate as possible, using all of our senses when engaging an exhibit. We want to be sure to note those characteristics we think are important and these choices, of course, depend on our knowledge of

Figure 10.2
Using Field Notes at the Museum

Field notes can be taken using this double-entry format.

Observations	Reflections, Questions
Jot down your observations—what you see, hear, touch, and smell. Be objective and include words that describe names, shapes, sizes, colors, ages, materials, functions, textures . . .	Record your impressions, questions, feelings, meanings of observed phenomena . . . Draw a picture

where the specimen fits into a larger frame of reference. (Remember Stephen Reynolds's field notes in Chapter 5.)

"Find Something You Want to Remember"

Maritza Macdonald is director of professional development at the American Museum of Natural History. She wants students who come to the museum to take something with them that is meaningful and personal. "I want them to focus on something they want to remember. Find something interesting" (personal communication, April 2001). Using Maritza's suggestion, I have taken teachers on tours of various halls in the museum in this fashion. I give them an overview of the highlights—for example, of the Hall of Planet Earth. This hall is organized around several questions: "How has the Earth evolved? How do we account for continents and ocean basins? How do we read the rocks? How does climate affect life on Earth? And what are the origins of life?"

After the general overview tour, I ask visitors to select an area they want to remember. "Go spend some time in that part of the hall you want to remember or where you already have some questions." I give them field note guides similar to those in Figure 10.2 and perhaps a ruler and a magnifying glass.

Then after 20 minutes of their small group investigations, we bring everybody back together to share what they have found. These are like expert groups in a jigsaw cooperative learning experience. Everybody shares what excited them and, invariably, there are questions:

- About life deep down at the mid-ocean ridges where there is no sunlight: "Are the spider crabs like any other animals on Earth's surface? That would help us study them if we could make comparisons."
- About plate tectonics: "What energizes the plates? What makes them move?"
- About climate: "How do ocean currents affect climate?" (Visitors were fascinated by representations of El Niño and La Niña.)
- About the 3.96-billion-year-old gneiss rock from the Acasta Shield from northwestern Canada: "How do we know it's that old?"
- About the Earth's oceans: "How did fresh and salt water separate?"

There are so many questions when we afford visitors opportunities to spend some time with "something they want to remember," as Maritza Macdonald suggests.

Some of these questions lead to discussions, for example, about the movement of tectonic plates and the nature of convection currents. "Abundant heat, which drives convection, is generated throughout the mantle by radioactivity" (Bunge, 2001, p. 71). We compare temperatures during the winter close to the ceiling of a room and how frozen foods are often stored in supermarkets—in open displays where cold, dense air just sits on the food, not going anywhere. One of the major themes of both the Hall of Planet Earth and the Hall of the Universe at the museum is that we can come to understand what occurs on Earth and out in space by using the laws of physics as they affect phenomena observable here.

We need to remember that museums are informal learning settings where we should give ourselves ample opportunities to freely explore what we are interested in. Again, I chafe at the sight of students only copying down text about a famous meteorite or potlatch ceremony and not having time to let their imaginations roam over the magnificence of the other exhibits. They need to find information in order to understand what they are seeing, yes, but let's give them a few moments to wander, to explore with their eyes and their hands the marvels that they encounter with every step! Let them become curious about what they find interesting.

Strategies: Observe, Think, Question

Cheryl's students and my museum visitors are actually using a strategy called Observe, Think, and Question (Barell, 1992, p. 19). In both instances, visitors are making close observations of the objects, noting color, texture, shape, any aroma, size, relationship to other objects, functions, and the like. Then we relate these observations to what we think we know about such objects and their environments, noting any surprises or discrepancies in our expectations. And these reflections naturally lead to questions.

On one occasion Amy O'Donnell of the American Museum of Natural History staff presented these kinds of challenges using the museum collection of birds' nests. We spent several minutes alone and with partners examining closely the materials used, shapes, depth, colors, and density of the nests. Some birds make the kinds of robin's nests we are used to, but others build nests that look like socks hanging from a single branch with an opening at the top. One thing that really surprised me was that some birds use a wide variety of building materials, including twigs, human hair, and newspapers.

Amy asked us to make our observations and then think of questions we might have. These questions come from our being able to relate what we see to what we know and what we expected to find in a bird's nest. For example, I examined a nest that was so finely crafted of what looked like human hair with much open space between the curled-around strands that it was puzzling. It didn't look like what I knew about birds' nests: What kind of bird built it? Where? How long would it last? Could it hold the birds' young babies?

Observation is the key to all scientific work. We must have precise field observations.

"Looking for Evidence"

On other occasions Amy leads her students in to the Egyptian and African Halls where they observe cultural artifacts—pottery, water systems, masks, dress, weapons, tools—and attempt to draw reasonable conclusions about their construction and use. But her students are not merely passively observing. They are gathering information and then using it in very creative fashions:

> Create a diary entry which starts with your discovery of the Forest Treasure object and finishes with your observations from this assignment. You can write as if you are watching indigenous people using the objects or you can create a story line in which you actually come in contact with the indigenous people yourself. IMPORTANT: This is an exercise in weaving facts and detailed observations into a story line. Include all of the rich vocabulary from object observations in your journal entry. (O'Donnell, personal communication, July 2001)

Try your hand at making observations of the objects in Figure 10.3. Use the field note double-entry form if you wish and jot down your observations and questions, reflections, feelings, and connections in the right-hand column.

Figure 10.3
Illustrations for Observation

Image no. 2271
American Museum of Natural History

Image no. 2852
American Museum of Natural History

With students, you might try the following:

- Compare what each person observed. This will be most enlightening, because all of us see objects and phenomena through different sets of lenses. If you each drew a picture, what did you notice or emphasize and why?

- Discuss the process of observation: what you noticed first, and then later on as you spent more time with the object or illustration. What were your thoughts? What did it remind you of? What feelings did you experience as you observed?

- As the discussion proceeds questions will naturally arise. For example, in examining the pink flamingo we notice, of course, the neck—its color, length, and shape. So many questions arise: Why is it so long? What adaptive purpose does it serve? Do all flamingos have such a neck? Is it in any way related to other long-necked animals, for example, the giraffe?

One thing that seems important is to give some attention not only to the observations and questions generated, but also to the thinking processes associated with each. How were they similar to or different from others? What can each of us learn from others' thought processes? From the feelings we share about our engagement with the objects?

"Will Our Brains Shrink as We Evolve?"

A high school principal from Brooklyn, New York, posed this question after Ann Prewitt led an in-depth investigation of 18 hominid and primate skulls representing a time frame of about 3 million years ago to the present. This principal and others had come to the museum to experience the kinds of inquiry-based activities their teachers and students might engage in. Some of Ann's skulls were real, and others were casts made for the American Museum of Natural History. She had laid them out on a table in random order for all the school principals to see and began to ask these kinds of questions:

- "Most of these are casts. Can you identify the two real skulls among the group?"

- "Why are most of these casts rather than the real thing?"
- "There are two nonhuman primates in this group. Which ones do you think they are and why?"

Now the principals arose and came forward to the table, which had beige, brown, and varicolored skulls of different sizes. They handled the skulls to find those features that might distinguish the two groups.

Then Ann said, "Now, see if you can arrange them in a logical, evolutionary sequence within their groups, from the oldest to contemporary times." This called for careful examination of the features of each skull, the size, shape of face, and eyebrows and eye sockets, among other things.

Once the principals had completed this task, Ann asked them to identify their criteria for placing the skulls in a specific order. Here the participants were challenged to reflect on their critical thinking, their drawing conclusions in accordance with specific criteria: "We looked at size of the brain . . . at the eye sockets . . . at the brow ridges . . . flattened face . . . the size and shape of the teeth we see . . ." and so forth.

After this 30-minute investigation, Ann then modeled her own inquiries:

"How do we know that what I have here is an accurate likeness of what early humans looked like? You notice that much of the skull parts were missing when the scientists reconstructed the skulls. What do you think the probability is of getting a correct reconstruction of hundreds of pieces of smashed bone, knowing that there are many fragments missing? You were reading the features as if they were anatomically correct. One of the most exciting aspects of science is that new findings change our ways of looking at the past and we then reconstruct our models to reflect new information. We are continually challenging our assumptions with new research. What were your assumptions and how might they change?"

Then we asked our principals for their own questions:

- "Because we use such a small portion of our brain power, is it likely that our brains will shrink in size over the next 2 million years of evolution?"

- "Is there a relationship between the size of the eye socket and the ability to see?"
- "Now that men and women are engaged in basically the same kinds of work, would we expect to see a diminution of gender differences in skulls over time?"
- "How have geographical environments affected our development?"

These questions would form the basis of a wide variety of investigations that educators or their students could make—supplemented, of course, by the teacher's core concepts and questions.

What Ann and I were attempting to model for the principals was a way of taking complex, intriguing, and puzzling concepts from their curriculum and fashioning an Observe, Think, and Question inquiry approach. This demonstration used systematics as its core—that is, the scientific process of identifying species by their characteristics and attempting to classify them, find relationships among them, and, if necessary, create new categories.

When I asked these educational leaders what elements of our demonstration they would look for in their own classrooms, they responded with a variety of comments: ". . . real stuff to investigate . . . time to observe . . . students asking their own questions . . . hands on investigations . . . it was interesting—related to who we are. . . ."

What I loved about this investigation was the principals' involvement, intellectual, emotional, and physical, in a meaningful investigation. My hope is that these educational leaders were able to transfer from this hominid inquiry the elements we need to see within our own classrooms: teacher modeling of inquiry, stuff that's interesting to investigate with time to poke and prod the heart of the curriculum, and opportunities for students to pose their own questions, which they can then pursue.

I now wonder how Ann's display and discussion might differ when she can include a cast of the skull recently discovered in Chad, dating from nearly 7 million years ago! There may be questions about "the fateful moment when the human and chimpanzee lineages went their separate ways" and how a hominid that old could have a braincase comparable to a modern chimp but "more human like than the 'Lucy' species, *Australopithecus afarensis*, which lived more than 3.2 million years ago" (Wilford, 2002, F1, F2).

This investigation will be something to behold!

Surprise Discoveries

As with any expedition there will be surprises along the way. For example, exploring the ocean floors has given us many a scientifically fascinating discoveries. In 2000, on an undersea expedition to map the Gakkel Mid-ocean Ridge, a mountainous ridge that runs about 1,100 miles down the middle of the main Arctic basin, scientists made an amazing discovery. "Buried in sonar readings taken by a Navy submarine to create a map of the ocean floor, the scientists discovered two large volcanoes that had recently convulsed the Arctic seabed" (Broad, 2001, p. F3). Said one scientist, "People had predicted that we wouldn't see any eruptions here. But there they were." Such eruptions seem to be more common than anyone had imagined. Because we know that creatures exist at mid-ocean ridges in the Atlantic and Pacific oceans, there was speculation that life might exist two miles beneath the North Pole as well. Animal life (about 300 different species, including crablike creatures as well as tube-worms) at these mid-ocean ridges exists in the absence of sunlight and survives using chemosynthesis (chemical synthesis) rather than photosynthesis.

On any expedition, we will make discoveries of strange, unknown phenomena, like the Arctic volcanoes, or the discovery in 1841 by Captain Sir James Clark Ross of Mt. Erebus, the southernmost active volcano in Antarctica, only 900 miles from the South Pole.

So we encourage visitors to the museum to have a purpose, yes, but also to plan time to wander around, allowing their various interests to lure them toward different exhibits. There ought to be time to explore, not just to answer specific questions and then leave. Exploring opens the mind to the strange and mysterious. Recall Heidegger's description in Chapter 2 of the thoughtful person as "open to the mystery" of life in the natural world (1966, p. 55).

One observer likens families visiting museums to a "hunter-gatherer team actively foraging in these rich settings to satisfy their curiosity about the topics and objects that interest them" (McManus, 1994, p. 91). Some parents might object to this characterization of them and their children, but the point is that families do travel around museums in a constant search for exciting experiences from the wide variety of exhibits. All of these are bound to stimulate curiosities, like "How come we don't see any dinosaur skins?" "What does the prefix 'paleo' mean?" and "How could the Big Bang happen without having a specific location in space? That's impossible!" Perhaps not.

One day I was conversing with three parents in the Rose Center for Earth and Space. One asked me a question about the little creatures swimming around in our large, enclosed biosphere. I found out later they were a kind of shrimp. When I asked them how they were enjoying the museum, they all said they were chaperoning a school trip and were so delighted that the teachers had given their middle school children so much time to explore on their own. "Thank goodness there are no worksheets to fill out!" one exclaimed. I looked over at three of these students and they were excitedly examining the exhibits about stars like our sun and supermassive stars like Rigel in the constellation Orion. No pencils, no worksheets. All they had was the luxury of exploring what fascinated them with their friends. There needs to be sufficient time for such open explorations.

Back at Home in the Classroom

There is such a wide variety of ways of building on the curiosities stimulated by a visit to any of the many halls in a museum. Visitors who posed the questions above about plate tectonics, the oceans, and dating rocks have so many options for following up on their curiosities. They could do any of the following methods:

- Check out Internet sites on the topics, for example, www.refdesk.com ("Ask the Experts"); www.amnh.org; www.britannica.com; www.nationalgeographic.com; www.askjeeves.com; http://imagine.gsfc.nasa.gov

- Use megasearch engines like www.google.com; www.north-ernlight.com; and www.profusion.com
- Conduct informal research using books, articles, and newspapers
- Call or write curators of the halls that have stimulated your curiosity to ask them one or two of your most important questions
- Try the same on e-mail
- Interview a resource person (scientist, historian)
- Find an older person (in school or elsewhere) who knows something about the topic from previous studies

It may help to visit the museum gift shop to find a book, video, or toy that can continue our enjoyment of what we found interesting.

If we are returning to a classroom, specifically, we could consider these kinds of experiences:

- Review our field notes. Ask: "What impressed you? What did you notice the most? Find most fascinating, puzzling?"
- Identify specific questions to research on individual/group basis
- Follow the KWHLAQ format
- Conduct research using the wide variety of resources available, including the World Wide Web, and then plan for sharing results through these kinds of creative experiences: Group/individual oral/written reports—write stories involving the findings; imagine being a character making significant discoveries; imagine yourself using the discoveries of science in novel situations; host a panel including skeptics to discuss findings; or create video or PowerPoint presentations that demonstrate what you understand about your findings
- Post findings on an Internet site: for example, www.angelfire.com or www.geocities.com
- Send findings to a museum or scientist for expert feedback
- Curate your own exhibit of artifacts you've collected—in school or in your community center

■ Represent your findings through drawings, models, sculptures, or other forms

Linda D'Acquisto of Shorewood, Wisconsin, has created a program for students to research, design, and curate their own museum exhibits (D'Acquisto, 2001). Known as "Kid Curators," Linda's program recently engaged 5th grade students in the Maple Avenue Elementary School in Sussex, Wisconsin, in planning their own exhibits on the American Revolution. The teacher, Christina Garley, and Nancy Gin, a parent volunteer and the school secretary, worked as a team with Linda. They developed "focus questions" for the students' inquiry, such as "How did the war begin?" "What was it like to be a patriot, a loyalist?" and "How did the revolution affect families?" These focus questions, though broad enough to allow for student inquiry, also addressed important content standards teachers were responsible for within the curriculum.

The process Linda uses includes an introduction to the topic in school—an opportunity to become fascinated with the subject—and visits to a local museum to meet with museum staff to learn about curating an exhibit. This behind-the-scenes look at museum work is something most people are fascinated by!

When a local television station filmed the exhibit, Christina observed, "The kids had so much fun. It's the first time I've been able to teach social studies and the kids cheer, 'Yes! Social studies!'"

In addition to the research and critical thinking involved, students played the roles of docents and explainers of their exhibits, providing them with opportunities to share their understandings and respond to their parents' and guests' questions.

What might set this kind of experience apart from the kinds of projects most elementary school students engage in is, of course, the interaction with museum staff and the extensive research they had to conduct. One student, Adam, said, "When you work with it so long, it sticks with you." Another student, Tesa, said, "With a regular class you just read about what you're learning in a book. But this sticks with you. When you get older, you can look back and say, 'I made that'" (O'Donnell, 2001, p. 13).

Inquiry-Based Science

"Scientific literacy means that a person can ask, find, or deter-mine answers to questions derived from curiosity about every-day experiences" (National Research Council, 1996, p. 22). It also means that we know how to deal with the kinds of results others and we derive from experiment and/or observations.

As we proceed with investigations in the field or at a museum, we are bound to formulate conclusions. We may per-form experiments and arrive at results we think are impressive. When we tour the museum, we encounter exhibits where scien-tists make assertions such as: "This slab of gneiss from the North American Acasta Shield is 3.96 billion years old. We think it was once part of a continent" (Ed Mathez, personal communi-cation, October 2000).

When the curator of the Hall of Planet Earth, Ed Mathez, first said this to me and a group of other students, I asked him, "Well, how do we know it was a continent?" He gave a good explanation that ended with his admission, "We don't really know."

There are many concerns we ought to have with scientific data. When someone on radio or television tells us that 8 out of 10 people prefer one cola to another, or when we hear that arsenic in so many parts per billion is not harmful to our health, we should start asking questions. Here are some good ones:

- "How do we know?"
- "How certain are we of the results?"
- "Is there an alternative scientific explanation for the one we proposed?"
- "Do we need more evidence? Is our evidence adequate? Objective? Representative? Reliable?"
- "What are our sources of experimental error?"
- "How would we account for results different from ours?" (National Research Council, 1996, p. 174)

Such questions reflect McPeck's definition of critical thinking as "a certain skepticism" about what to believe (1981). Whenever we read in the papers about some amazing discovery of science—be it of a 7-million-year-old humanlike fossil or of a new solar system—we usually read the counter point of view: "Some scientists have different explanations for the same data . . . . A few dissenters continue to dispute these findings . . . . Others say it is too early to draw reasonable conclusions—we do not have sufficient data." When a meteorite in Antarctica was said to provide evidence of life on its originating planet, Mars, there were scientists who found other explanations for the evidence presented. This is as it should be.

Scientific reasoning, says my museum colleague Adriana Aquino, leads us to hypotheses, such as the classification systems of all vertebrates. These hypotheses are continually being challenged and not presented as final truths. A cladogram setting forth evolutionary development of vertebrates is as much an hypothesis as are the skull reconstructions Ann Prewitt used with the high school principals. Science proceeds by hypothesizing, dissenting, discussing, concluding, and always being open to revision. We can say the same for thinking in the humanities.

Remember Carl Sagan's two goals for education: to promote curiosity and wonder, and, with that, a healthy skepticism about all the possibilities we might accept and their meeting rigorous standards (Sagan, 1996).

Again, we return to my mother's question: "Well, how do you know?"

Conclusion

Why do we go to museums and to other venues, such as science fairs, zoos, botanical gardens, and nature centers? John H. Falk notes: "Adults go to science centers to satisfy their curiosity and to fulfill their needs for fun and intellectual stimulation. They take their children because they feel that such experiences are worthwhile and educational, as well as fun" (2001, p. 3). He refers to such visits as "free-choice science learning" experiences that are "non-sequential, self-paced and voluntary . . ." (p. 7). Such visits contrast with learning experiences in schools where there is a tighter structure and a more formal set of learning experiences often directed by an adult without students' input.

Museums are not places of dead stuff, nor are they amusement parks we dash through from one thrill to another. They are invitations to explore the riches we have found to be important in the continuing quest to make our lives meaningful. Every day I work at the American Museum of Natural History, I try to take time out to visit my favorite halls to learn something new: that the island on which I live is composed mostly of a metamorphic rock known as "Manhattan schist," that this rock is striated with deep gouges left by the glaciers of thousands of years ago, glaciers 1,000 feet thick!

I learn about the nature of supermassive black holes, how they form a point at the center of a huge galaxy, where matter equivalent to millions of times the mass of the sun is so condensed that light cannot escape the force of gravity; but that they power quasars, the most brilliant objects in the universe, brighter than hundreds or thousands of galaxies. How can this be? How can these objects, some 12 billion light-years out in space and back in history, tell us about the "dark ages" of the universe and the time when stars first began to shine?

A visitor to the museum recently toured all the major exhibits in one day and concluded with this observation about our being in the universe: "Man isn't lost as long as he's inquisitive" (Martin, 2002, p. E45).

References

Barell, J. (1992). *". . . EVER WONDER . . . ?"* Columbus, OH: Zaner-Bloser.

Broad, W. J. (2001, February 20). Under icy Arctic waters, a fiery, unexpected find. *The New York Times*, p. F3.

Bunge, P. (2001). Mantle convection. In E. Mathez (Ed.), *Earth: Inside and out. An American Museum of Natural History Book.* New York: The New Press.

D'Acquisto, L. (2001, June). *Kid Curators.* Shorewood, WI: Kid Curators LLC. Available: ldacquisto@www.kidcurators.com.

Falk, J. H. (2001). Free-choice science education: Framing the discussion. In J. H. Falk (Ed.), *Free-choice science education: How we learn science outside of school* (pp. 3–20). New York: Teachers College Press.

Heidegger, M. (1966). *Discourse on thinking.* New York: HarperTorchbooks.

Lipman, M. (1988). Critical thinking: What it can be. *Cogitare, 2*(4), 1–2.

Martin, D. (2002, January 4). A brief walk through time. *The New York Times*, pp. E39–45.

McManus, P. (1994). Families in museums. In R. Miles and L. Savala (Eds.), *Towards the museum of the future: New European perspectives* (pp. 81–97). London: Routledge. Quoted in G. E. Hein & M. Alexander (Eds.), 1998. *Museums: Places of learning* (p. 23). Washington, DC: American Association of Museums.

McPeck, J. (1981). *Critical thinking and education.* Oxford, England: Martin Robertson.

National Research Council. (1996). *National Science Education Standards.* Washington, DC: National Academy Press.

O'Donnell, T. (2001, March 27). Fifth-graders learn by creating museum. *Sussex Sun,* Sussex, WI, p. 13.

Pasachoff, J. (1983). *Astronomy: From the Earth to the universe.* New York: Saunders College Publishing.

Sagan, C. (1996). *The demon-haunted world: Science as a candle in the dark.* New York: Ballantine Books.

Wilford, J. N. (2002, August 6). Redrawing humanity's family tree—two skulls found in Africa and in Europe challenge theories of human origin and migrations. *The New York Times,* p. F1, F2.

Chapter 11

How We Assess
Our Inquisitiveness

Inquisitiveness is nothing other than gentle questions in the morning.

—High School Student

Many years ago I was conducting qualitative research on high school students' imaginative thinking (Barell, 1980). This study provided me with opportunities to sit in classrooms and observe their behavior. The students had no idea what I was looking for so I could follow up my observations with a wide variety of questions to attempt to understand what they were thinking about during classes.

My definition of imaginative thinking was based on the nature of play as a developmental phenomenon that involved intrinsic rewards (fun!), internal reality (you can make a block into a truck or a doll), and internal control (you were in charge and could create anything you wanted). My theory (derived from Erik Erikson) was that playing with blocks and toys in childhood became internalized during adolescence to consist of playing with ideas, exemplified by Einstein's "combinatory play with ideas" (Koestler, 1964, p. 171).

Part of what I saw was students asking a lot of questions in and out of class. The questions that seemed most playful were the "What if . . .?" questions that challenged conventional think-ing and that took us "outside the box" into new dimensions. The question that I remember most vividly was posed in a history class by a student named Betsy. The teacher was one of her favorites, and she loved history. During a discussion of the causes of World War II, Betsy asked, "Was Hitler the Kaiser Wilhelm of World War II?"

I was amazed at that question, not because it came from Betsy, but because it put the two German leaders in a playful, imaginative juxtaposition I'd never considered before. Here was a perfect illustration of Einstein's combinatory play with ideas.

Betsy's teacher responded to her statement by remarking, "No, I wouldn't say that." And that was it. After class I asked Betsy how she came up with this metaphoric statement. From her responses and those of the other five students, I learned something about how we make content meaningful—partly by taking facts and ideas and, as Einstein had done, reconstructing them imaginatively in our minds into meaningful patterns and relationships. Hence the title of the book that emerged from this work, *Playgrounds of Our Minds* (Barell, 1980).

During this study I had occasion to ask one or more of the teachers about the efficacy of having the students pose ques-tions. All agreed that it was important. When I asked if they ever assessed students on this ability to pose meaningful questions—that is, on their inquisitiveness—each of them replied, "No."

When working with some college faculty on the nature of crit-ical thinking in their subject areas, I encountered a chemistry professor whom I asked to list for me the important intellectual tasks that chemists undertake (Barell, 1988). He mentioned observing, collecting, and analyzing data and then said, "Good chemists need to ask good questions."

"When do we teach students to ask good questions?" I asked.

"Not very often," he replied.

"Why?"

He thought for a few seconds and then responded from behind his lab table, "Because there isn't enough time." Not enough time to teach and then assess what may be one of the most distinguishing characteristics of any good scientist, historian, teacher, doctor, or lawyer: asking good, significant questions.

So here is part of the dilemma as I see it: Most of us would think that inquisitiveness is, indeed, important. But there hasn't been much emphasis on including it among the many criteria we think are important to foster, develop, and assess as students learn. We do not seem to make getting better at asking good questions a high priority on evaluations of students' work.

And, at the time of this writing (August 2002), there is such a press among some educators and politicians for what we call high-stakes testing of students that I see more of a movement away from assessing those skills and dispositions that can help develop a responsible citizen capable of engaging in meaningful problem posing and resolving.

Reflective Pause

If you agree that assessing inquisitiveness is important, how would you suggest we go about doing it? What kinds of experiences would you create with and for students? How would you assess the effectiveness of the assessments themselves?

Defining Inquisitiveness

First, we need to identify what it is we're talking about. We need to ask what "inquisitiveness" looks and sounds like, and we can certainly do this with our students from just about any age. Figure 11.1 gets us on our way by using a framework developed by the Tahoma School District in Maple Valley, Washington. Based on the fine work of Arthur Costa in defining intelligent behavior and dispositions, this is a good analytic tool to use with children and older students (Costa & Kallick, 2000).

We can expand this list by considering other observable behaviors. Additions to "What Inquisitiveness Looks Like":

- Student persists in examinations and observations
- Seeks out a wide variety of resources for projects

Figure 11.1
The Nature of Inquisitiveness

What inquisitiveness looks like:

- Student looks closely at things, explores

- Observes using a variety of senses (touch, smell)

- Shows enthusiasm in facial expressions

- Seeks out new ways of learning or things to learn about and creates own problems to solve

What inquisitiveness sounds like:

- Student asks a variety of questions: "Why?"; "How come?"; "What if?"

- Seeks additional information: "Tell me more"; "Where else can I get information?"

- Makes analogies: "This reminds me of . . ."; "It's like. . . ."

- Statements reflect an "I enjoy" attitude: "This is fun!"; "I'd like more time to learn more!"; "How exciting!"

Source: Tahoma School District; Adapted from a checklist by Arthur L. Costa
http://www.tahoma.wednet.edu/teachlearn/perfinquis.htm.

- Is open to a wide variety of interpretations or points of view and ambiguities

- Has respect for factual information, attempts to clarify issues

- Evidences a healthy skepticism about claims, judgments, and generalizations, searches for underlying assumptions and biases

- Thinks of multiple ways to solve problems or approach issues

- Pokes, prods, and examines objects and phenomena at length

Additions to "What Inquisitiveness Sounds Like":

- Questions such as "I wonder . . . ."

- "Do you suppose?"

When Mary Wallace and Chuck Dolan of Thomas Jefferson Middle School in Fair Lawn, New Jersey, asked their 8th graders what inquisitiveness *sounded* like, they responded with questions including: "How do you know? What makes you think that? What happened? Why did it happen? Why not?" and statements like: "I don't get it."

When Mary and Chuck asked them what inquisitiveness *looked* like, some of them replied, "Puzzled looks . . . searching eyes . . . acting antsy . . . wandering around . . . engrossed . . . focused . . . attentive . . . eyes wide open with arched eyebrows. . . ." At the high school level, mathematics and computer education teacher Barbara M'Gonigle (Dumont High School, Dumont, New Jersey) found that students *saw* inquisitive persons as "a person who scratches their head a lot . . . a person who will succeed in life because of their ability to ask, 'Why?' . . . a person who looks at all things, simple and complex, for a long time to understand them . . . a person who is more argumentative, more annoying. . . ." (Mary Wallace & Barbara M'Gonigle, personal communications, April 2001).

M'Gonigle's high school students *heard* cries of "Ooh, what about this? . . . How'd you get that? Where'd you think of that? What made it do that?" and "Why is it like that?"

When we are satisfied that we have a workable set of indicators for inquisitiveness, we can begin thinking about how to include them in some of our assessments. Here is one story of how some young thinkers observed their own thinking processes that we might use as a model of how to assess their questioning.

"Were We Good Thinkers Today?"— Assessment Strategies

Many years ago, I had one of the most enriching experiences ever in a 1st grade classroom at the Richard E. Byrd Elementary School in Glen Rock, New Jersey. Here Mary Mulcahy worked her magic with students of "average" ability during their reading sessions. She spent a lot of time with them focusing on problem solving—trying to figure out how to help a student who had a broken arm to do homework, and to stop the writing of graffiti on the school's bathroom walls. The students were marvelous in their generation of solutions. Someone suggested installing a video camera in the bathroom, and immediately a friend noted, critically, "Why would you want to see all of that?" End of that proposed solution.

At the conclusion of their sessions, where everybody, including me, was seated on the carpet around Mary, she would ask, "Were we good thinkers today?" Her students had spent a lot of time problem solving and had generated a list of what "good problem solvers" do (see Figure 11.2).

Mary Mulcahy's students had a guide for good problem solving, and they could use this to reflect on their own behavior. On one occasion, a boy named Thomas said, "I don't think I was a good thinker today, because I usually think of more ideas." A classmate named Evan noted that his thinking was not so great, "because I was sort of copying other people's ideas." And another student added, "When you are copying others' thinking, you are not really thinking for yourself" (Barell, 1995, p. 45).

Figure 11.2
"Get to the Main Problem"

Ten Things Good Problem Solvers Do

1. Think!
2. Take the parts out of the problem that you don't really need—get to the main problem.
3. Make the problem littler and littler.
4. Make sure you know what you're trying to figure out before you start to do anything.
5. Look at the problem from a different angle.
6. Make sure the problem makes sense.
7. Work it out on a piece of paper—write it down in order, then list the best and worst solutions. This gets it better into your mind.
8. Ask someone to help you if the problem is too big.
9. When you're discussing a problem and you disagree with what someone else is saying, just jump in and argue. That helps everyone think.
10. Break up the problem; solve each piece and then put it back together. . . .

Adapted from Barell, 1995, p. 168.

Both the children's list of strategies and their reflections on their own thoughtfulness have always amazed me. Their rules for problem solving are so practical and, what's even more amazing, they reflect the best research adults have done on problem solving. For example, good problem solvers analyze a complex issue and break it down, or reduce it, to manageable parts (Hayes, 1981). Mary's students generated this list entirely from their own experiences and from Mary's structuring of their problem-solving reflections and deliberations. They had no formal, direct teaching about what constitutes good problem solving.

One of the lessons I learned from Mary's groundbreaking experiences is that our students can analyze highly complex issues and articulate rules for how to proceed with their inquiry. Another lesson is that students can reflect on their experiences at a young age or at any age and be quite analytic and constructive.

So it makes sense that if Mary Mulcahy's students can analyze their problem-solving abilities, they could also determine the nature of curious classmates and generate a list like that presented in Figure 11.2. And it also seems evident that students from the 1st on up through the 12th grade and beyond can determine the importance of being curious, wondering, and asking good questions in the face of life's significant challenges, such as problem solving and critical analysis of complex issues.

Mary's students have presented us with a model of how young people as well as learners of all ages can become articulate partners in the assessment of those goals and objectives that call for specific, observable behaviors. This should include almost any teacher's entire set of curricular goals! Ask our students, "Were we good problem solvers, inquirers, critical thinkers today? Are we behaving as a community of responsible citizens? What do you think our final projects should look like? What do you think good scientists, historians, mathematicians, writers do and how can we see it in your work?"

They'll tell us!

The Untold Story of Mrs. Claus—Another Strategy

Christine Burt taught English at Dumont High School in Dumont, New Jersey. In one of her journalism classes a few years ago, she

was teaching her students how to ferret out important information and compose a good story. She taught them about the major
questions a journalist asks: "Who, What, When, Where, How, and
Why?" Christine gave them plenty of experiences analyzing others' stories in the major New York metropolitan newspapers. The
students in Christine's class wrote stories and peer edited them
for accuracy, depth, and organization.

On one occasion Christine told me she had invited a guest
speaker in to test her students' abilities to ask good questions.
What Christine was especially interested in was not the initial
"Who, What, and Why?" questions, but how her students followed
up on their initial queries. Could they pose good probing questions
of the guest and then weave them into the stories they filed later?

Christine was, in fact, engaged in an authentic assessment of
students' abilities to ask better questions and compose a story.
Her guest was "Mrs. Claus," Santa's wife. Christine prepared her
students with a press release about Mrs. Claus that told of her
recent book, *Claus and Effect: The Untold Story of Mrs. Santa.*

The teacher playing the role of Mrs. Claus sat in front of the
class and briefly introduced herself, giving some background on
her book and on life with Santa.

What I saw were students posing their initial questions to get
the major points of the story, and what I was listening for were
the follow-up questions. I also attempted to jot down who asked
what kinds of questions.

At the end of the session, Christine and I compared notes on
who asked what. She, of course, knew the students far better
than I did and was able to discuss whose questions reflected
some level of growth. She knew who had developed her or his
ability to probe more deeply into a story and not merely accept
initial descriptions without attempting to elicit more background
information. Some students sought out the underlying assumptions, while a few others asked questions to gain deeper understanding of the overall issues involved.

Christine had structured this session to observe (by taking
notes and videotaping the session) how her students were able
to think on their feet. She knew that sitting in a classroom reading news articles is one kind of reality, but when you are in the
midst of an interview you have to be able to think clearly and

sometimes quickly and spontaneously. Of course, preparation for a session like this is important, but Christine wanted to see if students could take what they were hearing, analyze it, and find the puzzles and ambiguities.

After the session, students reflected on their behavior just as Mary's did and, eventually, they watched the videotape and were able to analyze their individual and class behavior more closely.

Reflective Pause

What do you think of Christine Burt's assessment experience? When and how have you attempted such an assessment? Under what circumstances might you try this kind of challenge in the future—or an improvement upon it—and how might you handle it differently?

I am now amazed at recalling this episode because I think it is the only one in over 35 years of teaching where I saw an assessment of inquisitiveness—the only example of a teacher's wanting to know specifically how her students were getting better at being probing inquirers. It is remarkable also because Christine Burt created an authentic kind of setting for this assessment: an actual interview that would result in a news story.

Once again, we note the thoughts of Grant Wiggins on authentic assessments; these are ones that are

1. Realistic;
2. Require judgment and innovation;
3. Ask the students to "do" the subject;
4. Assess the students' ability to efficiently and effectively use a repertoire of knowledge and skill to negotiate a complex task; and
5. Allow appropriate opportunities to rehearse, practice, consult resources, and get feedback on and refine performances and products. (1998, p. 22)

How could this interview experience have become more authentic?

Christine's interview experience meets all of these criteria, just as Cheryl Hopper's World Bank assessment in Chapter 8 did.

In all authentic assessments, we are challenging students to use their acquired knowledge to think through a complex issue, not merely repeat what they have memorized. They must, in effect, think on their feet and adjust their performance after receiving feedback from a variety of sources.

Assessing the Quality of Our Conclusions

We have defined inquisitiveness as a set of mental operations and dispositions. We can use this kind of chart developed by the Tahoma School District as a neat form of self-assessment for students and faculty. But there is more we can investigate. It's not just the numbers of questions we ask; it's also the quality of those inquiries that matters.

Quality can be defined as that which reflects excellence, superiority, or something of high value. It is not enough just to ask more questions. We want students, as a course or school year progresses, to pose more meaningful questions of the kinds we have suggested: "Why?"; "What if?"; and "How do we know?"

We want to see, as Christine Burt attempted to, that students move from posing simple to more complex questions. We would also want to help students to ask the kinds of self-reflective questions suggested in Chapter 4: "What is my goal?"; "How well am I doing?"; and "How satisfied with the results am I?"

But how do we know if students' curiosities are leading them toward high-quality intellectual conclusions? How can we assess the quality of their final products? This will depend on how we define "quality" and can be reflected in the scoring rubrics we use for the final projects.

For example, in asking junior faculty ("student teachers") how they want to self-assess their portfolios, they often generate criteria such as organization, originality, presentation, use of resources, and reflection of critical thinking. When we ask what each of these "looks like" in a portfolio, we begin to get an idea of what quality in this instance is. For example, an indicator of quality could be originality of thought. What students who want to be assessed by this criterion often say is that originality looks like something that is "creative . . . innovative . . . different. . . ." And then we notice that these words are synonyms for "original." We must dig deeper to find the indicators of originality. Again, what does it look like in a portfolio?

Then we begin to develop more observable indicators:

- New strategies used in the classroom
- Novel artwork
- Questions posed that are novel, different from all the others
- Occasions when a different perspective or point of view on a subject was taken
- A new way of looking at a problem—novel problem identification

Perkins (1981) determined that such flexibility in thinking is more conducive to original thought than is the mere generation of many ideas. Such flexibility ought to become one of our curricular objectives—to help students ask, "How can I see this problem or situation from a different point of view?" (See Figure 9.1.)

So a student portfolio can reflect a quality product if it shows some evidence of new ways of thinking about a subject. Quality rests in how we think about it.

Another criterion would surely reflect understanding of major concepts, ideas, and principles within the subject.

Checking for Understanding

What does deeper understanding look like in a final project? The best assessment for understanding I ever conducted challenged students to use any art form to demonstrate that they understood the major conflicts and characters in *Othello*. I was delighted to receive a long poem, a cartoon depicting Iago, and an original violin sonata, along with many collages (Barell, 1995, pp. 278–283). Accompanying each work of art was a brief explanatory essay stating just how the symbols presented represented the major themes of the play.

If we are studying the U.S. Constitution, for example, what kinds of intellectual challenges, embedded within various kinds of aesthetic and more formal formats, might we be looking for that provide evidence of students' deep understanding of this complex document?

Here are some possibilities. Students could do the following:

- Explain various provisions/articles.

- Relate/compare/transfer concepts such as Separation of Powers to similar concepts in other subjects, in own experiences.

- Create models/metaphors for our federal system.

- Design a new constitution for your class using basic principles of the U.S. Constitution, for example, federalism, equality under the law, or proposing of amendments.

- Generate hypotheses to explain why constitutions in some countries are not as long lasting as ours.

- Generalize from data to broad principles/ideas and concepts.

- Create a poem, a play, or a picture depicting the major concepts and themes.

- Respond to questions about their product. For example, "What if we didn't have a strong executive branch?"

- Teach concepts/ideas/information to others. (Barell, 1995, p. 278)

These are some ways in which we all demonstrate that we understand the fundamental principles and provisions of the U.S. Constitution. This is a sure indicator of quality.

Of course, there are so many different kinds of assessment experiences that we could engage to elicit the mental operations listed: debates, video stories, artworks, research papers, model building, and role-playing scenarios. The goal is to let students help in designing the experiences they will use to demonstrate the depth of their understanding and the quality of their reasoning through which they find answers to their own questions.

What, you might ask, does all of this have to do with assessing the quality of inquisitiveness? I suggest that if we are using some of these strategies to assess students' understanding of content, and if their final products are the result of their own curiosities and our helping with these final projects, then we are gathering evidence that students have asked good questions that lead to the creation of meaningful products. As we all know, it's not enough to ask a good question; we hope that these questions lead to deeper understanding of our content.

Assessment Using Subject and State Standards

All subjects have ways of acquiring new knowledge, sometimes known as methods of inquiry or "ways of knowing." In science, for example, we expect students in grade 4 to be able to "ask a question about objects, organisms, and events in the environment." Then we expect they should be able to "plan and conduct a simple investigation" (National Research Council, 2000, p. 19).

In grades 9 through 12, we expect students to be able to "understand the use of hypotheses in science (for example, selecting and narrowing the focus of data . . .)." Furthermore, we intend that a student "designs and conducts scientific investigations" (McREL, 2001).

Our experiment or investigation needs to collect data that is objective, representative, unbiased, and so forth. Our conclusions need to be able to be replicated by others for validity and reliability.

Marzano, Pickering, and McTighe (1993) have set up a scoring rubric for such scientific investigations:

Experimental inquiry involves testing hypotheses that have been generated to explain a phenomenon. It includes four components that can be assessed:

1. Accurately explains the phenomenon initially observed using appropriate and accepted facts, concepts, or principles.

2. Makes a logical prediction based on the facts, concepts, or principles underlying the explanation.

3. Sets up and carries out an activity or experiment that effectively tests the prediction.

4. Effectively evaluates the outcome of the activity or experiment in terms of the original explanation. (p. 81)

In 1967, Edwin Fenton wrote this about inquiry: "Physicists, historians, and teachers of literature should all challenge their students to develop and test hypotheses—tentative explanations adopted provisionally to explain certain facts and guide the investigation of others—and to learn the rules of logic which govern the process" (p. 11).

In the humanities, we become intrigued by some puzzle, problematic situation, doubt, or uncertainty, such as one that I heard a student ask once: "Did FDR know about the attack on Pearl Harbor beforehand?" We can develop a working hypothesis or explanation and set about how to arrive at a conclusion by assembling all the relevant documents or passages for interpretation. We search for clues, relate those that seem relevant to each other, weigh the preponderance of evidence, and arrive at tentative judgments.

General Assessment Guidelines

In assessing student performances in the sciences and the humanities, we are looking for how they conduct their investigations. To assess their work, we can use the scoring rubrics suggested by Marzano, Pickering, and McTighe. We can also ask how well a student does the following:

- Identifies a problematic situation worth investigating. Recognizes the puzzles, the complex and ambiguous situations that suggest questions to be asked.

- Designs and conducts a scientific investigation (for example, formulates hypotheses, designs and executes investigations, interprets data, synthesizes evidence into explanations, proposes alternatives for observations, critiques explanations and procedures) (McREL, 2001).

- Keeps an open mind about the process and all relevant evidence. Analyzes data for accuracy, reliability, and relevance.

- Identifies assumptions on which his or her investigations are based. Examines the issue from a number of different points of view. Takes opposing sides of an issue.

- Maintains a healthy skepticism about results and conclusions . . . . Distinguishes between actual observations and
  preconceived notions about what was observed. Asks
  "How do you know?" about conclusions and results.
- Seeks alternative explanations for one's conclusions.

These questions may help us and our students reflect on our
progress in conducting inquiry in the sciences and the humanities.

In addition, we want students to reflect on what they have
learned about the inquiry process, with themselves as investigators, working collaboratively with friends, and we want them to
ask themselves what they might do differently next time.

These questions can be answered as a class group or, perhaps more reflectively and at first, in journals on one's own. Too
often we neglect the learning process itself: the act of being a
member of a team of inquiring minds searching out answers to
puzzling situations.

One 6th grade student reflected on his inquiry process and
noted: "I learned that first you have to make a plan. Next you
have to ask yourself questions. After you do that, the whole thing
makes sense." Some might reverse the order of questioning and
planning, but he makes the important point: meaningful learning
results from effective inquiry.

Another student wrote: "If you really think about all of the
steps in our plans, then we can figure out why the plans suc-
ceeded or why they did not succeed." Here the observer realizes
the value of reflecting on the whole process, leading to the strategic uses of various learning experiences. She is now in more control of her own inquiry for the future (Barell, 1995, p. 266).

Conclusion

After Mary Wallace and Chuck Dolan, 8th grade teachers at
Thomas Jefferson Middle School in Fair Lawn, New Jersey, asked
their students about the look and sound of inquisitiveness, they
went a step beyond. They also asked the students what it *felt* like.

Here's how some of them responded: "An adrenaline rush . . . your brain races . . . you explode if you don't know . . . a sense of desperation . . . tense . . . anxious that you don't know . . . excitement . . . helpless that you don't know . . . ."

Another of Mary's students commented that she felt "open minded to possibilities . . . ." And that's what inquisitiveness is all about—being open to lots of possible mysteries, solutions, and explanations, all of which we search for with persistence and critical reasoning.

How do we know if we're getting better at it? Let our students tell us how well they are doing. They're the best observers of their own behavior.

References

Barell, J. (1980). *Playgrounds of our minds*. New York: Teachers College Press.

Barell, J. (1988). *Opening the American mind: Reflections upon teaching thinking in higher education*. Upper Montclair, NJ: Montclair State College.

Barell, J. (1995). *Teaching for thoughtfulness: Classroom strategies to enhance intellectual development*. (2nd ed.). New York: Longman.

Costa, A., & Kallick, B. (2000). *Discovering and exploring habits of mind*. Alexandria, VA: ASCD.

Fenton, E. (1967). *The new social studies*. New York: Holt, Rinehart and Winston.

Hayes, J. (1981). *The complete problem solver*. Philadelphia: Franklin Institute.

Koestler, A. (1964). *The act of creation*. New York: Dell Publishing Company.

Marzano, R., Pickering, D., & McTighe, J. (1993). *Assessing student outcomes: Performance assessments using the dimensions of learning model*. Alexandria, VA: ASCD.

McREL (2001). *K–12 standards*. Aurora, CO: Mid-continent Research for Education and Learning. Available: http://www.mcrel.org/compendium/Benchmark.asp?SubjectID=2&StandardID=12.

National Research Council. (2000). *Inquiry and the National Science Education Standards: A guide for teaching and learning*. Washington, DC: National Academy Press.

Perkins, D. N. (1981). *The mind's best work*. Cambridge, MA: Harvard University Press.

Wiggins, G. (1998). *Educative assessment: Designing assessments to inform and improve student performance*. San Francisco: Jossey-Bass.

Chapter 12

THE POWER OF LEADERSHIP

. . . . nothing about museums is as splendid as their entrances—the sudden vault, the shapely cornices . . . the broad stairs leading upward into heaven knows what mansions of expectantly hushed treasure.

—JOHN UPDIKE (1981, P. 17)

The American Museum of Natural History in New York has such a "splendid" entrance off Central Park West. You climb broad steps surrounding a weathered statue of Theodore Roosevelt, pass through revolving doors to enter a grand mansion with a high, vaulted ceiling supported by massive coral-colored terrazzo pillars.

Here the spirit of inquiry resonates around the great rotunda, where a towering model of the dinosaur *Barosaurus* stretches her neck 80 feet above the marble floor. We think this plant-eating dinosaur lived about 140 million years ago on what were the plains of western America. Her natural enemy, depicted in the exhibit, was *Allosaurus,* a cousin of the fierce carnivore, *Tyrannosaurus rex.*

Children and adults come in to this magnificent space, so open and invitational in its vaulted dimensions, with a sense of awe and wonder. As I stroll through this hall on my way to meetings or when I come just to look at this magnificent reconstruction made out of fiberglass, I am continually reminded of the museum's provost, Michael Novacek, who wrote eloquently about the construction of this model:

> Sauropods [like *Barosaurus*] with their massive trunks, lofty necks, and pillar like legs, seem to defy gravity. These gargantua serve well as examples of the challenge and ambiguities of reconstructing dinosaur behavior. First of all, how can an animal with this much mass walk, feed, and, for that matter, breathe on land? The question has long been pondered. . . . Whether sauropods were partial to watercress salads or tree-top foliage, the question concerning the manner in which huge, absurdly small headed beasts ate invariably comes up. . . ." (Novacek, 1996, p. 188–190)

Novacek goes on to discuss the controversy over the decision to depict *Barosaurus* with her head raised 80 feet above the museum floor. Would it have been possible for her to stand like this? "The question of sauropod posture has given rise to one of the more notable controversies concerning dinosaur lifestyles. Some claim that to hold the neck erect for prolonged periods of time would be a physiological impossibility" (1996, p. 191). They have asserted that this creature did not have strong enough muscles and ligaments for this posture. Others have asserted that to get blood that high up to the brain would have required "an 800-pound heart to pump its blood to its extremities" (p. 191).

Novacek concluded his inquiries in this fashion:

> We believe that all the erudite discussion about what *Barosaurus* could or could not have done does not exclude the possibility that these animals occasionally reared up. Indeed, sauropods must have been able to go bipedal in some instances—mating would have been impossible without this ability . . . . Arguments for a certain behavior of a fossil creature are often as consistent with scientific evidence as arguments against the behavior. The *Barosaurus* display at the American Museum dramatically illustrates the point." (p. 194)

What Novacek illustrates is the spirit of active inquiry about one particular domain of scientific work—paleontology. He poses the question: Could dinosaurs like *Barosaurus* have raised their heads up 80 feet above ground to defend their young? There's evidence on both sides of the question, but, as he concluded, there's nothing definitive that proves the *Barosaurus* could not. This is often how science proceeds: by setting up possible hypotheses and then treating them with McPeck's "certain skepticism" (McPeck, 1981, p. 6) to see which we can disprove. The hypothesis that remains standing is often the one we come to believe.

Why have I introduced an example of inquiry from a paleontologist to illustrate leadership in schools? My reason is simple: Wherever we find adults engaged in the energetic pursuit of finding answers to their own questions, there we have good models of inquiry from which we can all learn.

Every time I pass *Barosaurus* in the museum's rotunda, I think of Novacek's curiosities about this creature. Novacek is an excellent model of active inquiry and a teacher for all of us. As the leader of so many expeditions to the Gobi Desert in search of dinosaur fossils (magnificently chronicled in *Dinosaurs of the Flaming Cliffs*, 1996), he is an example of a scientist consumed with the passion to discover and to find answers to his questions and those of others.

This is what we need in schools if they are to become models of Carl Sagan's twin goals for education: developing a sense of wonder, awe, and curiosity about the world and, simultaneously, fostering a healthy sense of skepticism about what to believe (Sagan, 1996, p. 306).

By comparison, when I stroll into most schools, if I see any evidence of achievement or the spirit of the school, I usually see it in a trophy case full of silver and brass medallions in honor of student athletes. These are fine; but where are the 80-foot *Barosaurus* indicators of leaders' and students' inquiry, of their persistent curiosity about our world and their lives?

Leaders Who Model

Michael Novacek is one leader who has put his inquiries on display for all to see, read about, and, in the spirit of inquiry, to dispute and lay claim to alternative conclusions.

Where are the leaders in our schools who model for their students, faculty, and the community the searching questions they have about education? I know this may sound idealistic, because I think of several principals with whom I've worked over the years. I know how extremely busy they are with all sorts of issues, problems, and conflicts—about student safety, management of the curriculum (flexible bell schedules and block schedules), legal matters related to students' behaviors, attendance policies, improvement of the physical plant, student achievement on standardized tests (so-called high-stakes tests), prevention of violence on campus, and so many more.

But every principal is a leader manifesting what is important to her or him. Some stress the smooth operation of the class schedule; others stress high achievement for all their students in standardized tests; and others emphasize the differentiated ways in which children learn.

Reflective Pause

What do you think leaders can do to foster inquiry within the school community? What has your experience taught you about leaders' model strategies and practices?

If we wanted to stress developing students' inquisitiveness and their abilities to persist in searching out answers and thinking critically about information they have discovered, then we could do lots of different things in our schools, as was suggested in Chapter 3. Here are some suggestions:

- Developing with faculty, students, and parents a vision of what students need to succeed in the 21st century
- Publishing this vision
- Working during professional development experiences toward instructional and curricular strategies to implement it
- Communicating these intentions to the community and enlisting people's support
- Finding examples of students' achievement and performance that exemplify the goals of the vision, and sharing and publishing these for the entire community

Through these and other measures, we communicate a sense of the culture of the school—what it values and deems significant. There are so many channels of communication open to those in leadership positions. Like any American president, leaders have a bully pulpit from which to spread their message.

And the best place to proclaim a message of the value and importance of being curious throughout life is in the classroom. Here is where the principal and the head or lead teacher can make a big difference.

Mrs. Bonaventura and Her Dolphins

Consider this scenario:

Mrs. Bonaventura, speaking to Mrs. Talbot's 4th grade class: "Good morning, boys and girls. I'm Mrs. Bonaventura, the school principal. I've met some of you as well as your parents, and I look forward to getting to know all of you very well!

"This morning I'd like to share a story with you. When I was a little girl in school, just as you are now, I read a book about dolphins and it captured my imagination! After reading it I had so many questions on my mind that I determined to find some answers. I went to our library and found other books on dolphins; then my mom got me a few videos about marine biology and my dad took all of us to Disney World, and while there we went to SeaWorld, and I just loved the dolphin show.

"As I worked through school I continued to be fascinated by dolphins and then by sharks and rays and other sea creatures, including one of my favorites, whales. How many of you enjoy seeing and reading about whales? Yes, so did I. I was amazed that they could dive down so deep in the ocean and wondered how they could do that. Do you know?

"Well, when I got to college, I decided to major in marine biology to answer some of my questions and I got to go on some amazing expeditions my school sponsored. Here are some photos of me working with dolphins a few years ago.

"Now, why am I telling you all of this, do you suppose?"

Ben: "So we'll grow up to be scientists?"

Mrs. Bonaventura: "That's a good possibility."

Betsy: "So we'll always be curious?"

Then Jason asked: "So if you were so curious about dolphins, why did you become a principal?"

Mrs. Bonaventura smiled broadly and responded, "Aha! Yes, what a question. Who has an idea?"

Noah: "Because you got tired of it?"

Mrs. Bonaventura: "I still have loads of questions about sea life and take my own children to the aquarium whenever I can."

Emily: "Because you wanted to tell us all about it, so we'd grow up curious like you?"

Mrs. Bonaventura continued to smile and nodded her head in assent. "I want all of you to grow up to have lots of questions on your minds—questions that fascinate you, that you'll want to investigate and that may change your life as they did mine. And to get that started, Mrs. Talbot and all of our teachers have agreed that we need to challenge you all to ask your own good questions. So we're going to start sharing your own questions about the books you read out in the hallways and in our lobby, and during our final Spring Celebration we're going to feature your projects, those that present answers to the questions you've posed."

Is this a fantasy? Yes. Unlike all the other scenarios in this book, this is an imagined experience. Is it a possibility for our schools? I think so! Principals speak to their classes all the time. Why wouldn't they be able to share a scenario from their own lives with children, tell them stories about what kinds of curiosities they've had growing up? There's no reason why not. Every adult was once a curious child. Every adult was once an adolescent who had significant questions about what he or she saw happening in the world. We all have stories about growing up as curious persons who sought out our own answers. Some of us consider ourselves as grown up children who still have so many questions about life and the world! Why not share them, as I've tried to do in the Preface and elsewhere in this book?

There's nothing more important than to have the lead teacher communicate those educational priorities she deems most significant. And we do communicate our priorities, if not directly as Mrs. Bonaventura has done, then by so many other verbal and nonverbal means.

The emphasis in this book is that developing what makes us who we are—our inquisitiveness and our searching for meaning in the world—is what schools can and should be about. Leaders can make the difference in this quest.

Reflective Principals

Can you imagine a group of principals congregating on a regular basis to discuss how they got into education? What motivated them? What were their separate pathways toward working with children, and what excited them then and what motivates them now about teaching and learning?

Well, such conversations do take place, according to Tim Lucas, director of curriculum in Glen Rock, New Jersey. Tim described to me these meetings among New Jersey suburban and urban principals, where they shared their stories about their origins, hopes, and dreams. Eventually, Tim said, someone would start to raise a current problem, and all would lend the benefit of their considerable years of experience (Tim Lucas, personal communication, May 2001).

The benefits of such storytelling is that, according to Lucas, participants are engaged in what he called "double-loop reflection," a process that looks not only at what we have done with what success, but also examines the underlying structures of our actions. Here Lucas and his principals were examining their basic assumptions about education and these would naturally lead to their visions and their mental models, all elements in a systems approach to education and change (Senge, Cambron-McCabe, Lucas, Smith, Dutton, & Kleiner, 2000, p. 95). This "double-loop reflection" involves reconsidering our basic assumptions, reconnecting to new possible approaches and perspectives, and reframing our guiding principles and ideas. (You can see here the similarities with our discussion of students' challenging underlying assumptions of their learning processes using the Sarason model in Chapter 7.)

Now, imagine if these principals shared their self-questioning with their teachers and thereby modeled their own inquisitiveness. And imagine if teachers formed their own study groups to share their stories while reading Robert Coles's *The Call of Stories: Teaching and the Moral Imagination* (1989). And imagine, too, that these teachers shared their personal journeys with students and that such stories led students to consider what they wanted to get out of school and what their underlying models of good teaching and learning were. That's a most powerful model that could lead to the kinds of questioning of the status quo and what Tim Lucas calls the "deep structures" of our teaching patterns suggested in previous chapters (Senge et al., p. 26). We might have principals leading the way in their questioning of why we do the following:

- Teach most subjects the same amount of time during a week or year
- Ask students to learn in certain ways
- Consider books our primary sources of knowledge
- Assess student learning in the ways we do
- Keep teachers isolated from each other
- Expect teachers to be in front of a group of students most of the time (rather than working alongside them, for example, in solving authentic problems)
- Use only "licensed" supervisors as teacher coaches for improvement of instruction most of the time
- Expect principals to give up teaching

Addressing these kinds of questions under the principal's leadership could help create a community of inquiry that would have long-term positive effects. There is no doubt that principals and other administrative leaders send out the most powerful messages about inquiry and intellectual achievement by the ways in which they interact with teachers and students.

"How Did the Mayans Build Their Pyramids?"

This question came from Margaret Schultz, principal of PS 238 in Brooklyn, on a walk through the Mexican exhibit at the Museum of Natural History. Accompanied by her colleagues, Bruce Wallach, principal of PS 288 (both K–8 schools) and Barry Fein of the District 21 office and a principal himself, Margaret wondered about the relationships between the Mayan architects and those in Egypt. Soon all four of us were standing in front of the white models of the Mayan architecture of Chichen Itza in the dim lighting of the hall. How do you explain the similarities in construction? How could these peoples have communicated? Are there platonic ideas in our heads of perfect geometric figures that each civilization might separately have drawn on? Could the Egyptians have sailed west before Columbus? Were the Mayan pyramids constructed by visitors from outer space?

These questions swirled around the hushed treasures of the Mayan and Aztec exhibits on the crisp January morning these District 21 leaders came to the museum to plan learning experiences for their teachers and students for the following year. "This is amazing," I observed, "how the objects speak to us from the past and generate so many curiosities."

Maritza Macdonald, director of professional development at the museum, noted later in our conversations, "You folks are the kinds of leaders we seldom see here. Usually, it's a 4th or 9th grade teacher who provides the energy and commitment." Too often we have principals who are so consumed with their administrative duties that they spend little time focusing on the kinds of inquiry they want their students to participate in.

"We want our students engaged in science projects starting in the fall and culminating in the science fair in the spring," Margaret said. "We want our teachers to come here and feel comfortable with science so they can enthusiastically communicate their interest to students," said Bruce. "We want them to become comfortable with inquiry in the classroom."

Here are educational leaders who first came to the museum to establish a partnership with us, one that would last for several years. These are not "one-shot deals" for professional development. District 21 wrote a grant and received funds to supplement existing budgets for instructional materials to establish first-rate science programs.

These three leaders are special because they are the principals, because they came to the museum to explore its many mansions full of silent treasures, to savor the fun of intellectual curiosity and then share that with their teachers. In the best spirit of planned inquiry, the teachers of PS 238 and PS 288 sub-sequently came to these and other exhibits to plan for the expeditions of their students in the spring.

The way to lead in any endeavor is to get out in front of those in the organization, to set the example, to model the vision, not to push from behind.

Teacher Professional Development

Principal modeling is fine, but we need more. We as educators need experiences that help us grow beyond the levels of professional skill we possess when we first start teaching. Sometimes these come in the form of monthly or bimonthly meetings organized by the district office or our supervisors—events that we have to attend. At other times we attend workshops presented by an outside consultant or by a teacher in the district.

What has, in the past, governed many of these kinds of experiences is the "one-shot" phenomenon: We have one opportunity to learn something new, and next month, semester, or year, it's something entirely different. Too often these prepared sessions have little to do with what we are experiencing in our classrooms.

Reflective Pause

In your experience, what have been the most powerful and effective professional development programs that have really helped you grow? What do you think are necessary elements for such programs in your schools?

What follows are two models of professional development, both initiated by teachers and supported by administrators who recognized their value in affecting how students in their schools learn.

"Why Do We Have to Do This Geometry?"

The most impressive kinds of professional development experiences have always seemed to me to emanate from the teachers' identifying the needs of their students. Research (Barth, 1991;

Fullan, 1993) tells us that successful professional development programs that work toward changing life in the classroom commence with a clear definition of a problem, perceiving a need related to students' learning.

Roland Barth writes eloquently about working as a school principal to help teachers identify the questions they are most concerned with, rather than initiating change from above and finding all sorts of clever ways to sell these ideas to sometimes reluctant and resistant teachers. (How vividly I remember, as a young English teacher just starting out in New York City, trying to convince my colleagues of the efficacy of using videotape technologies in their classrooms! Nothing happened until one teacher, after working with me on a film, saw a need in her classroom, and that made all the difference.)

The best professional development can begin with teachers' real concerns and questions about helping students learn.

I have seen excellent professional development strategies initiated by teachers. For example, teachers of mathematics at Paramus High School in New Jersey, under the leadership of Deanne Supchak-Stigliano, noticed that a lack of interest was affecting long-term retention of important concepts. These were also students who continually asked, "Why do we have to do this? Why do we have to learn geometric forms or memorize ways to solve algebraic equations relating to time and distance problems?" These are students' deeply felt, but often ignored, inquiries about how the subjects we teach relate to the worlds they experience. Too often we merely reply, "You'll need this in college or next year in Algebra II," forgetting that one of the cardinal principles of learning is that students construct meaningful connections between subject matter and their own lives.

Deanne started a program of helping her geometry students achieve deeper levels of understanding by creating projects that involved their applying as many as 15 geometric concepts, first to floor plans for an ideal residence and then to constructing three-dimensional models. Every time I entered her room at Paramus High School I could see evidences of students' carefully constructed three-dimensional models of expensive homes on display for everybody to admire. By doing this, she made geometry authentic for her students: they were solving problems found in the real world of work (Deanne Supchak-Stigliano, personal communication, April 2000).

In discussing her projects with others in the math department, colleagues identified the same need and they became involved in creating similar projects with their students. Eventually, they all shared their experiences and student models with colleagues in a faculty meeting where the theme was problem-based learning in all subjects. (See Chapter 8 for Cheryl Hopper's Africa unit, also on display at this faculty meeting.)

With the support of their supervisor, Peter Nicholson, Deanne convinced a member of the mathematics faculty at Montclair State University to join them during the year to think through how to evaluate these projects. They developed a rubric for assessing students' work. Subsequently, because Paramus High School was a Professional Development School (where I worked for 3 years with an undergraduate cohort of junior faculty in field-based courses), Deanne and the others applied for grants through the university and received a fair amount of funding to expand this project further into math and science classes, where Sandra Antoine, science supervisor, supported their endeavors.

Deanne subsequently has been asked to share her knowledge with teachers in districts that are part of the New Jersey Network for Educational Renewal. She has taught courses on problem-based learning in mathematics to help others identify significant student needs that we can meet with the kinds of authentic projects her students created.

This is an excellent example of professional development that simply began with a question: "How can we help our average (and classified) students succeed in geometry?" This inquiry led to the best kind of professional development; it commenced with real classroom needs and resulted in observable and strategic changes in the teaching of mathematics. Too often, educational change exemplifies the conclusion presented by Sarason (1982) and Fullan (1993) that nothing of consequence changes in how students learn and behave in the classroom as the result of large-scale innovation efforts. If we want meaningful change in how our students learn, we must challenge them as Deanne and her colleagues have—by changing the actual teaching and learning practices they experience daily.

Deanne's students saw the value of these projects:

- "We learn in class then use it in the real world."
- "Math has gone from a 4 letter word to a 3 letter word— FUN."
- "[The project approach] opens different opportunities to explore careers related to math, things I never thought of."

"How Do We Teach Our ADD Kids?"

Another example comes from a middle school faculty in Caldwell, New Jersey, in which an administrator actively participated as part of the study group investigating how to apply certain principles of learning.

These teachers, led by Jane Kinkle (1999), decided they wanted to know more about how to apply multiple intelligences (MIs) to their classrooms. They set up a study group that decided on a novel strategy, using an electronic journal powered by their weekly questions.

Keeping an electronic journal is like participating in an online course. There are many organizations that provide opportunities for students to take courses online. Colleges and universities have entered this arena in a significant fashion, and Massachusetts Institute of Technology (MIT) announced that it was offering its entire curriculum materials online for free in its OpenCourseWare project at http://web.mit.edu/ocw. Classroom Connect (www.classroom.com) is but one private organization that serves as a platform for courses (among which are the Seminars on Science created by the American Museum of Natural History).

Participating in what is called an "asynchronous environment" is quite a novelty if you haven't tried it. Using technology that allows you to post a message at any time or place and respond whenever you want, it's just like keeping up with your e-mail, except that everybody can read all of the messages that the others have posted in something like an electronic forum.

Jane and her colleagues applied for and received a modest grant from the New Jersey Network for Educational Renewal (based at Montclair State University under the leadership, at that time, of Ada Beth Cutler) and began their electronic questioning of each other about applying MI theory in practice.

Here are excerpts from their "threaded discussions."

Marcy wrote on March 3: "How can we teach our very social, disruptive and ADD [attention deficit disorder] kids (who are often very interpersonal and bodily-kinesthetic) to use their intelligences in a more positive way in the classroom and how can we as teachers gear our lessons toward the utilization of these intelligences? I think this is a tough one. I can't wait to read your replies . . . ."

Then (March 8) one of the administrators in the group (bless him!), C. R., joined the discussion: "Marcy, I was thinking about your question when I observed a more traditional teacher last week. This person was having the students do a complicated repetitive task over and over for 45 minutes. I began to think of some of the workshop activities . . . . If the students need to practice a skill, then maybe stations placed around the room are one answer . . . I remember when I did my brainstorming lesson in your class [administrator modeling!] and I mentioned that the carousel exercise did not engage their bodily kinesthetic intelligence but you said it did get them moving and they need that. Perhaps the answer is in your insight . . . ."

And on March 16, Mike e-mailed his colleagues: "I really feel that the MI approach was made for the ADD, social and/or disruptive child . . . . Recently, I did a lesson where the kinesthetic intelligence played a big role in learning to remember facts . . . one usually disruptive child really got into the actions associated with the list and when it came time to recall them he was right on the mark . . . . When a student is disruptive I really feel that they are crying out to move around so maybe we can let that be the gauge on when we need it . . . ."

Jane came on board March 16: "Marcy, to respond to your question: I have to tell you that disruptive kids are not my forte. Contentious kids have given me nightmares in the past . . . but I have found that with my new MI perspective, my discipline problems have been kept to a minimum this year. For one thing, I split most of my classes into two parts. We start off with a quick review of the lesson or discuss a "science in the news" item. This usually takes about 20 minutes. Then everyone gets up and goes over to the other side of the room where we do our labs for about 35 minutes . . . . For the super social interpersonals, talking time during a lab is encouraged (I know scientists talk about last night's football game . . .). I've abandoned the "fill-in-the-blank-with-the-right-answer" worksheets in favor of science lab journals. Each lab requests some kind of artwork: diagram, illustration, cartoon, etc. I've discovered that many of my super social students like to draw, so that engages them even more . . . ."

Then, interspersed with answering Marcy's question of March 3, came this question from Pat on March 10: "It's my turn to come up with a question. We have addressed changes in our interpretation of intelligence after studying Gardner's theory on the eight different intelligences. We have discussed the changes in our teaching, as well as any difficulties we are experiencing. What if we look at MI from the students' point of view. What are their feelings, both pro and con, about the MI strategies we are implementing? Do they enjoy working in their less developed intelligences as well as their stronger intelligences?"

Pat (March 22): "We need to create an 'exit' survey for our project."

Before getting to the students' feelings, several teachers exchanged their own stories about how they liked to learn and how some students had struggled in the past with their preferred teaching styles.

Reflective Pause

What do you think are the benefits and drawbacks of such an electronic journal form of professional development? How do you think Jane, C. R., and their colleagues might have grown from these kinds of "asynchronous discussions"?

I'm sure you have seen the benefits to teachers of using this kind of e-mail journal as a professional development strategy, energized by the real questions posed about applying an educational theory to their own classrooms. Several lessons are striking:

- This was a teacher-initiated endeavor.
- The fact that the teachers were joined by an administrator, C. R., is amazing and all too uncommon. I have had the pleasure of presenting a variety of workshops for the New Jersey Network for Educational Renewal over the years and was always delighted when C. R. was there, satisfying his own curiosity and modeling an administrator's inquiring mind for all. Administrators participating in teachers' professional development experiences can, however, be as rare as snow in New York City in July.
- The effort was driven by faculty questions about application of MI and how students benefited and felt about the whole process.
- From reading the transcripts (of which this is only a brief taste!), you can tell how engrossed teachers were in their own inquiries and how meaningful the whole process was for them.
- Teachers can focus on any instructional need of significance.
- We might assume that Jane and her colleagues at various times sat down together to discuss what they were learning.

What we can glean from this "threaded discussion" for professional development in the electronic age is that we can do a lot with face-to-face discussions and nothing will replace them for delivering messages and expressing ideas. But the electronic sharing of ideas, as we've witnessed with Jane and her colleagues, is not the future. It is here now, and we need to take advantage of this marvelous technology to help all our community members grow.

Powered by their own inquiry, students, teachers, administrators, and community members can establish their own visions, design strategies, and work toward the accomplishment of real change for students. So many schools now have extensive Web sites where they exchange information with all members of the community. Jane's "threaded discussion" could have included community participants and, perhaps in the future, some such discussions might include students as well.

Conclusion

It all comes down to leadership of the sort presented here by teachers like Deanne Supchak-Stigliano and Jane Kinkle and administrators like Mike Novacek, C. R., Tim Lucas, Margaret Schultz, Bruce Wallach, and Barry Fein.

This is the future—teachers taking more control of their own professional development inquiries through experiences like those of Deanne and Jane. And this is the future, too: leaders modeling their own inquisitiveness for all in the organization and using that love of inquiry to foster a culture of inquiry within their schools.

Leadership is not about pushing people from behind. It is not the result of taking public opinion polls. Leadership is about being in the forefront of issues and ideas, often when others are of a contrary point of view, and providing full resources to accomplish goals. Furthermore, it requires a continued sense of awe and wonder about the natural and interpersonal worlds.

American Museum of Natural History Provost Mike Novacek recently reflected on his feelings of exploration and discovery: "I often feel this typical wanderlust thing. When I get back from the field, I say, 'I'm not going anywhere for the next 10 years.' But then the months go on and you find yourself jumping, ready to go. Again." Perhaps in search of that "out-of-body" experience that accompanies a truly great discovery in the Gobi Desert (Dreifus, 2002, p. F3).

Leaders open new mansions full of hushed, splendid treasures for our exploration and discovery.

References

Barth, R. (1991). *Improving schools from within: Teachers, parents and principals can make the difference.* San Francisco: Jossey-Bass.

Coles, R. (1989). *The call of stories: Teaching and the moral imagination.* Boston: Houghton Mifflin.

Dreifus, C. (2002, January 8). A paleontologist retains his sense of wonder. *The New York Times*, p. F3.

Fullan, M. (1993). *Change forces: Probing the depth of educational reform.* Philadelphia: Falmer Press.

Kinkle, J. (1999). *Accommodating multiple intelligences in the middle school classroom.* Unpublished manuscript, Caldwell-West Caldwell, NJ, Public Schools.

McPeck, J. (1981). *Critical thinking and education.* Oxford, England: Martin Robertson.

Novacek, M. (1996). *Dinosaurs of the flaming cliffs.* New York: Anchor Books.

Sagan, C. (1996). *The demon-haunted world: Science as a candle in the dark.* New York: Ballantine Books.

Sarason, S. (1982). *The culture of the school and the problem of change.* Boston: Allyn & Bacon.

Senge, P., Cambron-McCabe, N., Lucas, T., Smith, B., Dutton, J., & Kleiner, A. (2000). *Schools that learn: A fifth discipline fieldbook for educators, parents, and everyone who cares about education.* New York: Doubleday.

Updike, J. (1981). *Museums and women, and other stories.* New York: Vintage.

"CITIZENS OF THE COSMOS"

We have come to a resting place on our journey of inquiry.

For me this journey began with my grandfather posing so many fascinating questions about the universe—for example, "Why do you think the sun setting on the horizon appears so much larger than it does at its zenith?"

This question confronted me at a very young age with a model of what fosters curiosity: a situation that seems strange and mysterious with respect to what we would normally expect. The vision of two suns—one very much larger than the other—set his mind and mine to wondering, and for as long as I was privileged to be his grandson, we shared a common fascination about the world.

Now, so many years later and transformed and chastened by the events of September 11, 2001, this journey has taken me far beyond wondering about the events in the heavens to become more wide awake to the world we live in at the start of the 21st century. It is without doubt so different from my grandfather's world, but then he served as a volunteer during World War I and lived through the Depression and the attack on Pearl Harbor. Those were no times for complacency and apathy.

Today, we can ill afford the kinds of apathy that are reflected in our voting patterns. In the last election for President, fewer than 50 percent of eligible U.S. voters went to the polls.

Today, we live in a "new normalcy," where all of us need to be alert and vigilant. This is one reason why this book, I hope, is making a contribution.

But as I have tried to make clear from the outset, our need for inquisitive minds far transcends noticing who is taking flying lessons and not wanting to learn how to land or take off. Becoming an inquisitive person is one prerequisite for growing up with the potential for living an enriching life. Remember the words of Samuel Johnson in 1751: "Curiosity is one of the permanent and certain characteristics of a vigorous mind."

Inquisitiveness may be the beginning of meaningful learning, but, beyond that, it is one permanent and certain characteristic of citizens of a thriving democracy who seek self-enriching worlds of scientific, aesthetic, and humanistic exploration and discovery.

A society that squashes a child's curiosity is one doomed toward the lives of those living under Dostoevsky's Grand Inquisitor, lives lived "like cattle," being led around by those in authority. Questioning authority is never easy, but that is what the times demand.

Let the 21st century in America be marked by the education of children and adolescents who relish the roles of questioner. Let it also be known as the century where we educated teachers to fulfill the grand vision of Anatole France, "The whole art of teaching is only the art of awakening the natural curiosity of young minds for the purpose of satisfying it afterwards."

Let us awaken all the minds of all the children with whom we work. Our reward is their continued flowering into mature adults who are responsible, contributing, and enriched citizens of our democracy and citizens of the world.

And if, as astronomers now assert, "We are star stuff," meaning we are composed of matter that is generated from exploding stars—carbon, oxygen, calcium, iron, for example—then we can perceive our task in its cosmic context. We are educating young people to grow up to be enlightened "citizens of the cosmos," capable of continuing to figure out our place in the vastness of the observable universe stretching out to 10 to the 26th meters (Druyan & Soter, 2000).

At the end of our journey of inquiry, I saw youngsters gathered beneath the gigantic Hayden Sphere at the Planetarium of the American Museum of Natural History presenting their experiments to be launched on the Space Shuttle in the summer of 2002. These young people were full of curiosities about the cosmos: how would extreme temperatures and radiation affect plant seeds, magnets, mold on bread, and bacteria. They even sent up their bus and subway MetroCards! Here were the adventurers of tomorrow, sending their inquiries on a space mission that would travel seven million miles (www.nasa.gov/kids.html and www.wff.nasa.gov/sem).

Here were the future creators of our civilization disturbing the universe with their questions.

Stepping back from these enthusiastic elementary and middle school students—all from New York—I marveled at the vastness of our universe and the wonders yet to behold. And I'm still full of curiosities.

How could the expansiveness of this universe—13 billion years young—have been generated in the Big Bang from a bubble of space smaller than an atom, creating space and time, stars and galaxies, black holes, and life as we know it?

This is our challenge—to continue wondering and planning journeys into the vastness of the universe as well as deep into the recesses of our souls.

Reference

Druyan, A., & Soter, S. (2000). *Passport to the universe.* (Space show). New York: American Museum of Natural History.

Appendix A

Current and Valuable Web Sites

As of publication date, the following Web sites were active. However, you may find that some have been discontinued.

Educational Resources

www.refdesk.com—A wonderful site for access to current newspapers, anthologies, almanacs, and texts full of information. See "Ask the Experts."

www.bartleby.com—Access to extensive resource and reference texts such as *The Columbia Encyclopedia*, *The Encyclopedia of World History*, and more.

http://lcweb2.loc.gov/ammem/ammemhome.html—Home page of the American Memory project from the Library of Congress.

www.pbs.org—Public Television site.

www.education-world.com—A comprehensive site with plans, curricula, discussion of current issues, and technology strategies.

www.britannica.com—The *Encyclopedia Britannica* online.

www.askjeeves.com—Find answers to your questions.

www.yahooligans.com—A Web site for kids including "Ask Earl."

Assessment of Web Sources

These are two excellent sites presenting evaluative criteria:

http://lib.nmsu.edu/instruction/eval.html

http://www.ithaca.edu/library/Training/hott.html

Explorations of Space

www.imagine.gsfc.nasa.gov—Excellent space site, complete with extensive definitions and examples of quasars, superactive galaxies, black holes, and so forth.

http://spaceplace.nasa.gov—Good introduction to NASA activities for younger scientists.

www.windows.ucar.edu—An interdisciplinary Web site on the earth and space sciences.

www.chandra.harvard.edu/edu/index.html—Source for educational programs about space sciences.

http://www.seds.org/hst/—The Best of NASA's Hubble Space Telescope.

American Museum of Natural History, New York City

www.amnh.org—Museum home page with links to all its programs, expeditions, faculty, and online resources.

www.amnh.org/education/resources—Resources for Learning provides access to museum-created curricula, profiles, and learning experiences.

www.ology.amnh.org—Learning all about science and scientists, including astronomy, paleontology, and genetics.

www.amnh.org/exhibitions/expeditions—Site devoted to amazing expeditions all over the world.

www.amnh.org/learn/pd/sos—Online seminars on science in astronomy, geology, ichthyology, paleontology, genetics, and other subjects.

www.amnh.org/learn/biodiversity_counts—A curriculum for middle school students.

www.amnh.org/learn/musings—A Web newsletter for science educators published by the National Center for Science Literacy, Education and Technology.

www.amnh.org/nationalcenter/expeditions/blacksmokers/black_smokers.html—Site devoted to an expedition to recover hydrothermal vents at the bottom of the ocean.

www.amnh.org/nationalcenter/youngnaturalistsawards—Winning entries in national contest (grades 7–12) where students go on expeditions and share findings.

General Resources for Educators

www.oops.bizland.com—One of the best portals to teacher resources, including Kathy Schrock's Guides for Educators.

www.kn.pacbell.com—Excellent source of educational resources, PLUS an amazing search engine called BLUEWEB'N (projects in many subjects) and Filamentality (create Web linkages for your learning experiences).

Webquests

http://webquest.sdsu.edu—The WebQuest page.

www.manteno.k12.il.us—Very good source for school-based Webquests at all levels.

www.spa3.k12.sc.us—Webquests with extensive scoring rubric.

Projects Online

www.spaceday.com—Problem solving on the International Space Station.

www.gsn.org—An excellent project Web site.

www.jasonproject.org—Site for multidisciplinary expeditions across the Earth created by Robert Ballard, founder and head of the Institute of Exploration in Mystic, Connecticut.

http://quest.arc.nasa.gov—National Aeronautics and Space Administration (NASA) site for sharing its "authentic scientific and engineering pursuits."

www.passporttoknowledge.com—Interactive learning experiences in life, earth, space, and physical sciences (NASA, NSF, NOAA).

www.exploratorium.edu—Webcasts and adventures from Antarctica, Rain Forest, Hubble Space Telescope, and many more research sites.

www.surfaquarium.com—Home page with extensive project information.

www.school.discovery.com—Extensive lesson plans and Kathy Schrock's guide to all subjects.

www.bigsignal.net—NASA explores remote terrains on Earth with robots.

www.classroom.com—Go here for current Quest expeditions. Sponsored with the American Museum of Natural History (AMNH). Go to "Connected University" for excellent courses on pedagogy and "Seminars on Science" created by AMNH.

www.thinkquest.com—An international collaboration of students, teachers, parents, and technologists conducting research.

Problem-Based Learning

www.samford.edu/pbl/pbl_main.html—Center for problem-based learning studies.

www.imsa.edu/team/cpbl/cpbl.html—The Illinois Mathematics and Science Academy source of significant problem-based learning studies.

Service Learning

www.kidsconsortium.org—Many wonderful service learning projects with students planning their own projects within the community.

Online Interest Groups

http://groups.yahoo.com—Share photos, files, and newsletters.

Communications with Classroom and with Parents

www.eboard.com—Post homework and assignments.

www.schoolnotes.com—Post notes for your class.

Students Communicating with Other Students

www.epals.com—Opportunities for students to e-mail other students in many languages.

Directories with Databases

www.yahoo.com
www.altavista.com
www.lycos.com
www.hotbot.com

Mega Search Engines

www.google.com
www.profusion.com
www.metacrawler.com
www.northernlight.com

Create Your Own Web Site

www.angelfire.com
www.myschoolonline.com
www.geocities.com

Appendix B

Contact Information for Educators

I hope the ideas, strategies, and stories in this book have brought to mind more questions than it has been able to answer. Should you wish to communicate with me or other educators mentioned herein, please feel free to contact us at the addresses given below.

John Barell, 444 E. 82 St. 10A, New York, New York 10028 (jbarell@nyc.rr.com or johnbarell@hotmail.com)

Cathy Brophy, Hampton, New Hampshire (cbrophy@sau21.k12.nh.us)

Christine Burt, 605 Mountain Rd., Kinnelon, New Jersey 07405

Rose Cohen, PS 238, 1633 East 8th St., Brooklyn, New York 11223 (klady207@excite.com)

Linda D'Acquisto, Kids Curators (ldacquisto@kidcurators.com)

Chuck Dolan, Fair Lawn, New Jersey (Dolanch@aol.com)

Cheryl Hopper, Montclair State University (moonhop@intac.com)

Jane Kinkle, Caldwell-West Caldwell, New Jersey (Jkinkle@cwcboe.org)

Tim Lucas, Glen Rock, New Jersey (lucasrps@aol.com)

Barbara M'Gonigle, Dumont, New Jersey (mgonigleb@nni.com)

Amy O'Donnell, American Museum of Natural History, 79th Street and Central Park West, New York, New York 10024

Ann Prewitt, American Museum of Natural History (prewitt@amnh.org)

Stephen Reynolds, University of Arizona (sreynolds@asu.edu)

Margaret Schultz, Principal, PS 238, 1633 East 8th St., Brooklyn, New York 11223 (margtschultz@aol.com)

Deanne Supchak-Stigliano (Desupchak@aol.com)

Mary Wallace, Fair Lawn, New Jersey (Fairlawn@aol.com)

Ann White, Jackson Academy, 106 Prospect St., East Orange, New Jersey 07017

School Inquisitiveness Inventory

	Seldom	Often	Usually
1. Our school is a community of inquiry.			
2. Teachers and administrators model their own curiosities.			
3. Our goals and philosophy stress developing students' powers of inquiry.			
4. There is time during faculty meetings for questions about instruction, curriculum, and how we teach students.			
5. Teachers ask most questions in class.			
6. We encourage students to ask good questions about content.			
7. We provide many, varied ways for students to conduct formal/informal investigations.			

	Seldom	Often	Usually
8. There are models of inquisitive persons within our content.			
9. Students feel comfortable posing questions of texts, the teachers, and other authorities.			
10. We challenge each other with questions during class and during faculty meetings.			
11. Students' research projects are the result of their own interests and curiosities.			
12. We attempt to assess the quality and development of students' inquisitiveness or curiosity.			
13. There is time during class for wonder, speculation, and asking good questions.			
14. Teachers often work together (in study groups) to investigate their own curiosities about teaching and learning.			
15. The school and its community value the inquiry process.			

Appendix D

Personal Inquisitiveness Inventory

1. Did you grow up being a very curious person?

2. What experiences have you had that fostered or inhibited your inquisitiveness? In school? At home? At work?

3. Who were your models of curiosity? Who are they now?

4. Would you say that now you are a very curious person? What kinds of subjects or experiences interest you?

5. Think of today's headlines. What do you want to know more about?

6. Reflect on the last book you read. What questions would you ask the author?

7. In your personal relationships, what questions do you want to answer for yourself? How might you go about doing this? Who would help? What obstacles might you have to overcome?

8. At work, what supports and facilitates your posing good questions and seeking answers? What impedes your progress?

9. How might you go about enhancing your own inquisitiveness?

10. How might you work toward enhancing the community of inquiry within which you work?

Index

Note: Page numbers followed by *f* refer to figures.

About the Author

John Barell has been involved with inquiry ever since he read a book about Antarctic exploration. That book, *Alone* by Admiral Richard E. Byrd, led to questions about science, survival, and expeditions to the South Pole. Following a tour of duty with the Navy in Antarctica, he began teaching in New York City, continued at Montclair State University, and is now Professor, Emeritus at the university and a consultant at the American Museum of Natural History in New York City. At the museum, he helps develop and coordinate educational plans for teachers and students interested in expanding their curriculum offerings to include alternative, more informal settings where their curiosities can freely explore the wonders of our planet—both inner and outer spaces.

Barell's previous publications include *Playgrounds of Our Minds* (1980), "*. . .EVER WONDER . . . ?*" (1992), and *Teaching for Thoughtfulness* (2nd, 1995). He can be contacted through e-mail at jbarell@nyc.rr.com and johnbarell@hotmail.com.

Related ASCD Resources:
Developing More Curious Minds

At the time of publication, the following ASCD resources were available; for the most up-to-date information about ASCD resources, go to www.ascd.org. ASCD stock numbers are noted in parentheses.

Audiotapes
Celebrate Learning with Student-Led Conferences: Increase Student Accountability, Involve Parents, and Help Meet Standards by Susan Barnett and Barbara Benson (#200174)
Education: The Key to a Healthy America by M. Joycelyn Elders (#202133)
The Net: Teaching Zack to Think by Alan November (#202241)
Teaching Thinking to Multiple Intelligences and Diverse Student Populations (#294022)
Taking the Ho-Hum Out of Teaching: Strategies for Embedding Thinking Skill in the Curriculum by J. Robert Hanson and P. Robert Hanson (#200179)

Multimedia
Dimensions of Learning Complete Program (#614239)
Problem-Based Learning Across the Curriculum Professional Inquiry Kit by William J. Stepien and Shelagh Gallagher (#997148)

Networks
Visit the ASCD Web site (www.ascd.org) and search for "networks" for information about professional educators who have formed groups around topics like "Dimensions of Learning," "Problem-Based Learning," and "Teaching Thinking." Look in the "Network Directory" for current facilitators' addresses and phone numbers.

Online Resources
Educational Leadership: Do Students Care About Learning? (entire issue, September 2002) Excerpted articles online free (http://www.ascd.org/frameedlead.html); entire issue online and accessible to ASCD members (http://www.ascd.org/members-only.html)
Professional Development Online: *Dimensions of Learning*, among others (http://www.ascd.org/framepdonline.html) (for a small fee; password protected)

Print Products
Developing Minds: A Resource Book for Teaching Thinking, 3rd Edition edited by Arthur L. Costa (#101063)
Dimensions of Thinking: A Framework for Curriculum and Instruction by Robert Marzano (#61187040)
How to Develop Student Creativity by Robert J. Sternberg and Wendy M. Williams (#196073)
How to Use Problem-Based Learning in the Classroom by Robert Delise (#197166)
Problems as Possibilities: Problem-Based Learning for K–16 Education, 2nd Edition by Linda Torp and Sara Sage (#101064)
Schooling for Life: Reclaiming the Essence of Learning by Jacqueline Grennon Brooks (#101302)
The Soul of Education: Helping Students Find Connection, Compassion, and Character at School by Rachael Kessler (#100045)

Videos
Dimensions of Learning Video Series (six videos) (#614236)
How to Engage Students in Critical Thinking Tape 8 (#400050)
Problem-Based Learning Across the Curriculum by William Stepien (#297182)

For more information, visit us on the World Wide Web (http://www.ascd.org), send an e-mail message to member@ascd.org, call the ASCD Service Center (1-800-933-ASCD or 703-578-9600, then press 2), send a fax to 703-575-5400, or write to Information Services, ASCD, 1703 N. Beauregard St., Alexandria, VA 22311-1714 USA.